FORT STEELE

Gold Rush to Boom Town

Naomi Miller

Heritage
House

National Library of Canada Cataloguing in Publication Data

Miller, Naomi, 1927-
    Fort Steele

    Includes bibliographical references and index.
    ISBN 1-894384-38-5

    1. Fort Steele (B.C.)—History. 2. Frontier and pioneer
life—British Columbia—Fort Steele. I. Title.

FC3849.F7M54 2002   971.1'65   C2002-910224-3
F1089.5.F7M54 2002

First edition 2002

Heritage House acknowledges the financial support for our
publishing program from the Government of Canada through
the Book Publishing Industry Development Program (BPIDP),
Canada Council for the Arts, and the British Columbia Arts
Council.

Cover and book design by Darlene Nickull
Edited by Terri Elderton
Cover photo courtesy Martin Ross

HERITAGE HOUSE PUBLISHING COMPANY LTD.
Unit #108 - 17665 66 A Ave., Surrey, B.C. V3S 2A7

Printed in Canada

Contents

Acknowledgements

I consulted many resources during the preparation of this history of Fort Steele. I thank everyone who shared references or loaned books. My prime source for material was the Fort Steele Archives, but I also found other source materials ensconced in files in the Provincial Archives in Victoria. A major vote of thanks goes to Derryll White, archivist, curator, and "Keeper of the Keys" at Fort Steele, for his ongoing assistance, encouragement, and evaluation of the manuscript. Honourable mention goes to Marie Elliott of Victoria who volunteered to photocopy letters and documents that she noticed while she was doing parallel research on Barkerville and the Cariboo.

I also thank Patricia Leverre, who turned my handwritten notes into computer printouts, enabling the editors at Heritage House to publish this book.

I also wish to publicly acknowledge the contributions of Shelagh Dehart, Carolyn Cross, E.L. "Ted" Affleck, Winnifred Weir, the late Judge J.T. Harvey, Martin Ross, and, of course, my husband Peter Miller. Each has added to my collection of information and pictures, which are now woven into this presentation.

It has been my pleasure to share a little of this history with hundreds of summer visitors to Fort Steele Heritage Town. Now they—and others—can read many more details. My sincere thanks to all who have helped me.

Naomi Miller

Prologue

This is the story of a community that came into being because of a gold rush, grew to become a bustling city, then lost pride of place when the Canadian Pacific Railway was routed seven miles south through an estate with only a handful of residents. The story was gleaned from official records wherever possible, supplemented by the memoirs of Father Nicolas Coccola and Major Samuel Benfield Steele.

Fort Steele truly became a "community" in 1895, when the newspaper, *The Prospector*, began to give delightful week-by-week accounts of local activities, including building, mining, politics, businesses, social events, births, marriages, and deaths. The words from the items and columns in *The Prospector* made life in Fort Steele come alive for me. I augmented the facts obtained from the newspaper with in-depth research into the lives of some leading citizens, using government, church, and business records as well as correspondence now in various archives. By selecting from all of these sources, I have written this book to share the stories about life when the Europeans and Americans first settled in the East Kootenays. I chose to conclude this history at the time *The Prospector* ceased publication.

Fort Steele shrivelled and aged but never died. There have been loyal citizens in a few of the homes to the present day. The school operated until 1954. The Windsor Hotel served drinks in its beer parlour until 1958. When that hotel was to be demolished, Allan Wood Hunter purchased it. He joined forces with Allan "Dinty" Moore, the storekeeper in the old Carlin and Durick establishment. The two began an emphatic demand to the government of British Columbia. "This site must be designated and maintained as a heritage property!" Hunter

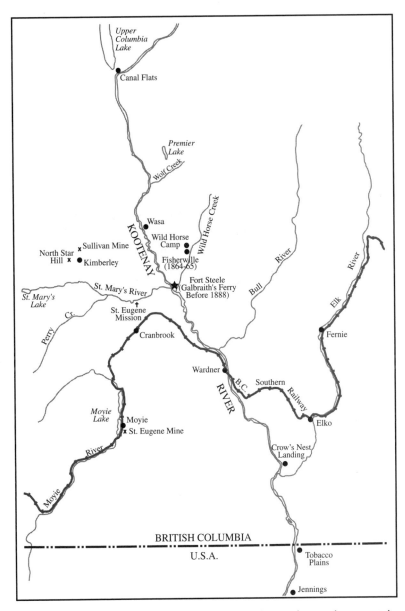

The earliest prospectors and settlers followed old Indian trails near the rivers. The north-south trails were improved in the 1860s and 70s. A trail to the West Coast—the Dewdney Trail—was cut through in 1865, just north of the international boundary. The B.C. Southern Railway, which came from Fort Macleod through Crow's Nest Pass, was built through Cranbrook in 1898, bypassing Fort Steele.

Aerial view of Fort Steele Heritage Town, circa 1986. To the left is Main Street, extending from the foreground towards the mountains. Slightly left of centre is the Windsor Hotel, which is on the corner of Main and Riverside, in its original location.

directed his persuasive message to many in high places. In March 1961 Fort Steele was declared to be a provincial park. Immediately a small staff began shoring up sagging buildings and cleaning up overgrown lots, not only for appearance but also for fire protection. An office centre was needed, so the Wasa Hotel was erected to serve in three ways: as an office, a museum, and an attractive tearoom.

The highway went along Main Street, down the hill, and across the bridge to Westport. A new bridge was needed, so surveyors laid out a new roadway to connect with a larger, higher crossing. Fort Steele townsite was divided! Some prominent historic buildings had to be relocated before the road was finally cut through in 1964–65. It was a major job, but at least the schoolhouse, two churches, and the Opera House were set on new footings because of this move.

Fort Steele was never a fort. It was "Kootenay Post," a barrack square occupied for one year by Major Samuel Benfield Steele and the men of the North West Mounted Police. The new caretakers argued that the site should be fenced, so they erected a log picket fence with gatehouse towers that conveyed a "fort" appearance. The gatehouse was replaced in 1997 with a large building whose exterior replicates the Fort Steele brewery that once stood across the river in Westport.

The early curators had the good sense to interview pioneers who remembered some details about this town and its people. They talked to some who had been students under the famous Miss Bailey. They found family members who had roots in Fort Steele, some of whom willingly donated heirlooms or pictures most helpful to restoring homes or businesses to 1890s vintage for public display. Gradually the old town was groomed with wooden sidewalks, a new water supply that made it possible to keep lawns and gardens green, and fresh paint or new roofs as needed. Certain buildings were replicated to fill spaces on Riverside Avenue. Each summer, costumed personnel make the town return to an era of formality with family activities and horse-drawn transportation, creating a "living history" museum.

The Fort Steele Archives carefully catalogued and stored photographs and other records. The collections provide tidbits of information that delighted me so much, I felt that they should be shared with others.

A final note: The modern spelling for the local First Nation is "Ktunaxa." Every reference that I consulted used "Kootenay," so I used the old spelling throughout. "Kootenay" is the Canadian spelling, and "Kootenai" is the American spelling of the word. Similarly, I have also used the word "Indian" to denote the Aboriginal peoples, as this is what they were called at this time in history.

Chapter 1

Kootenay Territory
(Before 1864)

Mountains and major waterways defined the homeland of the aboriginal Kootenays long before mapmakers drew lines on parchment. Their territory included the section of the Rocky Mountain Trench between the Big Bend of the Columbia River in the north and the Kootenay River loop in the south.

The Kootenays were tall, sturdy hunters and fishers with a language that bore no relationship to that of the tribes around them. They were the first people west of the Rockies to capture and use wild horses.[1] These people moved from fishing grounds to berry-picking areas to hunting camps. Four bands were named for the location of their respective winter villages: at Columbia Lake, St. Mary's River, Tobacco Plains, and Lower Kootenay (near the mouth of the Kootenay River). The Lake, or Lower Kootenay, Indians had sturgeon-nosed canoes—very different from any other native canoe but similar to those used in Siberia.

The district was also home to the Kinbaskets of the Shuswap band. They had settled on the east bank of the Columbia River, five miles below the outlet of Lower Columbia (now Windermere) Lake. The Shuswaps dug pits for storing food, and also built their winter homes primarily underground. These "kekullies" were perhaps 40 feet in diameter and 10 feet deep. There was a sleeping bench left around much of the perimeter. The roof of beams, arranged in a conical shape, had a central opening fitted with a notched tree to use as a ladder for entering and exiting the home. The roof was covered with sod, and a heavy mat was at hand to cover the opening whenever it rained or snowed. Where a hillside slope or soil conditions permitted there was also a side tunnel or "women's entrance." The cooking fire would generally be outside. The inner room was illuminated by burning wicks in grease. For heat, hot rocks were carried in, using cleverly woven green willow branches where the fork was braided into a loop. It was likely more snug and warm in a kekullie than in a lodge or teepee.

The first recorded white man in the Kootenay-Columbia Valley was David Thompson. Thompson came to Canada in 1784 as a teenaged apprentice to the Hudson's Bay Company (HBC). In 1797 he left the HBC to enter the service of the rival North West Company. The North West Company merged with the Hudson's Bay Company in 1821, and all employees became HBC personnel.

Thompson not only established new trading posts, but he also explored and mapped huge areas of our continent. In May 1807, accompanied by his wife and family, he crossed the Rockies by what is now Howse Pass. He proceeded up the Columbia River, chose a site almost across from the Kinbaskets, and built Kootenae House, the first trading post in Kootenay territory. This post did not attract Kootenay Indians to trade, so after 1811 it was abandoned. Each summer Thompson travelled by canoe, on horseback, or on foot, surveying and mapping. He befriended Kootenay and Kinbasket alike and depended on them to guide or paddle him through this unknown land.

On the Tobacco Plains, about five miles south of the Canada–U.S. boundary, David Thompson opened another small trading post called, "Kootenai Post." Despite the 1846 treaty declaring the 49th parallel as an international boundary, the Hudson's Bay Company operated posts in the Oregon Territory for another twenty years before regrouping on the British side of the line. HBC factor John Linklater had been at a Tobacco Plains post in Montana for several years before the gold rush of 1864.

The Roman Catholic Church sent Father de Smet into the Kootenays in 1845. He ranged north from Portland, Oregon to the Windermere area, where a Métis, Francois Morigeau, welcomed him. Morigeau asked the priest to formally marry him to his wife, then baptize his several children. After observing these baptisms, numerous Columbia Lake Band families asked to be baptized as well.

Various missionaries visited the district each summer until Father Leon Fouquet built the first mission here in 1874.

Chapter 2

The Gold Rush
(1864–65)

Fort Steele sits on a level bench high above a bend in the Kootenay River close to where Wild Horse Creek alternately rushes or trickles out of its twisted gorge in the Rocky Mountains. This was a place where deer and elk might find open grazing when nearby hills were deep in snow. Native peoples passed by on the way to their favourite berry patches. Only a handful of Europeans, wandering curiously through the district, would have trod here before the gold rush.

Late in 1863 a group led by Joe Finlay camped at the mouth of this then unnamed creek. Their horses were hobbled and set to graze. As one man prepared the fire to cook an evening meal, he saw a wild horse above, silhouetted by the setting sun. His partners tested the gravel at the edge of the stream. They were delighted when their panning produced large flakes of gold. In a short time they netted $700 worth of pumpkinseed gold. As they sat around the campfire, eating their supper, the visiting stallion circled their horses, paying close attention to the mare. Finlay muttered, "Guess we'll tether the mare to a tree so that eager stud horse don't take her away."

The weather was cooling, and supplies were running low. The prospectors had to continue trekking south to civilization for the winter. They broke camp at daylight and plodded downstream. It was easy to ford the Bull and Elk Rivers at this time, and over much of the way they found beaches and sandbars, allowing them to travel in comparative comfort. They chatted optimistically about returning to "Stud Horse Creek."

The prospectors paused at the Hudson's Bay Company post at Tobacco Plains. They showed John Linklater the impressive panning from the mouth of Stud Horse Creek. During their winter layover in Walla Walla, word got around that Finlay's group had found not one, but two productive gold creeks north of the newly marked boundary between U.S. and British territory. Groups of men, inspired by the recent California gold rush, spent the winter assembling supplies so that they could move north as soon as the old Indian trails were passable.

Two parties competed for the first stakings at the new bonanza. Bob Dore and his six-man team left Walla Walla on the morning of March 17, 1864. They went north of the St. Mary's River before attempting to cross the Kootenay River. Four of Dore's men stayed on the west bank of the Kootenay River and got to Finlay Creek. Jack Fisher, with fifteen companions, left two days after Dore, and managed to cross the Kootenay River and access Stud Horse Creek. They panned at the mouth, as Finlay's crew had done, whooped with joy, then picked their way upstream through the rocky canyon and patches of snow. Fisher's party chose to put their campsite on a level bench above the creek. Tents were pitched, and a log shanty was hastily constructed for storing supplies. On Sunday, April 10, 1864, the miners voted to adopt two clauses from the Gold Fields Act of 1859 and its Appendix of 1863.

> **First**: All Creek claims should be two hundred feet in length and running from "bank to bank" including all low bars.
> **Second**: All Hill claims shall be one hundred and fifty feet, facing the creek, running back the same distance of one hundred and fifty feet. These are called "Bench Claims."

Fisher was granted first choice for his placer claim. All others were registered as being either so many lots upstream or downstream of Fisher's initial staking. For a few weeks this registration was carried out on an honour system.

The tent town was named Fisherville. More miners came in every few days. Merchants arrived with the first supplies for selling. An eager entrepreneur began brewing beer, using water from a nearby side stream that is still known as Brewery Creek. Hastily constructed saloons were soon serving brew.

The Ferry Office, Fort Steele BC.
Built 1864.

Edward Goodall 1987

Courtesy Edward Goodall Estate and Canadian Gallery Prints Ltd.

The ferry office and John Galbraith's first home, built in 1864, was small but cozy.

Late one July evening some young Fenians bantered with several American veterans of the California gold rush. Banter changed to insults, and in the twilight shots rang out. Tommy Walker shot off the thumb of "Yeast Powder Bill" Burmeister. Burmeister reached for his revolver and blazed in return. Tommy Walker died six days later and was buried on a hillside about half a mile from the community. The miners convened a court. It was learned that others had pulled weapons. Burmeister was warned but could not be declared guilty.

British justice, in the persons of Gold Commissioner John Haynes and Constable Harry Anderson, reached Fisherville a few days later. Another jury was promptly assembled to try Burmeister, but there was still insufficient evidence to convict him. He was given one hour to get out of camp; he was packed and on the way in half that time.

Haynes and Anderson hurriedly threw up a cabin, and later, a jail. Haynes ordered that every man must buy a miner's licence for five dollars; no pistols were to be carried while the owner was on the creek; an export tax must be paid on gold being carried into the U.S.; and all businesses must buy a trading or liquor licence. Naturally, this created a lot of grumbling, and a few of the less successful prospectors left in disgust.

Meanwhile, John Galbraith had built a ferry just upstream from the mouth of Stud Horse Creek. He built a log cabin on the flat high above the river, the first building at what was to become known as Galbraith's Ferry and later renamed Fort Steele. Galbraith charged one dollar for a man and five dollars per horse or mule to come in, then raised the fee to five dollars a man and ten dollars a horse to leave. Galbraith made more money than many of the prospectors!

The government of the Colony of British Columbia wanted to learn more about the activity in the mines close to the Rocky Mountains; so, in August 1864 Colonial Secretary Birch and his registrar, Arthur Bushby, were sent from New Westminster to view the camp at "Wild Horse" Creek. (Government officials had declared that "Stud Horse" was too unseemly a name to enter on their maps.) They found that the first section of the Dewdney Trail, built in 1860 between Hope and Rock Creek, was already in disrepair, with windfalls blocking some places or with sections washed out by slides. Beyond Rock Creek they had to criss-cross the Kettle River and face a forest fire and other hazards. Their 500-mile trip took 26 days and proved to all that a lot of work needed to be done before merchants in New Westminster could arrange to deliver supplies to the Kootenays.

When the leaves started falling and Wild Horse Creek ran so low that panning was difficult, many prospectors trekked out to "civilization." A few, however, decided to improve their cabins and stay for the winter. Supplies were ordered, but the pack trains dispatched to deliver them were turned back by early heavy snowstorms. Those left in Fisherville found scant game and few fish to augment their foodstuffs. Spring of 1865 found the crew at the Wild Horse in a very emaciated state. Even so, some of them had spent the winter digging the Victoria Ditch, which was almost five miles of waterway—five feet deep and five feet wide, with wooden flumes on trestles over gullies. Water flowed; using a tiny fraction of the ditch's stream, prospectors were able to test hillside claims with their gold pans. The bench containing the shack town of Fisherville proved very productive. A few cabins were carefully moved, and some were demolished or torched, as yard by yard the area was dug up and worked with a rocker or a pan. Only the government office was left untouched.

The year of 1865 was an even busier year than when the first rush up the Wild Horse took place. The initial simple resolutions on "bank to bank" and "bench claims" had served well, but now the miners studied the Gold Fields Act to adapt to co-operative ownership.

> "Two discoverers shall be entitled to a claim double the established size."
>
> or
>
> "If the party consists of three men, they shall collectively be entitled to five claims of the established size."
>
> or
>
> "If of four or more men, such a party shall be entitled to a claim and a half per man."[2]

Further, all old-timers knew that to keep their claims valid they had to work on the property every day except Sundays, and such other holidays as the gold commissioner thought fit to proclaim. If a claim remained unworked by the registered holder for the space of 72 hours, unless in case of sickness or unless further extension was granted by the gold commissioner before the expiry of the 72 hours, it could be deemed abandoned and open to occupation by any free miner.[3]

Peter O'Reilly of Victoria was appointed gold commissioner at Fisherville for 1865. This feisty Irishman grumbled about the drafty building—thrown up by Haynes just a year earlier—and the grubby office designed for the gold commissioner and constable. At the first Sunday meeting of miners, O'Reilly jumped onto a bench under a flagpole flying the Union Jack. He loudly declared, "Boys, I'm here to keep order and to administer the law. Those that don't want law and order can git out, but those who stay with the camp, remember what side of the line the camp is on. If there is a shooting in Kootenay, there will be a hanging in the Kootenay!"[4]

American miners respected "Judge" O'Reilly, but they complained about the various tariffs collected. They arranged to celebrate the Fourth of July holiday. The Stars and Stripes was flown, and there were races, a parade, speeches, and lots of noise, but *no shooting*.

The camp at Wild Horse was below an almost naked hillside. Wood had been cut to create a few log buildings—some with neatly peeled logs and some with insect-inviting unpeeled logs—or to make frames for tents or lean-tos covered with branches. All dead trees had been used for firewood.

A few camp followers arrived in the district. They sized up the situation and built their houses halfway between the ferry and Fisherville. Madams with nicknames such as Axe Handle Bertha, Gunpowder Sue, Wildcat Jenny, and Madam Kalispell set up a cluster of brothels, which was soon dubbed Toneyville.

Early in 1865 Governor Seymour commissioned Edgar Dewdney to create a pack trail across the province: It must stay north of the 49th parallel, be four feet wide, less than 12 percent grade if possible, and be completed no later than September. Between 1858 and 1860 surveyors had marked the 49th parallel, which was agreed upon in 1846 as the dividing boundary between American and British territory. The Hudson's Bay Company had maintained posts in Oregon Territory until the gold rush, when it moved them north. About this time the earliest customs posts were opened on the U.S. side of the border, staffed by officers who charged duty on any goods passing through their territory. Whenever the earliest pack trains en route to Wild Horse from New Westminster—following existing trails—travelled a few yards or miles south of the border, these officers would charge them duty.

Dewdney surveyed a route and assigned various crews to sections of the road. He made William Fernie the foreman of a crew of 65 workers, who improved the trail from Wild Horse to Moyie and extended it past Goat River to the present site of Wyndell. From there they installed a ferry—used only during high water—to David McLoughlin's Hudson's Bay Company post, then cleared a good trail over the summit to Fort Shepherd on the Columbia River near present-day Trail. West of Shepherd the work party consisted of mainly Chinese workers, who opened a trail to Christina Lake.

The most difficult section on the whole route was the flooded flats below Kootenay Lake. It was accessed over soggy swampland that had to be filled with logs in "corduroy" fashion. Dewdney arrived at Wild Horse and was paid $2,500 in gold from Peter O'Reilly's summer collection of dues. Dewdney then travelled west, accompanied only by his Indian guide. During his third day on the trail Dewdney had to carefully pick his way across the Creston flats before starting up the trail beside Summit Creek. On that section he "met Sir Matthew Baillie Begbie en route to Wild Horse to hold his first court at that place. I advised Sir Matthew that the corduroy had not yet been laid and suggested it would be better for me to return and pilot him over the bad places. He jumped at this at once and asked me to camp with him that evening. The only difficulty was the gold dust for I didn't want to be packing it backward and forward on the trail."[5]

Dewdney and the judge's registrar went a couple of hundred feet off the main trail and cached the gold dust in a large buckskin purse down a hollow stump. They blazed the side trail slightly. The next day they got Sir Matthew and his pack train of fourteen animals safely over the soft road. Dewdney and his escorting Colville Indian, Peter, retraced their steps out to the hiding place. Dewdney reached in for the purse and could not feel it! In a cold sweat he unpacked an axe and chopped away a portion of the stump. The inside of the stump was so rotten that the weight of the gold had caused the bag to sink beyond his arm's reach. After a little work he was able to feel the bag and pull it out. He "returned to Fort Shepherd without delay and quickly deposited [his] treasure in the Hudson's Bay Company."[6]

Begbie went up the Wild Horse to conduct trials. Some sessions were managed inside the small government office, but when there were several witnesses, court was convened outdoors. Most of the cases regarded claim jumping, and Begbie insisted on walking the disputed area before handing down the ruling.

One such challenge laid before Judge Begbie was between Shirt Collar Bill and Scotty. Bill marked the boundary of his claim with a huge driftwood log over 100 feet long. After an exceptionally heavy rain, high water had moved the log downstream to Scotty's claim. Shirt Collar Bill went to work the ground, which proved richer than his upper claim. Scotty

F.S. 5 - 444

Old Chinese cabins on Wild Horse Creek. The large rocks in the foreground indicate that adjacent dirt had been dug and screened for gold.

was furious. Bill argued, "Doesn't everyone know that log marks the boundary of my claim?"

Scotty purchased all the gunpowder available locally, laid it under the log, and blew the offending marker into small pieces. Begbie suppressed a smile upon hearing the case, surveyed the claims, and gave his decision. The lower claim was totally Scotty's, but Scotty was to find another log to be used as Shirt Collar Bill's boundary marker.

The influx of miners to Wild Horse Creek dwindled each subsequent season. In 1867 Perry Creek was deemed the most promising stream to work, and the impatient Europeans and Americans left their claims on the Wild Horse. Chinese miners quietly acquired much of the Wild Horse, and soon Fisherville became a Chinatown. The district settled into a somnolent quiet for almost twenty years. There were no more instant towns. Pack trails were widened to wagon roads whenever it could be done easily, but the sections were not joined to make a recognizable, continuous road from Golden until 1892.

Chapter 3

Early Settlers in the District (1864–1880)

Prospectors came to the creeks and rivers each spring and went out in the fall. The Kootenay Indians roamed the wide trench and undertook their seasonal buffalo hunts east of the Rockies. But near and far changes were happening that slowly influenced life in the southeast corner of British Columbia.

During the Wild Horse gold rush British rule over the area was administered from New Westminster. By 1868 Victoria claimed the honours as the capital city. The infant colonial government negotiated with the eastern provinces, changing its status from that of a British colony to a province of the Dominion of Canada on condition that the West Coast be linked to the east by a transcontinental railway. Once the last spike was driven in November 1885, passengers and freight reached Golden at the north end of Columbia Valley with reasonable regularity from then on. To the east the prairies still bore the name of North-West Territories; the provinces of Alberta and Saskatchewan weren't created until 1905.

South of the newly accepted boundary of the 49th parallel, British Columbia faced Oregon Territory and Montana Territory. In 1883 the Americans laid the Northern Pacific Railway through those territories, and in 1889 Montana and Washington achieved state status. Idaho was similarly recognized in 1890.

The Canadian Pacific Railway in Canada and the Northern Pacific Railway in the U.S. were connected to the southeast of B.C. by waterways and trails, then roads and spur railroads.

Fort Steele was approximately in the centre of the evolving East Kootenay. The settlement slowly grew, but over two decades passed before it became the business and social hub of the area. This growth began with the earliest settlers, who set down roots and helped open up the district.

Dave Griffiths

Dave Griffiths came to the Wild Horse area in 1864 and called his hillside cabin home for the rest of his life. He struck it lucky with his earliest claim. There were years when he worked with partners and each netted between $1,000 and $2,000 a week. Dave bragged about spending large amounts each weekend in "town," playing poker or pool or perhaps visiting Toneyville. He ran a small store of miners' supplies, selling everything from tea and tobacco to rubber boots and axe handles. His home cabin stood beside Victoria Ditch, about a mile from Fisherville. Griffiths kept Victoria Ditch operational to supply water for his home and garden. The hillside nearby was logged for firewood and minor building projects.

Griffiths brought in some seedling apple trees that he carefully planted and watered until they were well established. For the first three growing years each tree needed a daily bucket of water, dipped out of Victoria Ditch and carried uphill. Four of those trees are still producing. Historical Society members have pruned these trees periodically. The fruit is a prime target for bears.

The monotony of bachelor life moved Griffiths to go south to court and marry a nice lady. Mrs. Griffiths came to Wild Horse in 1884 and spent the rest of her days as helpmate to this pioneer prospector, storekeeper, and local legend.

Mrs. Griffiths was proficient with her own axe or hatchet. She split blocks of wood into kindling, or gathered dead branches in a large basket to serve as fire starter. Griffiths built a fireplace and chimney with flat rocks and mud, which still stands today. This fireplace was Mrs. Griffiths' cooking fire until the pack trains were able to bring in a cast-iron stove that weighed about 250 pounds. The cost of the stove was less than the freight charges, but Griffiths had his hidden poke of gold dust from which to make the payments.

The predominantly male population welcomed Mrs. Griffiths. She became known for her hospitality, which included serving some baked goody or pie. Baking, as she had known it, included eggs, but to have eggs, one needed chickens. Her husband patiently constructed a pen out of slim poles, with an adjacent henhouse. He grumbled at the cost of importing chicken feed, but enjoyed the tasty treats his wife could now produce. The fencing protected the chickens from large predators such as coyotes, but one dark night there was a major cackling and clucking in the henhouse. Griffiths lit a lantern to go out to investigate. When he entered the henhouse, he witnessed a weasel sucking the blood from the fattest hen. The weasel retreated as he advanced; however, it managed to raid again, breaking and eating one or two eggs. Finally Griffiths discovered the hole through which the invader had entered, set a trap, and caught the bright-eyed thief. The hens settled down to their domestic egg production again.

Griffiths watched "his" creek for almost 50 years. He was ready to buy claims from miners quitting the creek, be they white or Chinese, but he was unwilling to sell goods from his store or water from his ditch to the Chinese. He observed the success of early groups using hydraulic monitors or "giants," and eventually invested in this "newfangled" and expensive equipment for his own claims.

Griffiths was a favourite visitor to Fort Steele when it became a bustling community. One year the Mining Association sponsored him to represent it at the Spokane Exhibition— necessitating him buying a new suit for his trip.

Michael Phillipps

The Hudson's Bay Company (HBC) maintained a presence during the 1864 gold rush. John Linklater of Kootenai Post at Tobacco Plains sent John Campbell to Wild Horse Creek with as many trade goods as he could spare. During the summer of 1864 Linklater took leave to go home to Scotland to seek a bride, and Michael Phillipps replaced him at Kootenai Post, moving north the following season. The HBC post, just south of the new border, closed as part of the negotiated retreat from the U.S.

In 1866 Phillipps married Rowen (Rowena), daughter of Chief David of the Tobacco Plains band. Phillipps was astute

F.S. 5 - 62

A group of pioneers was assembled for this picture in 1890. Back row, left to right: William Fernie, C.M. Edwards, Lemual Dole, Captain E.C. Parker, T.T. McVittie, J.E. Humphreys, William McCord. Front row: F. Freeman, F.P. Norbury, O.G. Dennis with Hazel Galbraith, and Michael Phillipps.

enough to build a store to sell HBC goods at Perry Creek when that creek became the busiest prospecting site in the district. He sent a suggestion to HBC headquarters in London, England, that 160 acres at Tobacco Plains be purchased to re-establish Kootenai Post north of the border. He pointed out that it would serve prospectors coming north each spring, as well as reaching the Indians of Kootenay Lake and Tobacco Plains. Many months later, the official answer came: The company did not wish to acquire land, but perhaps Phillipps would pre-empt the property in his own name.

So in 1869 Michael Phillipps and his family took up 320 acres half a mile north of the monument indicating the new Canada–U.S. border at Tobacco Plains. He paid for the supplies left in the old Kootenai Post and set up a small trading post on his new homestead.

In 1884, when Peter O'Reilly arrived to assign reservation lands to each band, Michael Phillipps was recruited as translator. Chief David, his father-in-law, originally asked for the whole continent for Indian peoples. Patiently explaining that that was impossible, Phillipps urged David to think in terms of his own band. Logically, David named a southern boundary in the U.S., with a northern boundary at the loop of the Columbia River. When the 1846 international boundary decision was explained to Chief David, he burst out, "White man say that that line runs right through the middle of my house. Why should you, without asking me or considering me, divide my property and also divide my children?" O'Reilly left Tobacco Plains early the next day without further consultation. He sent in surveyors shortly thereafter. As it happened, all of the residents were away at a food-gathering camp, and the survey laid out very poor ground. Chief David and his councillors criticized Michael Phillipps for failing to press for a better settlement.

Phillipps received newspapers in the mail that came in once a month. The November 1885 papers headlined the completion of the Canadian Pacific Railway. Reading this news, he envisioned regular passenger trains moving both ways across the continent, so he planned to visit his family in England. It took him four days' travel to reach Golden on the rail line. There, on December 19, he caught the last eastbound train of the winter. Snowslides had already closed Rogers Pass to the west. The train was crowded with railway employees who had been laid off for the winter. It proceeded with fits and starts. Passengers spent the night of December 22 in Winnipeg and hoped to be in Montreal before New Year's Day. They spent an exceptionally cold Christmas Day in White River; then, on January 3, they started walking. After a trek of 104 miles and six days, they reached a derailed engine and railway snowplow; eventually they found a train that took them to Portland, Maine, where they sailed on January 15. It took another twelve days to cross the Atlantic Ocean.

Phillipps visited his parents and other relatives, enjoying civilization and old-fashioned hospitality. He did, however, resist all suggestions that he might like to marry one or another of the English girls they were prepared to arrange for him to meet. He firmly declared loyalty to Rowena, who waited for him back in the Kootenays.

When Phillipps returned home he wrote a detailed letter to railway authorities and politicians. He decried the foolishness of putting the line through the avalanche-plagued Rogers Pass when—with very few extra miles—the route could have gone beside the Columbia River, with an easy grade and river transportation when maintenance was needed.

His property on Tobacco Plains was producing good crops of oats and vegetables. In January 1887, Inspector Herchmer was in the district to evaluate the need for establishing a Mounted Police post. He was convinced that their presence was justified, and arranged—wherever possible—to buy the post's supplies locally. He ordered 14,000 pounds of potatoes from Michael Phillipps and 100,000 pounds of oats from other growers.

Michael Phillipps' life became even more involved in 1887, when he was appointed as a magistrate, which meant he would have to sit and rule on cases of theft, assault, drunk and disorderly conduct, disputes over property lines, or other minor offences. He would have to study an official handbook to learn the suggested procedures and punishments. Next he was summoned to Kootenay Ferry to confer with Dr. Israel Powell of the Indian Affairs Department. Phillipps became the Indian agent for the Kootenays. This entailed visiting each of the five reserves to assist their transition to an agricultural society, to assess their health and well-being, and, of course, to write a detailed annual report for Victoria and Ottawa. At this first meeting with Dr. Powell, he promised to build a dwelling and Indian office at "Kootenay" so that he would be centrally located for the bands he was being asked to oversee.

In September of that same year he welcomed a young Englishman, Frederick Paget Norbury, referred by his sister to become his protegé. Norbury's story is told later in this chapter, and is woven throughout Fort Steele's history.

The Galbraiths

John Galbraith had tasted the rigours of the gold fields during the California gold rush. He followed rumours of new finds, and was in Walla Walla when the Finlay brothers boasted of their great discoveries north of the new boundary line between American and British territory. He joined Jack Fisher's team, which started north on March 19, 1864. Bob Dore's small party was ahead of them, breaking trail wherever snow lay on their route. When they reached the bank of the Kootenay River, Jack Fisher's party scouted for a possible ford. They managed to cross because the water level was low. They tested Stud Horse Creek, were convinced this was a great find, then made their way upstream, able to walk through the canyon due to low water. John Galbraith helped the team set up tents and a supply cabin, then he assembled the pack horses, leading them to the broad plateau beside the mouth of "their" creek, high above the Kootenay River. He knew his home cabin would be safe and dry when he could build on that plateau. He carefully surveyed the riverbanks and estimated the amount of cable that would be needed to establish a ferry. Then he headed south with the pack train.

At Walla Walla he recruited packers, bought a few more mules and horses, and purchased supplies. The weight of the cable was shared between four horses, each with a coil. Pulleys, hardware, and food supplies were also purchased and transported north. Within a few weeks a raft was built, connected to the cables, and Galbraith's ferry was in business.

Galbraith had helpers to erect a log building above the road from the ferry, and later to build his store. He brought in an anvil and farrier's tools. Among his earliest customers who needed their horses shod were Colonial Secretary Birch and Registrar Arthur Bushby. Bushby's diary notes, "Galbraith was awfully nice to us because he wants us to grant him a permit for his ferry." Even at this spot so remote from the coast, Galbraith was assessed $500 for a charter for the ferry.

John Galbraith made frequent trips south of the border. In 1869 he married Sarah Larue and brought her back to Galbraith's Ferry. As a bride and the only white woman in the district, Sarah had to do many chores, learn her husband's ways of bargaining and bookkeeping, and learn the rudiments of the Ktunaxa language.

John's brother James arrived in the district shortly after Sarah. He assumed major responsibility for operating the ferry. An addition to the ferry office was made in a different style to the original.

Shortly after James settled here, Catherine (Galbraith) Clark arrived with her husband and infant son. Charles Clark became postmaster at the Kootenay Post Office.

A younger brother, Robert Leslie Thomas Galbraith, arrived and soon began to make his mark on the district. Robert worked

F.S. 8 - 532

Robert Leslie Thomas Galbraith, seated, is shown here with his sister, Maria Bert Clark, and her husband, James Clark. Mrs. Clark became a school monitor when the school expanded to two rooms.

with brother John's pack train to familiarize himself with local circumstances, then bought his own string of animals. Robert Galbraith's pack train was employed by Walter Moberly, surveying for the Canadian Pacific Railway route in 1871 near present-day Golden. Robert also won a contract to pack in supplies for the crew slashing the route into Rogers Pass.

The brothers both memorized the trail from Galbraith's Ferry to Walla Walla (or Wallula, on the Columbia River). They had to know where good feed could be found for their horses, and arrange to camp at these places approximately twenty miles apart—a suitable day's travel for man and beast. One horse in each string dominated and insisted on being leader. Other horses chose their place in line, and each persisted in staying in the same order when the train moved again. If, for example, a packer inadvertently put the fifth horse in front of the fourth horse, there would be jostling until positions were rearranged. On a narrow trail the "impostor" might be pushed down a bank to allow Number Four into her rightful position. Then the packer would have to repack the shifted load on Number Five—and no doubt would memorize the existing line-up for the rest of the trip.

Robert Galbraith was an alert, eager businessman. He anticipated the needs of future newcomers and was in a position to invest in property, trade goods, or equipment. He observed the way incoming prospectors handled their own horses, and he hired the ablest handlers and packers for his own pack train.

The brothers acquired the Hudson's Bay Company stores at Perry Creek and on the Wild Horse. Michael Phillipps planned to pre-empt 100 acres close to Galbraith's Ferry. Upon learning of his plans, the Galbraiths paid cash for the property, making Phillipps alter his settlement plans and move to Tobacco Plains.

John and Sarah Galbraith moved to Victoria early in 1886. Robert was left to greet the North West Mounted Police when they came into the district. By that time James Galbraith had moved to Idaho, but another Galbraith sister, Maria, with her husband James Clark, arrived at The Ferry.

Galbraith's Ferry never had a post office of that name, despite the dominant family presence. Early documents refer to Kootenay, or Kootenay Ferry, or The Ferry, and within weeks of the arrival of the Mounted Police troop, the locals dubbed the locale "Fort Steele." Kootenay Post Office changed its name to Fort Steele in September 1888.

When John Galbraith passed away, Sarah opted to return to Fort Steele with their adopted daughter, Hazel. She co-operated with Robert in some business ventures, but was affluent enough to winter in warmer climes.

The Mathers

The Mathers were a well-known pioneer couple in the early years of the district. Robert and Mary Jane were both children of sea captains. They met in Victoria in the fall of 1881 and were married in Port Townsend in January of 1882 at the home of her parents, James and Janet Delgardno. Robert assembled a pack train of supplies and brought his bride to the East Kootenay, where he had established a miners' supply store at Galbraith's Ferry.

Robert pre-empted 1,000 acres at Cherry Creek, where he pastured a herd of Scottish long-haired cattle. These cattle were a gift from his father, who delivered them to Hope on the Fraser River. Robert hired some Kootenay Indians to then drive them over the Dewdney Trail; they brought the animals through without losing a single one.

The Cherry Creek property was surveyed to become Dalgardno City, but there were no takers for lots there.

Robert erected a sawmill and was relatively successful with it. Some of his lumber was used to construct a hotel at Fort Steele—the Dalgardno. For a short time the Mather family homesteaded at Cherry Creek, leasing out the hotel. The family home was destroyed by fire, so they moved back to Fort Steele and became prominent participants in the growth and activities of the bustling town.

Mary Jane went out to Winnipeg at the time the Mounties were moving south from Golden. Her eldest child, Mabel, was born in Winnipeg. Upon their return almost three months later, Mary Jane was met at the train in Golden by an Indian "nanny," who carried baby Mabel home in a papoose carrier. Mary Jane went to Port Townsend to have her next two children. Again, the new babies came back to Fort Steele in an Indian papoose pack.[7]

Robert Mather also ran a pack train. He kept his horses working through the winter, a time when Galbraith chose to pasture his horses for their well-being and safety.

The Mathers were very sympathetic to the Chinese and co-operated with them in every possible way. Their pro-Asian stance annoyed Dave Griffiths tremendously, but it didn't stop him from taking a room in Mather's hotel when he was in town overnight.

Thomas Thane McVittie

Thomas Thane McVittie was born in Barrie, Ontario, in 1855, educated in Upper Canada College, and came to British Columbia in 1879. In 1888 he was made a justice of the peace (JP), and served longer in that role than any JP in the province.

Tom McVittie was one of the earliest surveyors in the East Kootenay. He built a log cabin on what would become Riverside

Avenue in Galbraith's Ferry. McVittie laid out numerous mine sites, mapped the district, and surveyed every townsite *except* Cranbrook.

His two brothers, Archie and Harry, also lived and worked in Fort Steele. Tom was a favourite neighbour of Robert Galbraith. The name McVittie appears frequently in the story of Fort Steele.

J. E. Humphreys

This resident lived on Wolf Creek Road at Wasa. He built a stopping house with one new building in 1886 and built a second house in June 1888. Humphreys had a herd of cattle that was put up near Premier Lake for spring grazing, Bummer's Flats for the summer, and near his home during the winter. His diary indicates that he had a succession of helpers who assisted with ploughing, fencing, irrigating, driving cattle, and cutting hay. His place was called "The Grange," and was not only an overnight stop for passengers on the stage, but also a pleasant retreat for the elite of Fort Steele and Cranbrook.

Humphreys suffered extensive losses to his herd of cattle due to harsh weather in the winter of 1889–90. There was about two feet of snow with a heavy crust on it. The only available feed was brush willow in the lower meadow, but Humphreys and his helpers were able to get hay to the upper meadow. Fred Aylmer assumed responsibility for the place, and, with a co-worker called French, carried on for over a year as Humphreys visited family in England.

Captain Parker

Edwin Parker retired from the British army at age 33 and bought 300 acres of land at Fish Lakes, eight miles inland from the Kootenay River. He soon became known as a good host and hunting guide. He participated in road-clearing and bridge-building projects nearby to earn a bit of money. Grooming and managing the ranch proceeded at a much faster pace when Frederick Norbury joined Parker. Even so, it took a year to complete fencing of the property. They raised chickens, hogs, and cattle.

On Sundays, Parker and Norbury would go fishing or hunting, or into Fort Steele "to get a good square meal," presumably at the hotel dining room.

Frederick Paget Norbury[8]

Frederick Norbury came to the Fort Steele area as a young remittance man. Over the years he matured, found intermittent employment, and became independent. He was a well-respected community leader, and his absence was surely felt when he returned to England to handle family affairs in 1899.

He arrived in Golden on September 4, 1887, and travelled south up the Columbia River on the *Duchess*. The "ugly duckling" of a sternwheeler had been pumped out, refloated, and repaired after an accident in July. Captain Armstrong navigated the *Duchess* safely to Windermere, where passengers boarded the stage—an open passenger wagon—for the rest of the journey to Kootenay Ferry. There, Norbury met Michael Phillipps, who had numerous duties for him. They left Wild Horse Creek on Saturday, October 1 around one o'clock. and travelled about 22 miles before making camp. With horses to saddle and pack, they were up at dawn and on the trail at 7 a.m. Norbury admitted he was "frightfully stiff from sitting in the same position" until 5 p.m. that evening.

The new arrival was put to work digging potatoes at Phillipps' ranch. He admitted that his hands were soft and his wind a bit short, but he kept at it. Three weeks later he accompanied Phillipps to deliver these potatoes to the Mounted Police. Phillipps brought his middle son to do the cooking. The three travellers took three days to travel the 65 miles from Tobacco Plains to Kootenay Ferry.

Phillipps brought an Indian lodge for use on the trails. Norbury describes it as follows.

> [It is] a little bigger than an ordinary Bell tent. It is put up with twelve poles inside. In the middle of the tent you have your fire so you can do your cooking without getting out into the cold. It is not in the least smoky inside. The draft of the chimney is regulated by the projecting ears, which you can move with the two poles

outside. These ears are always kept facing in the opposite direction of the wind. Before you go to bed you arrange some chips and wood underneath your blanket, and without getting out of bed you can light the fire so that by the time you want to get up there is a good fire going.[8]

By November 1887 the potato digging was completed, and Phillipps had no further employment for the newcomer. Norbury wrote, "P. says the ranch seven miles north of here is open for me to take if I like it." Phillipps had staked off 320 acres (one mile by one-half mile) for his oldest son. The son declined to follow up on the pre-emption, so Norbury decided to take it, writing about the details of his obligation to his father: "The price is $1 per acre payable over a four year period, started by filling out a form stating that you have taken up the land, are a British subject, and paying a registration fee of $2."

In this letter, Norbury also stated that he had hired John Campbell to build a cabin. (Both men were living in the guesthouse on the Phillipps ranch.) He noted that no registration could be made until January 1888 because no government official would be in eastern British Columbia until then.

Norbury prepared a list of anticipated expenses in Canadian dollars, further defining his request with the instructions: "Divide dollars by 5 to get pounds sterling."

Putting up cabin	$ 60
Plough	30
Harness	30
2 work horses	130
Riding horse	60
Saddle & Bridle	35
2 axes, spade, scythe, saw, hammer, chisel, auger	25
Cooking & eating utensils	15
Dutch oven	5
Sundries	20
Total	**$410**

He had moved into a cabin, fenced a few acres, and started a small garden and field of oats when he had to take time off to travel to Golden to meet his younger brother, Billy.

Bill resented his parents' decision to send him to work with Frederick (who was known as "Tommy"). He learned how to make good bread, but that seemed to be his only accomplishment in pioneering. He deliberately tortured Tommy's favourite horse. He said he had mended a fence around the oat field but made absolutely no effort to do so. (The oats were eaten.) He deliberately spilled food all over the cabin to make it smell and annoy his brother. After one major argument Tommy gave Bill ten dollars and told him to leave and get work elsewhere. Bill went to Fort Steele, played billiards, drank, and "loafed for a fortnight," charging everything in his brother's good name.

When summoned to Fort Steele, Norbury met with his younger brother—who seemed duly contrite—and paid the $25 debt, negotiating a promise from Bill for better behaviour. The brothers went back to Tobacco Plains. For a few days Bill did indeed perform housekeeping or outside duties cheerfully and efficiently; however, whenever Tommy was away for two or three days at a time, Billy would do nothing and his brother would always came back to a filthy house. On July 3 when Norbury went north on an errand, Bill vandalized their home; he took every bit of money ($26), a horse worth $60, a saddle worth $14, a $7 blanket, and left. Detective work soon proved that Bill went through the Crow's Nest Pass[9], sold the horse to a farmer at Pincher Creek, and was seen walking to Fort Macleod. Two North West Mounted Policemen had talked to him. They said it was his intention to try to enlist in the police force, but Major Steele was unlikely to accept him without consulting his nominal guardian.

In late July a rancher in Pincher Creek, E.M. Wilmot, notified Norbury that Bill was staying with him. The rancher also wrote to the brothers' mother in England, politely saying, "It is a great pity he couldn't have stayed in B.C. but if his brother couldn't make any use of him, I am sure no one else would." Norbury thanked Wilmot, and sent enough money so that Billy could return to England via the colonist car and steerage rate with $15 to cover his meals en route.

Reality fast tempered the optimism of this novice rancher. The oats and garden grew very well during the summer of 1889. His 24 head of cattle were thriving. Norbury had occasional jobs on a steamboat, or packing supplies for a survey party. Just before harvest time, his cattle broke down the fence. "My oats and ricks gone, and every potato, onion, carrot and cabbage eaten. I had a fine crop of onions and expected to sell them at $7 per 100 wt."

Therefore, in October, Tommy summarized philosophically:

Three things this year has taught me:
1. That if I worked a lifetime I could never make this a good ranch because the land is not here. If I cleared every inch of good land I could not get more than 15 arable acres. I am also hemmed in by Indian Reservation.
2. That a man by himself can not do more than one thing at a time. If he intends ranching, his individual attention must be given to it. If he intends running a steamboat, he must give up his ranch.
3. One man by himself can not make ranching a success.[8]

So he sold his Tobacco Plains property to Phillipps for four head of cattle and a yearling filly. He then made a fresh start by buying half of Fairfield Ranch and going into partnership with Captain Parker.

Chapter 4

Grohman and His Canal Dream (1882-1890)

A frequent visitor to Fort Steele was William Adolph Baillie-Grohman, whose name is remembered in both East and West Kootenay. He was born in 1851 to British aristocracy. His mother was a cousin of the Duke of Wellington. His paternal grandfather, a noted botanist, had an estate in Austria. He spent his formative years with private tutors, alternating between the family homes in the Tyrolean Alps and Tipperary, Ireland. He reputedly shot his first stag at the age of nine. He was well versed in the art of mountaineering. This early love of sport brought him across the Atlantic in 1878 to visit the hunting grounds of North America in the Rocky Mountains of Wyoming and Idaho. In 1882 he came to the Kootenays, ostensibly to hunt mountain goat. He came to Sandpoint by train, and hiked over the Pack River Pass to Bonner's Ferry. There he hired two Kootenay Indians to paddle him onto Kootenay Lake.[10]

While travelling down the slow-moving Kootenay River Baillie-Grohman became intrigued by the potential of the rich alluvial soil on what we now call the Creston Flats. He was informed that this bottom land was flooded each year from early June to mid-July. He spent the rest of the summer exploring Kootenay Lake and the Kootenay River.

Baillie-Grohman envisioned reclaiming the flood plains of the Creston Flats for agriculture by diverting the Kootenay River into Columbia Lake at what is now called Canal Flats, and widening the outlet of Kootenay Lake just below present-day Nelson. He arranged to have a home built at McGillivray's Portage at the south end of Columbia Lake. (His own activities changed the name of that isthmus of land to Canal Flats.) And, being worldly wise, with background experience gained while working briefly in a lawyer's office, Baillie-Grohman applied to the British Columbia government for permission to start work on his proposed projects.

In the summer of 1883 the chief commissioner of lands and works dispatched A.S. Farwell to the Kootenays to evaluate the situation. (He was also given a second task to do while in the district: The Department of Indian Affairs asked him to take a census of the Indians and their horses and cattle.) Accompanying him was Mr. G.M. Sproat. Farwell and Sproat took this trip before the Canadian Pacific Railway was operating, so they travelled on the Northern Pacific Railway from Portland, Oregon, to Sandpoint, Idaho Territory. On July 19 W.A. Baillie-Grohman, who had promised to provide transportation, met them at Sandpoint. They travelled through Pack River Pass to Bonner's Ferry. The timber en route was described by Montanans as "lush," but Farwell sneered that no logger from Burrard Inlet or Vancouver Island would waste time setting up a camp there. They carefully noted the river's flow and depth, the few elevated "islands," and the flow into the main lake. Farwell observed that the Kootenay River was navigable from Bonner's Ferry to the boundary (50 miles) and to Kootenay Lake (30 miles) further on.

Baillie-Grohman next took them down to the outlet of Kootenay Lake (down what now is called the West Arm). Visibility was severely impeded by smoke from a forest fire. Grohman's boat took them through the narrows below present-day Nelson, and down to the first falls in the series of drops between Kootenay Lake and present-day Castlegar, where the Kootenay River merges with the Columbia River.

Baillie-Grohman's proposal to dredge the narrows and blast any protruding rocks would be possible, but very expensive. Yet, they agreed, removing 300,000 cubic yards of gravel plus a few rocks *just might* lower the level of Kootenay Lake. Farwell and Sproat were then taken north to the Hot Springs (Ainsworth) and all the way to the Lardeau district, then down the east side of the lake to view the lead outcroppings at the Bluebell Mine.

The trio returned to McLoughlin's, which was now smoke free, and closely examined the valuable bottom lands of

Creston Flats, taking more measurements. Farwell philoso-phized that even if Kootenay Lake could be maintained at a lower level, the spring run-off from the Kootenay River would still flood these flats.

Then the three men went up the Goat River and along the Moyie Trail to Finlay Creek and then Columbia Lake. They observed that even in September the Kootenay River was "up to their horses' bellies" as they negotiated the ford when southbound. They discussed whether the whole flow of the Kootenay River, or just the flooding overflow, would be diverted into Upper Columbia Lake.

But what of the additional water in Columbia Lake? Would it flow down the Columbia River, submerging many riverfront flatlands? Would it raise the Columbia River enough to reach the newly laid railway line? Perhaps it would wash out proposed CPR railway bridges. Engineers of the CPR pressed the "Alert" button and waited.

Baillie-Grohman obtained a ten-year lease on 47,500 acres between the international boundary and Kootenay Lake. He hired a British engineer, who soon confirmed the feasibility of the whole scheme. Armed with the lease and the engineer's report, he returned to England, where he incorporated the Kootenay Syndicate Limited among his wealthy friends, with himself as managing director. With this promise of financial backing secured, he returned to Victoria and laid the full proposal before the provincial government. A concession of 73,000 acres in the Upper and Lower Kootenay for the purpose of reclamation and colonization was granted, dated September 7, 1885, on condition that the widening of the outlet of Kootenay Lake and the construction of a diversion canal be carried out.[11]

The success or failure of the entire project pivoted on one specific clause in the agreement of September 1885: "This agreement shall have no effect unless and until the Dominion of Canada shall authorize the diversion of the Upper Kootenay River." The final authority over inland waters belonged to the federal government as per the British North America Act of 1867.

When only a handful of settlers became justifiably worried about potential damages, they asked for "an environmental assessment." In March 1886 all 30 registered voters in the Upper Columbia Valley sent a petition to Ottawa and to

Victoria. They requested "suspension of works on the turning of the Kootenay River into the Columbia until a careful investigation of the consequences be made." The CPR voiced concerns to Ottawa. The federal government ordered the work stopped, and it voided the provincial concession.

Meanwhile, Baillie-Grohman protested the withdrawal of the concessions and requested financial remuneration for damages. The chief commissioner of lands and works in Victoria proposed that the Kootenay Syndicate Limited continue with its canal on the proviso that it be made a navigable canal fitted with a lock to accommodate the difference in elevation between the Kootenay River and Columbia Lake. Since the southern shore of Columbia Lake was a soggy slough that would be very expensive to clear for navigation, the provincial government agreed to do the work below the lock.

More delays ensued. The federal government agreed in August 1886 to permit the canal with a lock, but the provincial government stalled until December before permitting work to go ahead. Baillie-Grohman had a time limit of two years to complete the revised project. Work commenced in 1887. The Kootenay end of the canal was a large ditch 45 feet wide, 10 feet deep, and 6,700 feet long across the gravel isthmus. Heavy horses pulled scrapers along the bed of the canal. Chinese labourers removed the dirt, working rhythmically as a human conveyor belt, using side-dumping wheelbarrows.

Construction of the lock and floodgates was another matter. Some half-million feet of lumber were needed for the lock and pumphouses. A sawmill was ordered from Brantford, Ontario. In August 1887 it arrived by rail at Golden, but posed a challenge to move up the Columbia River. The SS *Duchess* had sunk. There was no road from Windermere to Canal Flats. Baillie-Grohman contracted Jack Hayes to arrange for the *Clive* to bring the machinery upriver, but Hayes was busy with NWMP freight. Finally, as the water level dropped late in the navigation season, it took 23 days to get the *Clive* and her cargo to Canal Flats.

The government specified the size of the lock as 100 feet long and 30 feet wide. When digging the lock, seepage water soon hit the site. Footings had to be much deeper, so steam pumps were brought in from the coast, further increasing the expense of the project.

During these activities in 1887, Baillie-Grohman went home to England to marry. He brought his wife to Canal Flats in good weather, but built her a home in Victoria, B.C., for other seasons. Mrs. Baillie-Grohman had their first child, a boy, in Victoria in 1888, and their second child, a girl, shortly after the official opening of the canal in July 1889.

There was some work done at the Grohman Narrows below Nelson. It achieved a small measure of control on the level of Kootenay Lake. Kootenay Syndicate Limited gradually dyked the Creston Flats between the years 1889 and 1890; then the concession was sold to the British Columbia and Alberta Exploration Company of London. Baillie-Grohman resigned as managing director in February 1891. Work continued on the Creston Flats until 1893. That same year, Baillie-Grohman divested himself of all property and interests in British Columbia and moved his family to Europe, taking his 23rd voyage on the Atlantic.

William Adolph Baillie-Grohman came to the Kootenays as a sportsman, but once there, he dreamed an ambitious dream and worked for eleven years attempting to change the face and fate of the area.

Chapter 5

Indian Affairs
(1874-1887)

In 1874 Father Leon Fouquet established the Roman Catholic Mission on the south bank of St. Mary's River, about seven miles from Galbraith's Ferry. This location was already the traditional winter campground for one band of the Upper Kootenay Indians. Soon the Kootenays built 50 log cabins adjacent to the mission building, which served as winter homes. Father Fouquet built a priest's house and a log church, where Mass was conducted at intervals.

The Kootenay people, who had moved from fishing grounds to berry-picking areas to hunting camps depending on the season, were apprehensive when the white settlers arrived. In turn, the new arrivals were uncertain about what to expect from their Kootenay neighbours. The newcomers put up homes and fences. Some of the white settlers made a point of learning the Kootenay language (Ktunaxa) so they could negotiate trades, work with Natives to guide or assist them, and to explain their own actions. John Galbraith purchased Joseph's Prairie from the Crown, assuring Chief Joseph, and later Joseph's son Isadore, that no fences would be erected and cattle from both communities could use the grazing area.

With reserves defined, Indian agencies were created in the late 1870s along the West Coast of the new province of British Columbia. South of the new Canada–U.S. boundary, the Flathead Reserve of 1.5 million acres and the Kalispell/Colville Reserve of 2 million acres had recently been defined. Chief Isadore and his followers anxiously awaited the arrival of a commissioner to allocate their lands. In July of 1883 A.S. Farwell was instructed to calculate the number of Indians and the size of their herds of cattle and horses so as to estimate Indian requirements in the locality.

Farwell later wrote that every white man in the Kootenay district "forcibly impressed on [him] the fact that the Indians are extremely dissatisfied with the unsettled state of their land affairs"[12] and would look on any government official with suspicion. Farwell travelled through the district, observing— but not approaching—the Indians, and gathering reports from old-timers. One particularly valuable informant was David McLoughlin, Esquire. McLoughlin had come to the area as a third-generation employee of the Hudson's Bay Company, doubling as a ferry operator on the Dewdney Trail just north of present-day Creston. McLoughlin now had a farm and a family 200 yards south of the boundary line. He knew the Lower Kootenay band intimately and had watched them attempt gardening and raising cattle. Their gardens were lost to floodwaters, and their cattle to gambling. The Lower Kootenays continued to live in teepees covered with reed mats or hides in summer and winter.

Farwell's estimate of the Kootenay tribe was 450 British Indians, 200 American Indians, and 150 who migrated south in order to collect annuities from the American government, but spent most of their time in British territory. The Upper Kootenay Indians had settlements at Tobacco Plains, Lower Columbia Lake, and St. Mary's Mission. Chief Isadore lived on the west bank of the Kootenay River, eight miles south of Galbraith's Ferry, where he wintered many horses and cattle.

The district was also home to the Kinbaskets of the Shuswap tribe that had settled on the east bank of the Columbia River, five miles below the outlet of Lower Columbia (now Windermere) Lake. They seemed to adapt to farming more readily than some of the others.

A former gold commissioner, Peter O'Reilly, in his new role as Indian reserve commissioner, left Victoria in 1884 for the East Kootenays. He travelled south first and then east from Portland, Oregon, on the Northern Pacific Railway to Sandpoint, Idaho. He made his way to Wild Horse Creek and asked to confer with Chief Isadore. Isadore and his council "made excessive demands," and the volunteer interpreter proved unable to facilitate communications, so the talks were briefly suspended.

O'Reilly then travelled to Tobacco Plains, 60 miles to the south. There he was able to secure long-time resident John Campbell as interpreter. Chief David of the Tobbacco Plains band made many objections and pointed to the generous settlement of lands and money given a few miles to the south. (This reserve was over a million acres and its American chief received an annual pension of $500.) David also complained that the Stoneys, Crees, and Blackfoot to the east of the Rockies were receiving seeds, farm implements, livestock, and more from the federal government of Canada. O'Reilly was at a loss to explain why Ottawa did not treat all tribes equitably.

Michael Phillipps, the only white landholder in Tobacco Plains, accompanied O'Reilly and Chief David on a ride throughout the district. Phillipps explained how the creek came out of the mountains but would disappear underground on the flat. The men observed that a flume could capture the water and transfer it to future gardens. Four acres were already being cultivated, but an adjacent twenty acres were deemed suitable for raising crops if some water could be brought to the area. Perhaps the Indian Affairs Department would help Chief David's people by building a flume?

On July 22, 1884, O'Reilly went back north to the Wild Horse Creek area to meet with Chief Isadore and his band. Isadore repeated his desire to have the whole valley from Boat Encampment (on the northern loop of the Columbia River) to the U.S. boundary on the south, and to the Rockies on the east, and Kootenay Lake on the west. Isadore seemed to understand the new political dividing line of the 49th parallel, but he refused to give a census of his people or the number of the group's stock. An appeal to Dave McLoughlin at Creston brought this old-timer over to assist with the talks. Isadore reluctantly gave a count of his people, his cattle, and their horses. After several days of frustrating verbal confrontation Isadore promised to accompany O'Reilly on a detailed examination of the land beside the St. Mary's River. The party rode for several days, criss-crossing the sparsely timbered hills, the gravel flats, and the hayfield that was under water each spring, observing grazing areas and already established gardens. At the mission, Father Fouquet had built a grist mill that turned local wheat into flour. There was a small church and the priests' own house. Father Fouquet had chosen this place because it was a traditional winter home to some of the Kootenay people. The presence of the good father inspired even more of the band to winter close to him. They learned the advantages of building log houses and abandoned their teepees during the winter.

The Number One Reserve fronted on the St. Mary's and the Kootenay Rivers; it contained 18,150 acres. Reserve Number Two at Tobacco Plains was 10,560 acres, and Reserve Number Three at Lower Columbia Lake was 8,320 acres. The Lower Kootenay Reserve near Creston was 1,600 acres, and the Shuswap Reserve 2,700 acres. O'Reilly ascertained that surveyors' markers were in place, with signs erected stating "Indian Reserve," where traffic was expected; then he returned to Victoria. No Indian agent was appointed. The Department of Indian Affairs did nothing further until 1887.

Meanwhile, Chief Isadore continued to set his cattle and horses to graze on Joseph's Prairie. This irritated Colonel James Baker, who could not communicate with the Kootenays; although his son, V. Hyde Baker, was trying to master the language.

Then Isadore challenged the lone provincial policeman for attempting to impose white man's justice on one of his band. Two American prospectors, travelling between Finlay Creek and Golden, had been killed in August 1884 near Brisco, at the crossing of Deadman's Creek. A suspect was Kapla, an Indian who travelled with another brave, Little Isadore, and a Kootenay lad named Baptise. Kapla was not seen at the mission or Galbraith's Ferry until March 1887. Constable Harry Anderson, a provincial policeman, arrested Kapla and held him in the rickety Wild Horse jail, awaiting arrival of a circuit judge appointed by Begbie. Chief Isadore, however, considered discipline his own prerogative, so on March 17 he rode up the Wild Horse with 25 of his best warriors and removed Kapla from the jail. He demanded that Anderson and Fred Aylmer (a surveyor and the other government representative there) leave the district. However, he promised to present Kapla at court whenever one should convene.

This second act of defiance against convention agitated Colonel Baker so much that he wrote to Ottawa, appealing for the North West Mounted Police to provide protection from the rebellious Indians.

Chapter 6

The Mounties Arrive (1887)

Colonel Baker claimed that he spoke for the whole district when he wrote to Ottawa in 1886, requesting assistance from the North West Mounted Police (NWMP). He cited the restlessness of his Native neighbours, and noted that there was a solitary British Columbia policeman covering the whole southeast corner of the new province of B.C.

Settlers in the East Kootenay had always felt apprehensive about the Indians, as the local bands were somewhat restless while waiting for their reservations to be laid out. After the division of the land in 1884, further tension occurred when Chief Isadore continued to turn his cattle out on Joseph's Prairie, which Colonel Baker now owned. John Galbraith had pre-empted Joseph's Prairie in 1882 and set up a small store at the south end, but he had assured the Kootenays' Chief Joseph that they could still run their cattle and horses on the rest of the flat land. This arrangement worked well until 1886, when Colonel Baker purchased Galbraith's spread and many adjoining acres. John Galbraith's health was failing, so he moved to Victoria to seek medical assistance, and passed away before the use of Joseph's Prairie could be settled.

In January 1887 Assistant Commissioner Colonel Herchmer visited the district and personally felt the tension. It was obvious that the single provincial policeman, responsible for the Rocky Mountain Trench from Brisco to Tobacco Plains, would be powerless in the face of organized Indian unrest. He recommended that the NWMP be sent to the area.

Herchmer's fear materialized shortly thereafter, in March, when Chief Isadore and his braves freed Kapla from the Wild

Horse jail. Isadore made it clear that if his man was guilty, punishment should be done within the tribe. He would not allow a member of his band to languish in a jail until a white judge came on circuit many weeks or even months in the future. Isadore also loudly proclaimed that no white man had ever been put in jail on suspicion that he had killed an Indian. And there had been a few dead Indians since white men came to Kootenay lands! Before the war party left with the released and happy Kapla, Isadore told Anderson and Aylmer to get out of the district.

Isadore told Robert Galbraith his story as the party passed through Galbraith's Ferry. Anderson and Aylmer hurried down to the small settlement, where they received scant sympathy. In fact, when Robert Galbraith got in touch with Colonel Baker and a few others, the white population concurred with Chief Isadore! They agreed that Anderson and Aylmer should leave the district as soon as possible, probably to avoid angering Isadore further.

The two went up to Golden, armed with a telegram to be sent from that railway community. The telegram, worded by Robert Galbraith, was an emphatic request for a troop of Mounties to come to the district to quell the Indian unrest. Colonel Herchmer returned in June. This time he checked possible sources of supplies for the NWMP troops. He was also advised that a camp might be set on Six Mile Creek, running through Bummer's Flat. It took several days' travel by riverboat, horseback, and stage for Colonel Herchmer to go from Golden to Kootenay, so he knew firsthand that the logistics of moving 75 men with their horses and supplies was formidable.

In the meantime, in June of 1887, the B.C. branch of Indian Affairs, also apprised of the restlessness, appointed a local settler as Indian agent. Indian Commissioner Dr. Israel W. Powell arrived in Kootenay (Galbraith's Ferry), and sent a message to Michael Phillipps at Tobacco Plains. Phillipps had lived among the Indians for over twenty years, speaking the language in his own household. Powell explained the duties of an Indian agent, urging Phillipps to accept the appointment. Phillipps thoughtfully noted that he would have to build a home and office at Kootenay to be readily accessible to those from the St. Mary's Reserve and still within reach of the other bands.

Commissioner Powell's report emphatically noted that additional farmland should be given to Chief Isadore, "even if it mean[t] buying a ranch from a white settler."[13] The North West Mounted Police would arrive before Isadore's complaints were settled.

Settlement of the Troops

The NWMP troops moved from Fort Macleod to near Calgary in several sections. Three remounts (horses) were transferred to "D" division from Calgary's "E" division. The train stopped at Calgary for the horses to be fed and the men to have dinner. The train delivered them to Golden at 10:30 a.m. on June 28. A camp was set up on the south bank of the Kicking Horse River, across from the small settlement near the railway tracks. They remained there, awaiting further supplies, and were joined by Inspector Wood, Sergeant-Major Lake, and Assistant Surgeon Aylen, who took medical charge of the division.

On July 5 Colonel Herchmer arrived in Golden on the steamer SS *Duchess*. He was travelling with Indian Commissioner Dr. Israel Powell and A.W. Vowell of the lands department. The SS *Duchess* was chartered at 75 cents per 100 pounds to move supplies on the Columbia River to the head of navigation on the Columbia just past the south end of Lake Windermere. Members of "D" troop, who had scant acquaintance with water transportation, loaded the freight on board with no thought for "trimming" the load. The *Duchess* left on the morning of July 6, but within a few miles she foundered and sank. The river ran yellow with oats and red with floating uniforms. Some troopers retrieved most of the cargo, but very little of it was useable even when dried out.

There was only one other river vessel at Golden. It was an awkward barge of a boat called *Clive*, owned by a scatter-brained fellow, J.C. Hayes. Sam Steele had to arrange, at one dollar per 100 pounds, to transport the supplies upriver. Hayes moved upriver behind schedule, delaying the planned supper hour at Hog Ranch at 5 p.m. to 10 p.m. The next day, the troop rode to Roger's Landing—this time taking rations for a full day. The *Clive* reached Roger's Landing at 8:30 a.m. the day after its expected arrival.

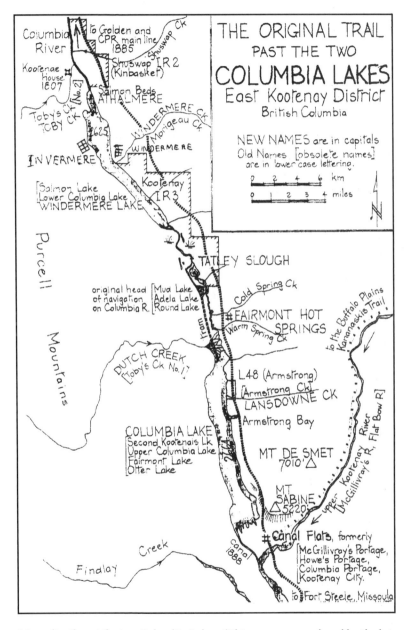

Map of trail past the two Columbia Lakes. (This map was produced by the late R.C. Harris, and is reproduced here courtesy of his wife, Rita.)

The third move took them to Lewis's place, probably near present-day Edgewater. Finally, on the morning of July 23, they arrived at the steamboat landing. Steele ordered Inspector Wood to return to Golden, "as it was evident that unless an officer was there to look after Hayes, there would be little chance of getting any work done by the steamer *Clive*."[15]

Other troubles befell the Mounties as they travelled to the Kootenays. On the morning after the *Duchess* sank, Division Sergeant-Major Lake shot himself in his tent because he was suffering a severe attack of neuralgia. By July 17 eight men were sick with fever and were left behind in Golden under the care of Staff Sergeants Fane and Mercer.

Once the *Clive* arrived at the steamboat landing, things began to improve. "Robert Galbraith was at the landing, ready with his pack train to take our baggage and supplies to Kootenay, as previously arranged by Colonel Herchmer. There was no further trouble as Mr. Galbraith was prompt and businesslike, and his pack animals in first class condition."[15]

The division reached Six Mile Creek above Bummer's Flats on July 30, 1887. Major Steele and his officers carefully examined the area and declared it unsuitable for several reasons: The ground was very uneven; the timber was too heavy for easy harvesting and building purposes; there was a much higher piece of ground across the creek, making the proposed camp vulnerable to attack; the flats below were flooded much of the year; and the creek supplying the site came through two swamps, making the surgeon condemn the water supply. Indeed, the suggested site was unhealthy.

Four Mile Creek was then explored, but no suitable spot was discovered. The next day Steele and Inspector Charles Huot rode to Fenwick's lower ranch, downstream from Galbraith's Ferry. There were objections to that locale, too, primarily because there was no wagon road connecting it to the Ferry.

Steele returned to the Ferry. He asked Robert Galbraith if he could look over his land for a suitable place. That evening it was arranged that the Mounties take ten acres on the high ground above the confluence of Wild Horse Creek and the Kootenay River. From a military point of view it was perfect, being inaccessible on two sides, and commanded the trails to Tobacco Plains, Moyie, and the Columbia Lakes. It was a central

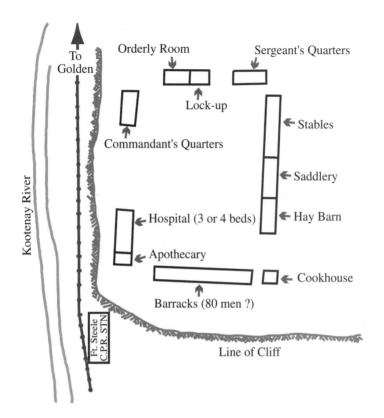

Sketch plan of old Fort Steele, drawn by Captain Stewart Dudley, M.C. on March 26, 1923, from information supplied by R.T.L. Galbraith.

point from which to communicate with the Indians or to shelter settlers in the event of an uprising. The water was clean, and feed for the horses was nearby. Camp was set up here on Sunday, July 31, 1887.

The men were assigned various duties. Some were sent to cut logs to build first a storehouse, then the barracks, stables, and smaller buildings. Some were sent on patrols, or to work bringing freight from Golden.

There was no connecting wagon road to Golden. As long as the waterways were open, freight came upriver from Golden by the reactivated *Duchess*—at 75 cents per 100 weight—to MacKay's Landing on Lake Windermere (Lower Columbia Lake). Then it went from MacKay's to Geary's on the north end of

Courtesy Edward Goodall Estate and Canadian Gallery Prints Ltd.

The officers' quarters at the NWMP barracks square, later used as the provincial police office. This original NWMP building is the only one to be moved to its new location when Fort Steele Heritage Town was created. Many of the other NWMP buildings were used to build the boarding school at St. Eugene Mission, soon after the NWMP troops left town.

Columbia Lake by wagon, then—at 50 cents per 100 weight—it went via small boats to Canal Flats. The trip from Canal Flats to "Kootenay Fort" was done by police pack train or wagons, Mather's pack train, and Galbraith's pack train. As winter set in, the steamer could not get south of Spillimacheen. Then the Upper Columbia Lake froze over, and Galbraith retired his horses for the winter. This meant the pack trains had to go from Spillimacheen to Kootenay Post on an old Indian trail that followed the east side of Columbia Lake. Major Steele growled that construction of a wagon road beside Columbia Lake had been stopped. "Petty jealousies caused the stoppage of work. One portion of the community wished the road on the west, the other on the east side—with the natural result that they have it on neither side as yet."[16]

Each stage of settling in presented challenges for Major Steele and his officers. The buildings were all made of yellow pine. The timber was very heavy and had to be hauled a considerable distance; about 1,400 logs at least 25 feet in length had to be hauled, peeled, and hewn. The roofing was of cedar shakes three feet long. The Mounties prepared some of these shakes; Mr. Cowan, who provided all the cedar blocks for the extensive project, split others. The floors were made of rough lumber that had been cut by Hanson's Mill at Wasa and rafted down the Kootenay to the ferry landing.

The barracks for the men contained two large rooms with a corridor between them. The beds were wooden, made of thin pole frames. Major Steele requested folding metal cots so that space could quickly be cleared for indoor activity, but his request was denied. There were nine other buildings plus a root house and latrines. The officers' quarters were 25 feet by 50 feet, containing four bedrooms, an ample office, a living-dining room, kitchen, pantry, washroom, and a storeroom— with space for the batman's small cot. The stable, including a saddle and harness room, was 25 feet by 70 feet, and could hold 75 horses. Adjacent to the stable was hay storage.

The sergeants' mess and kitchen and the staff sergeants' quarters were in another building of 25 feet by 50 feet. Similar buildings housed guardrooms and lock-up cells. There was an infirmary, a workshop shared by carpenters and saddlers, and a cookhouse. All of these buildings' eaves were nine feet high, and their roofs were of a quarter-pitch slope.

Chief Isadore's Land Settlement

In September, Indian Commissioner Dr. Israel Powell returned to the Kootenays with Indian Reserve Commissioner Peter O'Reilly and the Honorable F.G. Vernon, commissioner of lands and works. They set about surveying three additional reserves. They had hoped to ride through each tract of land with Chief Isadore to ensure that there was mutual understanding and acceptance, but Isadore and most of his band were in Sandpoint, buying their winter supplies. After the survey, O'Reilly and Vernon left to do a similar survey in the Chilcotin before the snow fell. Dr. Powell hoped to meet Isadore in about a fortnight, the predicted time for Isadore's group to return.

Major Sam Steele was prepared to co-operate with the Indian Affairs Department. On September 5 he convened court to hear the case of Kapla and Little Isadore, concluding that they were not guilty of murdering prospectors Kemp and Hylton.

At the newly established NWMP post, fourteen men were seriously ill with typhoid fever, including the resident doctor and assistant surgeon, Dr. Frederick H. Powell. Dr. Israel Powell had been requested to assume medical duties; a replacement doctor arrived three weeks later. Dr. Powell then met with Chief Isadore at Joseph's Prairie. The formal meeting lasted three hours. It was regretted that John Galbraith had been allowed to purchase Joseph's Prairie and then sell the favoured area to Colonel James Baker. Isadore claimed that John Galbraith repeatedly assured him that he'd taken up the land so no other settler could take up what would continue to be Isadore's property. John Galbraith couldn't be asked to verify this statement because he had died earlier in the year.

Powell pointed out that although Isadore had to remove his stock from the 40 acres on Joseph's Prairie,[17] he was now guaranteed his 680-acre winter ranch at Mayook, beside the Kootenay River. Colonel Baker had applied for—and had not been given—that excellent winter range to be part of his proposed 32,000-acre Cranbrook Ranch. Furthermore, Colonel Baker was also to pay Isadore for certain improvements on that land.

Isadore could see that the Kootenays had received more consideration than many tribes in other parts of the province, so he thanked Dr. Powell for the new lands, and upon learning that his defiant release of Kapla from the jail in March was forgiven, he thanked Powell and his commissioners for their mercy.

In November, Father Fouquet of St. Eugene Mission was leaving the district. Chief Isadore, who is described by Steele in his memoirs as "the most powerful chief I met in my forty years of service,"[18] brought Father Fouquet to Kootenay Post to present a farewell message and petition [at right].

On November 7, Sam Steele addressed a group assembled at the Mountie post by reading a long letter to them. The letter was written by the three commissioners involved in the Indian land settlement—F.G. Vernon, I.W. Powell, and P. O'Reilly—and was addressed to Chief Isadore and the Kootenay Indians at St. Mary's Reserve. In this letter they spoke of the chief's "duty" to "help the government when necessary" and observed that although Isadore had not "done his duty" in preventing his braves from breaking the jail, he had "admitted that he had done very wrong, and was sorry," and had followed through

To the officer of the North West Mounted Police, Kootenay, B.C.
Kootenay, B.C.
4th November, 1887.

Gentlemen,

Before leaving, I address you a few words in behalf of the Indians agreeably to the wishes of Chief Isadore, who gave for reason of his wish, the confidence he had in you.

During the thirteen years I have resided here, I have always found the Kootenays anxious to live on good terms with the whites. It has been always my personal opinion that although a brave and cool race, they would not go to war unless forced into it.

The first few years I was here, there had not been a case of drunkenness, and only four or five cases of light drinking known amongst the Kootenays. Not one case of robbery of any importance was heard of. But since the buffalo hunting has ceased, the Indians here have mixed more with Chinamen and whites, and since the authority of the chiefs have been lessened by various causes, the last four or five years there has been too many cases of drunkenness and gambling heard of, and some with shooting and fighting; half-breeds, whitemen, and Chinamen have been gambling with the Indians or supplying them with liquor.

It is my personal opinion that the missionaries, having no influence over these unscrupulous whitemen, half-breeds and Chinamen, will not be able to stop their evils, unless the Government checks these whitemen or Chinamen, and compels the Indians to say from whom they got the liquor.

I have the honour to be, Gentlemen,
Your obedient servant,

L. FOUQUET

on his promise to bring Kapla back to jail. They said that Dr. Powell had influenced the government in pardoning Isadore, but his behaviour would not be "forgotten, and should he at any future time be guilty of a breach of the law, he may rest assured that he will be severely dealt with, and no longer recognized by the Government as a chief."

The letter then observed the difficulties that Isadore had created in earlier land distribution discussions by wanting "the whole country, which ... [he] could not use," and changing his mind on land that was eventually agreed upon. It concluded that Isadore's reserve included much arable land that was not being used to its potential, and that with the additional lands recently granted, he would have "much more than has been allowed to Indians in some other places." Indian Agent Phillipps would "show [him] his lands and how to improve them."

At the conclusion of Steele's reading, Chief Isadore again protested the loss of Joseph's Prairie, but "left in good humour." A few days later he had his horses and cattle herded up and moved. He made his main home at his winter ranch, eight miles below Galbraith's Ferry. His widowed mother had her own house near the Kootenay River on this property. She had continued to live there comfortably, oblivious to the white man's land dealings.

Life Among the Troops

Concurrent with his settling of the Indian affairs, and readying the new police camp for winter living, Steele faced trouble within the ranks. A severe illness called "mountain fever" (presumably typhoid fever) had struck many members of the troops, starting about the first day in August. Four constables died and were buried at Fort Steele. Constables Lazenby, Mason, and Fisher died before Steele's year-end report was written. A fourth constable—named Mitchell—died later. The NWMP physician, Assistant Surgeon Frederick Hamilton Powell, contracted the fever on September 24 and had to be carefully nursed for several weeks. Indian Commissioner Dr. Israel Powell had volunteered to act as troop physician until a replacement, Assistant Surgeon Pare, arrived on October 10. Dr. Pare left Kootenay Post as soon as Dr. F.H. Powell was well enough to resume his duties. By that time the epidemic had run its course, and medical upsets thereafter were mainly injuries sustained by working in icy conditions.

Another problem was discontent among the Mounties: There were seven desertions and one suicide. There was a desertion in Golden by a constable facing imprisonment for being drunk and disorderly. A second went downriver in a boat to the U.S. on August 17.

A most embarrassing occurrence took place in September 1887. Three tourists, two of whom later published a book entitled *A Ramble in British Columbia, 1887,* arrived at the post via canoe. They were repeatedly assured that it would be safe to leave their two canoes in the bushes on the riverbank while they made a short visit to Colonel Baker's home in Cranbrook. Upon their return, however, the canoes had disappeared. The thieves were Constables Coles, Preston, and McDonald, who had used the canoes to reach American territory and desert. On September 27 Corporal Harrison and a party followed them, by trail along the river. Harrison was able to recover all stolen property by October 2.

Further desertions had taken place in late October. Sergeant Allen and a party were sent in pursuit but failed to catch the three deserters before they reached safety south of the border. All government properties—horses and tack—were recovered.

Two constables contemplated desertion in March 1888; however, they were cut off by an ice jam in the Elk River, which flooded the usual crossing site. Michael Phillipps, on his way back to Tobacco Plains, camped overnight with them. By morning a thin sheet of ice covered the water above the old ice. It was too dangerous to lead horses across, as the new ice would badly cut the horses' legs, so Phillipps gave the young Mounties his two horses, enabling their return to the barracks. Phillipps had to go a long way upstream before he could negotiate a crossing, proceeding home with what he could pack on his back.

On the whole, the discipline of the division, considering the varied circumstances under which it had been placed, was satisfactory. The great majority were "as fine and respectable a body of men as anyone could desire to command. They ... strictly attended the line of conduct laid down by [Steele]."[19] Their relationships with both the white and Indian populations had earned favourable comments and not a single complaint.

Patrols through the district went to Golden, 190 miles to the north; Tobacco Plains, 80 miles south; Colonel Baker's, 12 miles west; Wild Horse Creek Gold Camp, 4 miles east; and Fenwick's Ranch, 10 miles downriver on the eastern side. A non-commissioned officer and two constables were stationed at Fenwick's lower ranch to take charge of the horses. Except the ones kept at the barracks for daily use, the horses were all pastured there. Two men were stationed at Kootenay Crossing, 45 miles from the post, to receive and forward stores coming from Golden. Three men were similarly positioned at Sam's Landing near present-day Fairmont.

Meat and vegetables were purchased locally. The Indians appreciated the opportunity to sell cattle to the barracks for butchering. Steele purchased at least six animals from a Wasa rancher, J.E. Humphreys, after stopping overnight with this hospitable gentleman. Michael Phillipps was able to supply the requisite 14,000 pounds of potatoes, but because Colonel Baker and other growers had had their oat crops minimized by early frost, the Mounties' horses were maintained with 20,000 pounds of oats rather than the anticipated 100,000 pounds.

Hay was in short supply, and of rather poor quality. The Indians were reluctant to cut and gather winter feed for their animals. Hyde Baker loaned a mower to those at St. Eugene Mission late in the season, enabling some collection of hay for sale. In subsequent years Father Coccola purchased a mower for the use of his flock. The Kootenays wintered much of their herd at Bummer's Flat, a short distance upriver from Galbraith's Ferry.

Sam Steele's year-end report was written on December 1, 1887. Some buildings had been completed by that time, the Indian problem appeared to be settled, and the epidemic of "mountain fever" had subsided. Mail was also arriving reasonably regularly.

In his report, Steele estimated that his troops would be superfluous at the end of twelve months in the district. He described the Kootenays as "moral and industrious" and the Shuswaps as "so industrious and businesslike that they will not provoke trouble." A handful of braves with no property roamed far and wide, ready to take advantage of the absence of legal power. They had observed that only uniformed personnel would search out and imprison suspected criminals in the U.S., whereas in British territory the one and only constable recruited settlers—who up to that time had been friendly—as special constables in a posse. Major Steele therefore recommended leaving a half-dozen Mounties to assist a provincial commissioner or constable. He also advocated that this provincial officer occupy the officers' barracks and be responsible for the maintenance of the buildings in case it should be necessary to bring many Mounties there again. He expected that once the wagon road from Golden was completed, redeployment would be reasonably simple. When the Mounties did leave Fort Steele in 1888, provincial Constable O.G. Dennis was placed in the officers' quarters to fulfil the proposed arrangement.

During the winter of 1887–88 the NWMP men were thoroughly instructed in the duties of a constable. Inspectors Wood and Huot lectured every other evening on the contents of the *Constables Manual*. There was great interest, and prizes were awarded to the most efficient man in each subdivision. Drill and target practice were instituted in the spring, with drill from April 3 to mid-May, carbine shooting May 14 to June 2, and revolver practice June 4 to 12.

On June 7, 1888 orders were received to return "D" Division to the North-West Territories[20] in July. Arrangements were duly made about what to take and what to sell prior to departing.

A grand farewell party was planned. Robert Galbraith suggested some of the events and contributed prizes to be awarded for races and competition. The special event on July 2 was held at Four Mile Creek. Marquees were pitched under the trees, and an ample supply of food and refreshment provided so that no one need go home hungry. The program started with a parade and march past with Colonel Baker taking the salute. All the movements of a cavalry squad were performed before him, at all paces. On conclusion the whole of the visitors (white and Indians) joined the Mounted Police in three hearty cheers for the Queen.

Colonel Baker was appointed referee of the sports, with Mr. Galbraith and Mr. Norris (Collector of

Customs) as the judges, and myself as starter. The Indians proved very athletic, entering the events with enthusiasm. In sprints, the Mounties came first with Indians a close second; for long distance, the redskins excelled. Mounties refrained from entering the competition, Wrestling on Horseback, but the few excellent horsemen among the civilians who entered were hurled from their saddles by the Indians whose powerful limbs gripped their horses as if in a vice. That event inspired the admiration of all who watched. The concluding races were on horseback. In the mile race an Indian was on a buckskin—1 minute 50 seconds timed by *two* stop watches. The rider, Maiyuke, weighed after the race, tipped the scale at 197 pounds.[21]

In the evening Chief Isadore made an emotional speech, praising the men of the division for their manly and moral behaviour. He noted that when the troops first arrived, the Indians did not know what to expect, and naturally had considerable doubts. All that had changed. He observed that if in the future the Indians had any cause for complaint, instead of taking the law into their own hands, they would visit Fort Macleod to obtain advice from "the Great Mother's Redcoats."

Within a few days the departure plans were postponed. There had been considerable trouble with the American Kootenays just south of Tobacco Plains. Inspector Wood and Indian Agent Phillipps hurried to consult with the U.S. authorities. They discovered that some American Indians had murdered three white men, and friends of the victims had promptly lynched the guilty parties. A subsequent truce had been arranged with the avenging Kootenays, and it appeared that no military intervention was needed to enforce the peace. Calm routine living had resumed in the district.

The final sale of goods left behind by the NWMP was concluded on August 4, 1888. Among the items sold were four freight wagons and a buckboard, which could not be used on the pack trail through the Crow's Nest Pass. Michael Phillipps purchased one of the wagons plus a boat. Phillipps and his son took the river route home while Frederick Norbury drove the team with the wagon.

Chapter 7

The Mounties Leave
(1888)

Careful planning by Steele and his officers for the North West Mounted Police's departure from Fort Steele included sending two parties ahead of the main column. On August 3 Corporal Waite and Constable Eales were sent with a letter to Superintendent Neale at Fort Macleod. This letter requested that Neale send all available wagons to Old Man's Lake in Crow's Nest Pass, where the rented pack train could be dispensed with, as trail was widened to roadway east of that point.

Corporal Bunt and Constables Davis and Edgar were instructed to keep two days ahead of the main troop. Inspector Wood was to direct chopping out fallen trees and do general clearing of the trail.

Staff Sergeant Fane left camp on August 6 with five constables, carrying division stores such as ammunition and a safe. These were to be transported to Golden and then returned to Fort Macleod by railway.

On August 6, Robert Galbraith and ten packers arrived with their 54 pack animals and made up packs for loading at dawn next morning. Departure on the morning of August 7 was delayed, as some of the horses had strayed during the night. The horses of "D" Division were 10 team horses that were to be ridden by men of the division, 48 saddle horses, and 25 police pack animals. Three Mountie horses had eaten poisonous weeds and showed signs of weakness, so they were left in care of Fenwick, who lent three replacement animals. The first stop was at Lower Fish Lake at 11 a.m. The animals were unpacked and a cache of oats and biscuits retrieved.

On August 8 the troop marched at 5:30 a.m., following the trail and passing through beautiful, parklike country, watered by numerous small streams, timbered with fir, pine, and poplar. They crossed Bull River at 7:45 a.m. by a narrow but good bridge close to a magnificent waterfall. The trail turned west just after crossing the bridge and followed the east bank of the Kootenay River for several miles. The troop crossed another bridge high above a canyon and shortly thereafter found their second cache of rations. They had travelled eighteen miles.

At this place they found Inspector and Mrs. Wood and Assistant Surgeon Powell. Inspector Wood had sent his trail-clearing party ahead, as his wife was ill. The division doctor had been summoned from Fish Lake, and felt he should remain at the lady's bedside until she was out of danger.

The troop moved to Sand Creek before 8 a.m. the next day, with the pack train arriving at 10:45 a.m. Tents were set up, packs covered with tarpaulins in case of rain, and the men were freed from duties to go fishing or bathing in the creek.

Their travel on August 10 took them through thick timber, then occasional prairie meadows. As they turned east towards Crow's Nest, they passed the fork on the trail that led south to Tobacco Plains. They halted two miles west of the bridge over Elk River. Wild animals had disturbed their third cache of rations, but, water and grass were abundant. The saddle horses were left to graze until 9:45 p.m., then were tied up for the night.

The troops marched at 5:30 a.m., climbed a very steep hill, and crossed over—with a man at a time leading his horse—a narrow wooden bridge high above the Elk River Canyon. Up the very steep zigzag trail the Mounties continued on foot, leading their animals. When the trail descended again it crossed many side streams that were neatly bridged. The forest growth here was mostly huge cedars and large spruce trees. Shortly thereafter they passed through territory scarred by earlier forest fires. When they reached their next cache they stopped, but they did not pitch tents. The grass was lush but criss-crossed with fallen timber. Although the horses found good food, they had difficulty moving from place to place. The men were able to bathe in nearby Elk River.

Day six on the trail was slowed at the start when a bridge needed to be repaired. The countryside was hilly, covered with burnt timber, and the summits above were naked rock of "forbidding appearance."[21] Grass became scant, and the trail was fringed by a dense growth of raspberry bushes laden with ripe fruit.

After sixteen miles, the last three on the north bank of Coal Creek, they reached their next cache. Again, fallen timbers precluded them from setting up tents, but the weather was fair and the bivouac rather pleasant.

On August 13 the troop passed over a very rough section of trail. They followed Coal Creek over a summit to Marten Creek, past Ferney's Creek and cabin, then over the drift of Colonel Baker's coal claim, and finally made camp at Michel Creek. The day proved unlucky for one of Galbraith's pack mules, which fell over a steep bank near Ferney's, breaking its neck and one of its legs.

The way was through burnt timbers and windfalls. There was plenty of coarse grass for the mules and horses; however, the proposed campsite was full of logs. Since rain was threatening to downpour soon, they quickly moved enough of the logs to allow their tents to be set up. It poured rain most of the night. Corporal Waite and Constable Eales joined the eastbound Mounties here with news that seven wagons awaited them at the eastern end of Crow's Nest Pass.

The next morning the storm had passed, so they struck camp at an early hour. The party trekked across a very shaky bridge at Michel Creek, a lovely tract of beautiful timber, and mountain meadows with luxurious grass and magnificent scenery. Camped on a lovely mountain meadow they found Chief Isadore, who greeted them. Isadore had come from Kootenay and was on his way to visit some friends among the North Piegans. Once across the summit of the Rockies the trail began to descend, passing along the north bank of the middle fork of Old Man's River, past the Upper Lake. Soon they could see the Crow's Nest Mountains and the Lower Lake.

They camped at Lower Lake amid lush grass. They had travelled sixteen miles. After pitching their tents, the men went fishing in the lake and nearby river.

On August 15 the pack train met the police transport wagons. Robert Galbraith's pack train was unloaded, and a farewell speech given. Following three cheers for Galbraith's pack team, he and his packers led their horses back westward. The troop moved to "The Gap," where a small Mountie detachment was quartered. The road from Old Man's Lake to the Crow's Nest detachment was good during low water, with no bad hills and numerous safe fords over the Old Man's River. The troop moved twenty miles that day.

August 16 was highlighted by the difficulty of collecting all the horses. "The change from the confinement of the wooded pastures of British Columbia seemed to make them anxious for a run, and once off, the night being very dark, it was difficult to get them together again."[22]

Due to a late start at 9:45 a.m. the troop could only pause briefly for lunch, and by pressing the horses harder than on the trail, they reached Pincher Creek at 3:30 p.m.

At Pincher Creek some of the horses needed fresh shoes, so the teams pulling the wagons were serviced. The troop moved out at 9:30 a.m.; they had a two-hour dinner break at Scott's Coulee and reached Fort Macleod at 7:30 p.m.

The distance between Kootenay and Fort Macleod was 195 miles. It took Corporal Waite and Constable Eales four days to cover the distance. The mass exodus of horsemen and pack animals took eleven days. When passenger trains were running in the early 1900s, the same trip would take less than a day. The modern traveller driving on a paved highway can travel between these points in a leisurely three to four hours.

Chapter 8

Early Tourists to the East Kootenays (1887)

The white population of the East Kootenays was satisfied that Indian unrest was quelled when Sam Steele and "D" Troop of the North West Mounted Police passed through Crow's Nest Pass to return to the North-West Territories. (The provinces of Alberta and Saskatchewan were created years later in 1905.) The Mounties were in the area for one year plus one week, but had made a major contribution to the district. Chief Isadore had reached an understanding of the white man's rules, and he was accepting of those rules because Major Steele won his respect and confidence. Indians and settlers had enjoyed a market for their cattle, horses, and produce. Even once the police camp was reduced to four men, locals found that their herds and gardens could supply a large market.

In addition, all of the trails had been well maintained, with several new bridges built by troop carpenters. The bridge across Wild Horse Creek close to Fort Steele was partly washed away during spring run-off. It was repaired and reinforced. Bridges were also placed over the Bull and Elk Rivers for the use of the division leaving Kootenay en route to Fort Macleod. A bridge was built across the Kootenay River at Canal Flats, and a bridge to replace Galbraith's Ferry was started. Civilian carpenters completed it by late September of 1888.

Galbraith's charter for his ferry stated it was to be the exclusive transportation across the Kootenay River within ten miles upstream and ten miles downstream. However, even before the replacement bridge was built, Robert Mather had set up a ferry to access his Cherry Creek property from

Bummer's Flats. That ferry was subject to the vagaries of the river, especially when the eastern landing was under water. Mather's ferry was not part of an established trail; it was operated solely for his own convenience.

Mather's ferry was mentioned in J.A. Lees' and W.J. Clutterbuck's book *A Ramble in British Columbia, 1887*. This book attracted many readers in the "old country." Copies were sent to residents of the East Kootenay, who were pleased to see references to themselves. The authors travelled through the district with "Cardie," an American cousin, in the summer and fall of 1887. These early tourists not only left a most readable record of what they saw and who they met on that trip, they also created a fresh optimism for visiting other places. "Tourism" was suddenly considered in speculation about the future of the East Kootenay.

Lees and Clutterbuck visited many areas that were swept by forest fires. They observed the regeneration following these fires and accepted the scenery as "beautiful" despite scarification of hillsides. They could count the homes of permanent white residents in the valley on their fingers. The interruption of their travel plans (when their canoes were stolen by deserting Mounties) was treated as a lark.

Accompanied by "Cardie," Lees and Clutterbuck arrived at Golden and stayed in the Queens Hotel, a log cabin with three tiny bedrooms. Their canoes did not arrive on the same train, so they went upriver on Captain Armstrong's SS *Duchess* to the mouth of Canyon Creek. They camped for three nights at different sites beside Canyon Creek: first in a small clearing surrounded by fire-fallen timber that they remembered as "Mosquito Camp"; the second day in a log cabin they had found and were forced to stay in when a thunderstorm struck; and the third night in a pleasant mosquito-free setting above the canyon in a locale where they viewed white mountain goats romping nearby. On returning to the mouth of Canyon Creek they had the good fortune to arrive when the SS *Duchess* was passing by, headed upstream. Their canoes were already aboard, so they joined Captain Armstrong for lunch on the top deck (a deck with no guard rail). The *Duchess* churned to the Mounties' relay base at the south end of Windermere Lake to unload supplies, then docked overnight at Windermere.

The city of Windermere consisted of the hotel with two rooms, a kitchen and a loft, the store and the Government House with four rooms and a cellar. None, thus far, had chimneys. The kitchen of the store was outdoors.[23]

Clutterbuck and party explored Sinclair Creek, behind present-day Radium Hot Springs. There had been forest fires, so travel was dirty and impeded by fallen logs. A week later they worked their canoes from Mud Lake to Columbia Lake— a struggle that took over ten hours of hard work. The next day they were introduced to the luxury of a soak at the Fairmont Hot Springs. The day after they left George Geary's, a north wind forced them to beach for a few hours at Armstrong Bay. Cardie, leading their packhorse, travelled the footpath on the east side of Columbia Lake and set up camp at the southeast corner of the lake (near the current Canal Flats boat launch).

The canoes were portaged across to the Kootenay River. Cardie investigated a gold mine up nearby "Findley" (Finlay) Creek. The canoe trip to Skookumchuck took three and a half hours. They set up camp and relaxed until Cardie and the pack horse joined them.

The next stop was at Mather's ranch. Near noon the following day they observed, "On the left hillside was a pack train winding its way to the Police Camp. We met a boat poled by two men, a Swede and a Norwegian, who were making their living rafting lumber down to the great city of Galbraith's Ferry."[24]

They pulled their canoes ashore at the ferry "just opposite the mouth of St. Mary's River." The steep trail led up to a store at the top of the hill. There they found "a number of Indians and police, and the heterogeneous particles which go to make up a pack train."[25]

The highlights of their visit to Galbraith's Ferry were meeting Mrs. Clark, viewing the orderly NWMP camp, and being introduced to Hyde Baker. They described Mrs. Clark as "the first white woman we have seen since we left Golden more than a month ago, and one of the noble three who represent the sex in the few hundred miles which this valley contains."[26]

Colonel Baker's son had invited them to stay at his place in Cranbrook, so they parked their canoes in the bushes near the ferry landing, rented a pack horse, and, with a fellow named Richmond, set off westward. They described the trail from the west ferry landing: "[It] first crossed low flats covered with birch, dog willow and other small scrub. It mounts a steep hill and comes to a land of alternate prairie and forest. Fantastic fall colours—white alkali ponds, and a superb sunset."[27]

When they reached Joseph's Prairie, which was two miles of prairie grass, an Indian campfire could be seen to their right. In the twilight they could see before them a dim outline of buildings and could hear barking dogs and neighing horses. A door was thrown open, and they observed a huge cheery English fireplace and register book. The Chinese servant welcomed the travellers, but none of the Bakers were home. (The author noted he preferred the fireplace to the "square metal American stoves.")

That night they "went to sleep in real beds." They ate a huge breakfast served by the Chinese houseboy, then set off to visit Moyie Lake. The trail went on the west side of the lake. They camped at the south end, near a bridge. After four days of exploring and hunting they returned via the Peavine River trail. On a meadow nearby they marvelled at a camp of about twenty teepees "on dull brown grass, backed by yellow quaking aspens and golden tamaracks, dark green spruce and greying distant hills."[28]

They met the mailman from Golden when they arrived back at Cranbrook. "Cranbrook has mail once a fortnight in summer and once a month in winter. *No wonder the letters for this country are addressed B.C.* However, if they go on as energetically as they have begun, it seems likely that in the near future they will be entitled to date A.D. or perhaps even a little ahead of that."[29]

Returning to Galbraith's Ferry, where they expected to retrieve their canoes and paddle downriver, the trio soon learned that their canoes, *Lulie* and *Hope*, were gone. Indian Agent Phillipps told them that their canoes had been left just south of the U.S. border, where Corporal Harrison had tracked the NWMP deserters who had stolen them. As the canoes were now about a mile from Phillipps' home on Tobacco Plains, he "kindly lent two packhorses" to enable them to get down to *Lulie* and *Hope*.

F.S. 8 - 704

The beginnings of Cranbrook. This picture was taken in 1885 by George Mercer Dawson when he was in the district doing detailed geological surveys.

They started south on October 10, and came upon some prospectors who had created wing dams in the Bull River. These men demonstrated how they retrieved gold in the cracks of rocks now exposed above water. The travellers lingered quite some time, watching this unusual method of mining. When they moved on, they were forced to go past their intended campsite because it was stinking of skunk.

The three stopped at Elk River Camp for several days. They hunted and explored upriver. One feature at this campsite was an Indian sweat lodge, described as follows.

[It is] a circular dome-shaped cage of bent willow wands tied together wherever they come in contact with each other. When in use a small pool of water is made in the centre, and the whole cage having been covered in with mats or skins, the patient creeps in. A friend keeps him supplied with hot stones from the outside. These being dropped into the water make a very effective vapor bath. No large camping ground is without one or more of them.[30]

F.S. 34 -16

This Lower Kootenay Indian lodge, or teepee, covered with reed matting, was a year-round home for band members near present-day Creston. Note the external stick that adjusts the smoke flap. Other groups had teepee covers of animal hides, but they converted to canvas as soon as it was available.

They stopped at Phillipps' place, and were directed to replenish their supplies from a store just south of the border. They did so, but because ice had now formed along the river, it was no longer safe to travel by water to the new Northern Pacific Railway line, so they accompanied Phillipps and Norbury back to Kootenay Fort.

Phillipps set up a teepee for overnight stops during that trip. Norbury was fascinated by it, and Clutterbuck claimed it was "the very best moveable dwelling yet devised by the wit of man." He went on to give a complete description of it.

An Indian teepee or lodge used from ten to twenty poles. The poles, about fifteen feet long, were slim and straight, about two inches in diameter at the foot, one inch at the top. A smallish pine, lodgepole, which branched only near the top was a most convenient supplier of teepee framework. Four poles were joined together about a foot from the top, by a loose band of twisted withy (willow bark) and set up in a conical form. The base of the cone is fifteen or sixteen feet in diameter. The remaining poles are laid in the forks of the original four to complete the framework. The lower ends are set about three feet apart in as true a circle as can be managed. Over the framework is stretched the canvas, though in a few places skins, mats or bark coverings may still be seen. The covering is provided with two ears, one at each side of the opening which serves at the bottom as a door, at the top as a chimney. The space between these necessary two holes into a house was fastened with wooden skewers.[31]

Overnighters lay like wheel spokes around the central fire pit. Smoke vented neatly out of the top unless the wind changed. The ears atop the teepee were adjustable, each ear with its own pole. The ears had to be facing away from the wind to create the correct draft and remove smoke from within the teepee.

Lees and Clutterbuck left the Kootenays via Sandpoint, Idaho, where they caught the Northern Pacific train to Tacoma, Washington. They sailed to Victoria. After exploring and admiring the new capital city, they returned to the mainland to catch an eastbound CPR passenger train. They cursed the snowsheds in Rogers Pass for blocking their view of the dramatic scenery. At Golden they stayed overnight with Mrs. Green, the very good cook who hosted them in a new, larger Queen's Hotel that replaced the log hotel with only three rooms. The authors were home in England in time to spend the Christmas of 1887 with their families.

Their book was a detailed report of the exploration "of this little known country to test its capabilities as a home for some of the public school and university men who in this overcrowded old England of ours find themselves de trop."[32]

Chapter 9

St. Eugene Mission

With the establishment of St. Eugene Mission by Father Fouquet in 1874, the Kootenays soon adopted the Catholic faith and ceremonies, blending them with traditional tribal assemblies at Christmas and Easter. The early missionaries learned the Ktunaxa language so they could communicate with their neighbours; even their hymnals were worded in Chinook, the generalized language among Indians in Northwest America.

There is scant reference to Father Fouquet's years in the East Kootenay, but his successor, Father Nicolas Coccola, is documented in detail. Coccola was a Corsican, born in 1854. He arrived in British Columbia in July 1880, and was sent immediately to St. Mary's Mission on the Fraser River, where he joined the classes of Indian boys to learn some English vocabulary.[33]

The apprenticeship at the mission included gardening, making hay, and catching and preserving salmon for winter use. Two weeks before Easter 1881, Coccola and his classmate, Father Chiapini, were ordained by Bishop D'herbomez. They were immediately dispatched to the B.C. Interior. Father Coccola was sent to the mission at Kamloops, where he served until his transfer to St. Eugene.

The Oblates had been restructured, first in Oregon Territory and then in B.C., with stringent guidelines for enforcing the co-operation of Native peoples. In every willing Indian village the Durieu system created an administration under the supervision of local missionaries. The chiefs and sub-chiefs were responsible for keeping undesirable white men (for example, bootleggers) away from their people. Appointed watchmen, or strongmen, ensured that both adults and children attended religious instruction and services, that band policemen administered punishments, that catechists taught their fellow band members, and that bell ringers summoned the people to church.[34]

As part of his duties out of Kamloops, Father Coccola had organized the Nicola band to operate on the Durieu system, but when he arrived in the Kootenays, the system was already in place.

Nicolas Coccola initially had two helpers at St. Eugene. Brother Burns had been there many years with Father Fouquet. Father Ricard had expected to leave the Kootenays with Father Fouquet, but he was obliged to stay, as his intended replacement was urgently needed else-

Courtesy *Cominco Communicator*

Father Nicolas Coccola, founder of St. Eugene Mission School, and the priest who staked a rich mineral find near Moyie, which enabled him to build two Roman Catholic churches in the East Kootenay.

where. The Oblates believed in assigning their members in pairs to slowly developing communities. Their main obligation was to the Aboriginal population, but because there were no priests beyond Victoria and New Westminster, the nominal bishop of B.C. had pleaded that the Oblates also serve the spiritual needs of white people wherever and whenever possible.

Father Coccola arrived in the Kootenays at the same time as the North West Mounted Police—in the fall of 1887. He felt it his duty to befriend Major Sam Steele and his men. He arranged to say Mass at the police barracks from time to time, and kept the police informed about times of church services at the mission. The Mounties were accustomed to wearing their revolvers during every waking hour, and the Indians were alternately afraid and dismayed when weapons were brought into the church. The priest had to firmly insist that those entering a building for a religious assemblage wore no revolvers or knives.

Mrs. Colonel Baker, who was nominally an Anglican, was another white parishioner attending many of the services at St. Eugene. She befriended the priest and donated generously to a fund to buy a bell for the church. She also supplied decorations for the altar. The customs officer from Cranbrook, Mr. Norris, also became a parishioner.

The Catholic priests were obliged to do more than teach and follow spiritual practices. They had to be carpenters, gardeners, competent horsemen, able to prepare their own food, mend their own clothing, care for stock and chickens, and, overall, set an example as pioneers introducing an agricultural way of life. The Native peoples had been nomadic hunters and meat eaters who resisted vegetarian diets. They even became sickly when deprived of cooked or raw flesh. Some of the priests studied medical literature and were able to respond to calls from the sick and injured. Father Coccola was faced with some major emergencies. For example, one of the miners up Wild Horse Creek who was in a fight had the frontal bone of his forehead cut with an axe, and his brain begin to protrude. Coccola pressed the man's brain back in, and then treated the forehead with antiseptic and bandage. The patient was able to return to work within four months. [35]

The new priest deferred, in principle, to the senior Father Ricard. It was, however, Coccola who became the administrator, the planner, the lobbyist, and the director of expansion at the mission in the Kootenays. Immediately after the Mounties departed from Fort Steele, Father Coccola wrote to the Department of Indian Affairs in Ottawa to ask for a boarding school for the children. He cleverly stated, "After schooling the Indians would never again give any trouble to the Government."[36]

Mail was irregular and slow, but the answer was favourable. They scouted the new St. Mary's Reserve for a suitable location, but could not find one. The priest then offered 30 acres of land near the mission house and church. This was good land that could be irrigated by St. Joseph Creek. The federal government assisted the priest by donating many of the NWMP post's buildings. The barracks were dissembled, moved the seven miles, and erected as the dormitories and central structures for the use of the priests, nuns, and their pupils.

The school was finally readied in 1890. There were three buildings. The central building was for the staff, chapel, kitchen, and dining room. The two other buildings were dormitories and classrooms: one for boys, the other for girls.

Three Sisters of Providence and a white orphan girl, Mary Raunch, arrived by stage on August 15, 1890. Only their hand luggage arrived with them. Father Coccola scurried to a local store to borrow a dozen blankets for them. Three days later someone asked the Indians to bring some hay to make mattresses, so the ladies would no longer have to sleep on the bare floor.

Sister Pacifique was named the superior as she had been on staff at an Indian school in Walla Walla. Sister Adrien, a niece of Mother Joseph of the Sacred Heart, founder of missions in Washington Territory, was to be in charge of the boys. Sister Rita was a lively, happy 22-year-old woman who had mothered eight younger siblings. Mary was about to enter the order and was unsure of her capabilities.

While awaiting the school furnishings, the nuns cleaned the rectory, then the church. They washed, mended, and ironed church linens and the priests' personal effects. Robert Galbraith visited to extend a welcome from the community. Sister Pacifique pointed out some deficiencies in the arrangements, and Galbraith hastened to arrange for a laundry, a root cellar, and a fence around the schoolyard. To add to the sisters' joy he had a well dug.[37]

Weeks later the freight delivered furniture for the sisters. Life looked and felt better when each of them had a bed to sleep in. Government officials from Victoria and Ottawa inspected the new establishment. They were so favourably impressed that they rushed the needed furniture, paid for by the Indian Department, *and* they decided that—counter to the cautious plan to start with boys only—Indian girls would also be accepted as pupils.

It fell to Father Coccola to select the first class of boarding-school pupils. He visited each band and selected the children who he felt would be the best students. He had been to each camp twice a year, so he had visited many of the families who were cautiously optimistic about having their children attend a Catholic school. The Shuswap Reserve, near Athalmere, had the fewest members. Father Coccola had spoken their language before coming to the Kootenays, and admired their devotion to the church and their farms. He chose the chief's daughter, Amelia Kinbasket, and two boys for that opening year at St. Eugene.[38]

On October 16, 1890, Father Coccola, like the Pied Piper of old, arrived at the school with a throng of Indian children and their parents. Solemnly each couple presented their child to the sisters. "I give you my child. What is most precious to us now becomes precious to you. Do with him what you think best." The children gravely shook hands with their parents and said good-bye without a tear.

As soon as their parents had gone home the children were shown through the buildings. They were delighted at the prospect of living in such a palace, and of having a real bed all to themselves. Less pleasant was the experience of being bathed and of having their hair fine-combed, washed, and cut. The language barrier was also something to reckon with. Since the children were unaccustomed to being indoors sitting quietly, classroom instruction was quite limited. The girls were taught to bake, sew, cook, wash, iron, and mend. The boys were set to sawing and splitting wood, then carrying it in for the many stoves heating the three buildings. The boys did not take kindly to this task. At home it was women's work![39]

This school was described as an industrial school. It was a well-intentioned facility where the students learned the English language, to wear white man's clothing, and were immersed in the Roman Catholic faith. The girls became very good housekeepers and were able later to find employment as domestic help or seamstresses. The boys were instructed in carpentry, gardening, blacksmithing, harness repair, and the use of simple farm machinery. The boys abandoned the canvas skirt previously worn by adult Kootenay males, and were accepted in their "American trousers." The earliest pupils did not have summer holidays with their families. They struggled with everything new. It was especially hard when they were sick, with no mother or grandmother to comfort and care for them. There were, however, some happy interludes. Students took pride in their individual achievements. They left school upon graduation with an understanding of contemporary changes in the valley.

Courtesy Shelagh Dehart and F.S. 461 - 01

Girls at St. Eugene Mission School, circa 1902. All students were Kootenay Indians except Rosalee Kinbasket (third from left, back row) and her cousin Margaret (first right, front row).

Father Coccola watched the progress of his charges and rejoiced. His duties at first extended to white congregations in the West Kootenay communities of Nelson, Rossland, Ainsworth, Sandon, and Kaslo. When he travelled to the Indians at Tobacco Plains, he would sometimes answer calls from sick or dying Americans south of the border. Visits to the Upper Kootenays beside Lower Columbia Lake (Windermere) and his favourite friends on the Shuswap Reserve taught him that diligence in agriculture paid off even in these normally dry areas. The priest also enjoyed a comforting soak in Fairmont Hot Springs when visiting that district.

Complacency was never permitted. Father Coccola faced many minor challenges, which he handled with increasing expertise as he mastered the Ktunaxa language. He was startled, however, when he returned from a busy visit to the West Kootenay to find a restless brave waiting for him. Without pausing, this Indian—Pierre—declared, "You must leave the country! Three years ago we ordered the surveyors and provincial constable to leave, and they did or they would not be living today."

Thoughtfully Father Coccola answered, "If surveyors of land and a constable went, they did well. They had come here to make money and when they saw no money in sight and their life in danger, they left. But for myself I have not come for money or a good time, but to help the Indians to live well and show them the way to heaven. So long as I am living and there is an Indian who needs me, I shall remain in this country." Pierre threatened, "Then we shall *kill* you!" Coccola stood up, opened his shirt, and replied, "Go ahead. I shall not make a step back. No one can hurt me. The only one I fear is God." Pierre then retreated, and told those waiting outside, "That priest is an old soldier, has faced many guns, and can handle a gun better than any one of us. The whites love him, the Indians fear him, and God takes his word. [We] better leave him alone."[40]

Three years later, Pierre returned to see the good father. He threw a lump of mineral on the table. He answered questions vaguely when the father sought details. Father Coccola discreetly showed the ore to one or two white miners. The rock was assayed and found to be top quality, so he went to Fort Steele to obtain a miner's licence. While at Fort Steele he recruited the assistance of a good Catholic mining entrepreneur, James Cronin. After Mass on Sunday, Cronin and Coccola set off with Pierre to guide them. They had to be evasive with any travellers they met on the trail. Pierre showed where they could hide their horses without leaving tracks. The three scrambled up the hillside beside Moyie Lake and found rich outcroppings. Cronin coached them on the correct marking of each of five claims. These claims were duly registered at the Fort Steele government office the next day.

The St. Eugene Mine was developed and sold to an American company for $22,000. The CPR hastened to put a line to, and past, this new mine. With the money earned, Father Coccola directed the building of a special house for Pierre, who also received cattle and farm implements, and an honorary pension of five dollars a month from the Consolidated Mining Company. The money was also used to build a very beautiful church at the mission and a smaller church in the new community of Moyie.

Twice a year the Indians from the various reserves arrived at the mission for religious instruction and tribal meetings. A great number of teepees would be set up. Each day everyone assembled at the church to pray, to sing, or to have their catechism explained to them. The children from the school joined their families for many of the activities, coming in to the school for meals. The chief assembled his watchmen and catechists to receive reports on individuals who had been guilty of misdemeanours such as gambling, drunkenness, theft, or fighting. They then decided whether the punishment should be a fine or a whipping of so many strokes. Isadore and his four sheriffs seized all who had been guilty of any such offence. Each was stripped to a loincloth and laid on a robe with their hands and feet secured by rawhide thongs to stakes driven in the ground, and then flogged—regardless of age or sex. Despite anticipating his punishment, each culprit never failed to appear at St. Eugene at the feast of Christmas or Easter.[41]

Sister Pacifique and her staff watched the activities with great interest. The orderly coming and going of these hundreds of Indians during the week of preparation belied the rumours that the Kootenays were wild, warlike people. For Christmas service, all the Indians came—dressed in their very best blankets—to stand in front of the church, where in silence they awaited the first stroke of midnight. When the new bell rang, a procession of clergy and altar boys came out of the church singing. A volley of shots was fired in the air, then with all singing loudly to show their great joy, everyone entered the church for midnight Mass. It was somewhat easier for Indians to sing traditional praises in Latin than in English. Even tribal elders seemed to enjoy the chanting that accompanied a Roman Catholic Mass. As the ceremonies progressed, the people sang louder and louder, each one at his own speed. Sisters Adrien and Rita started to giggle about this unusual, unmusical rendition of the familiar hymns and carols, and Sister Pacifique glared at them.[42]

The week between Christmas and New Year's Day was given to visiting and feasting. A large tent was set up for dancing (though some years Chief Isadore forbade it). The women danced all day, and the men danced during the night, never having both sexes in the dance tent together. New Year's Mass was similar to the Christmas midnight service. After this Mass, all went to the Oblates' house, where the Indians all came to shake hands with the priests and the sisters, and good wishes were exchanged. It was after 2 a.m. when they went home and put the children to bed. The next day the chief entertained: A huge feast was laid out with goodies brought by each participating family. The pupils from the residential school ate their fill. Dancing went on. The Native policemen saw to it that the women did not leave their tents at night. Finally, a volley of shots was fired in the air, and the dancing ceased. There would be no more dancing till the next Christmas.

Easter preparation was serious. Attendance at this springtime observance fluctuated depending on whether their horses were healthy, whether they had sufficient food to contribute to the feast, or whether the trails to the mission were free of snow. Records indicate that the winter of 1889–90 was particularly bad. Cattle and horses could not move around in the crusted snow, and there was insufficient hay even if the animals could reach it. That winter Chief Isadore lost all his horses and 60 head of cattle.

The summer following gave good crops. Father Coccola brought a mower and seeder when he returned from a retreat in New Westminster. Colonel Baker loaned his thrashing machine to collect the bountiful grain crop. The grist mill beside the school ground the wheat to provide flour for bread at the school. The fall of 1890 they produced 10,900 pounds of first-class wheat, 3,400 pounds of second-class grain, and 3,200 pounds of third-class grain, as well as many tons of bran for feeding the stock or selling on the market.[43]

Chapter 10

The Indian Agency's Early Years

The Indian agent was instructed to visit the bands regularly, observing their general health and their crops, keeping a census of the people, their cattle, and their horses. The written reports by Michael Phillipps, the first Indian agent in the East Kootenay region, reveal the successes and frustrations.

The highlight in the early years was the building of the Kootenay residential school at the site of the Roman Catholic mission beside the St. Mary's River. Michael Phillipps made discreet statements such as, "The report on the school will be submitted by the principal" (Father Coccola), but his successor made frequent visits and waxed enthusiastic in every report.

Phillipps' main duty as the Indian agent was to assist each band so they could improve their gardens and farms. Seed oats, wheat, potatoes, and tools such as ploughs, harrows, and mowers were purchased and their uses demonstrated. Ditches and flumes were created to bring water for irrigation. His annual reports made comments for each reserve—noting frustrations such as flooding or frosts, or improvements in yields—and was submitted to the superintendent-general of Indian Affairs in Ottawa. These were accompanied by a summarized assessment of the whole province by a commissioner of Indian affairs in Victoria.

Indians were permitted to hunt for game in the mountains or fish in the rivers and lakes. The populations of both food sources were declining. Severe winters plus an increase in the number of hunters depleted the herds of deer and elk. American settlers at or near the mouth of the Columbia River established fisheries to supply new canneries. The Shuswaps had chosen land above the famous "Salmon Beds of Athalmere." The spawning runs dwindled to scant numbers. The Shuswaps and their Kootenay neighbours were deprived of their traditional caches of smoked salmon. Good hunters secured enough meat to feed their own families, but they did not share with their neighbours. It was increasingly important that cattle be raised, with hay cut for winter feeding, so that the health of the community could be maintained.

The winter of 1889–1890 was so severe that many horses and cattle died, especially those belonging to members of the St. Mary's band. The following winter was marred by illness— an influenza that lasted a long time, distressing residents on all four reserves. In an attempt to disinfect the homes of the stricken people, Agent Phillipps arranged for all Indian cabins at the mission to be whitewashed inside and out.

Agent Phillipps' report of July 1891 dealt with Indian disturbances in the U.S., south of Tobacco Plains. Troops and U.S. civil authorities arrested Chief Eneas and several rebellious braves. Four of them were executed, which, according to Phillipps, "had a very quieting effect on both sides of the line." Phillipps went on to speculate that the construction of the Great Northern Railway and a large influx of white settlers would stop these "Indian alarms" that had such a disquieting effect upon Canadian Indians.

The East Kootenay was considered in a depression until 1892. That was the year that large deposits of silver and lead were discovered, and were developed into the North Star and Sullivan Mines. Father Coccola showed a sample of galena to his parishioners at the mission, hoping that a find by one of them could be used to benefit the church. Some Kootenay women found good samples while picking huckleberries at the site of today's Kimberley Ski Hill. Rather than carry the heavy stones home, they showed them to a prospector, Joe Bourgeois. He staked the North Star Mine there. Although Father Coccola's plan had failed, maintaining the mission school occupied him.

The highlights within the Kootenay agency in 1892 were the arrival of a physician at Fort Steele, the death of Chief David at Tobacco Plains, the fatalities from pneumonia, and the exceptional advancements of the Kinbaskets on the Shuswap Reserve. The provincial government subsidized Dr. Charles MacLean to look after the Indians; however, when the Indians were fascinated by the white doctor's methods and medications, they thronged to his office with curiosity, so it became necessary for an Indian to check in with the Indian agent prior to visiting Dr. MacLean. This was the summer when F.P. Norbury replaced Phillipps for almost four months. Norbury wrote, "It is up to me to decide whether or not the person is shamming."

Michael Phillipps continued his duties as Indian agent until early 1894. The following passages are excerpts from his annual reports.

"Isadore, the Chief of the St. Mary's or main band of the Kootenays, has been improving his farm and working hard throughout the year. He sets a good example to his followers in point of industry; but does not like being troubled on Indian matters, and, considering his wealth, assists but little in relieving the poorer members of the band."

"The Columbia Lake Band of Kootenays have also done well during the past year. Their Chief Mooyais is growing very old—too old, in fact, to take any part or interest in the affairs of the tribe. The crop harvested on the Columbia Lake Reserve was above an average; the Indians, however, did not increase the acreage under cultivation."

"On this reserve they are not subject to the summer frosts that do so much harm on the St. Mary's; the Indians here have also a ready sale for their oats, which are shipped down the Columbia River."

"The small family of Shuswap Indians that reside on their reserve near the Lower Columbia Lake have shown their usual industry, and their farms are little, if at all, behind those belonging to the white settlers on the Columbia River. These Shuswap Indians receive neither seed nor farm implements from the Government, and prefer paying their own way in all things."

Some members of the Kinbasket band of the Shuswaps took an arduous trip to Missoula, Montana, to acquire a plough; however, they arrived home without the harness to pull the plough. It was too late in the season to either buy or create a harness, so the women of the band devised a way for eight of them to pull the plough, with one or two to guide it in furrows. The Kinbaskets were hard-working, stubborn people, who were descendants of one Shuswap Native couple. The Kootenay Indians did not intermarry with them, and they did not interact with their original Shuswap band, which they had left behind west of the Monashee Mountains, near Kamloops.

Amelia Kinbasket, the first girl chosen to attend St. Eugene Mission School, poses after her graduation in 1901, wearing a fashionable dress that she sewed herself.

Many of the Kinbasket daughters and granddaughters married white settlers. The children of Amelia (the first girl chosen to attend St. Eugene Mission School) and William Hobbs Palmer were considered Indian. All the daughters attended the mission school. It was intended that any sons born would attend a local school for whites, but there were none in that family. One of the Kinbasket daughters, Angelique, was considered so clever that for two years following her graduation from St. Eugene Mission School she taught at a Blackfoot school on the other side of the Rockies. The youngest daughter, Rosalee, became secretary for Chief Pierre after he lost his sight when he injured his eyes.

Michael Phillipps had worked very hard establishing good relationships between the Indians and whites in each part of his jurisdiction. There were no training sessions or workshops for government employees in those early years, so men such as Phillipps had to create an atmosphere of trust.

In the West Kootenay Valley the Flatbow or Lower Kootenay Indians, made use of injudicious and threatening language towards the men working on the diking and banking of the Kootenay Reclamation Company, a potato garden belonging to an Indian having been destroyed by the steam digger. Owing to the great distance of the work from the Indian Agent's Office, and the want of all communication between the Upper and Lower Kootenay Valley, a great deal of misunderstanding occurred, and, acting under bad advice, the Indians displayed a good deal of ill feeling towards the workmen of the Reclamation Company.

The general health of the Indians has been good; though consumption and scrofula seem to be much on the increase.

Formerly these Indians lived almost exclusively on a meat diet; now they use flour as their staple article of food, and the children are certainly less robust than formerly.

The crop of 1892 was a light one throughout the entire valley, much less than average. There was no rain for nearly five months. Not only was the potato crop small, but the grain and straw very inferior; the grass on the ranges was also burnt up.

The winter of 1892–93 will long be remembered, not only by the Indians but by the white settlers as a hard one. The cold was at no time very severe: 30° below zero at Fort Steele, 23° below at Tobacco Plains, marking the extreme of cold; nor did this extreme cold last for more than a few days. The snow, however, began to fall early in November; before the end of that month the depth was considerable. This snow remained on the ground without intermission until late in April.

The entire supply of hay belonging to both whites and Indians was exhausted early in March. At this time the snow generally disappears here. The loss of cattle and horses was very large; how any of the animals lived through the winter is surprising. Coming so soon after the hard winter of some two years ago, the loss was very much felt by the Indians: the applications for relief or assistance in the spring were, however, very few, less than for many years past, the marked good health throughout the entire tribe, in such marked contrast to the spring time of the last few years, being much in their favour.

The band of wild horses nominally the property of the chief died to the last one: more than half the band died two years ago. For some years they have ranged on the high table lands west of the St. Mary's Reserve, rarely coming out into the prairie land, and never of late years on to the lower lands near the river. Looked at in simply a practical light, their disappearance is not to be regretted. Riding or jack horses straying into the wild band became in a very short time as unapproachable as their wild associates.

The increase in the number of pupils at the Indian Industrial school sanctioned by the Government, was at once taken advantage of by the Indians; and the number of pupils at present is in excess of the fifty provided for by the Government.

The Indian children have made great progress, and many of them read and write well.

Although planted very late, the Indian crops look better than I have ever before seen them; and there is every prospect of a large crop.

I have the honour to be, sir,
Your obedient servant,
MICHAEL PHILLIPPS, Indian Agent   1 July 1893

Phillipps had met each challenge to the best of his ability and laid good groundwork for whoever would succeed him. He wished to concentrate his efforts with his farm and family back at Tobacco Plains.

Three applications were submitted to Victoria. Each gentleman had proven his ability to communicate in the Ktunaxa language. Norbury, the youngest, had handled the job briefly; Hyde Baker was popular with the local Indians; and Robert Galbraith was a Fort Steele businessman who had been in the district for over twenty years.

Robert Galbraith was awarded the job, and served in that role for many years. He discovered that the Kootenays had trouble pronouncing his name, so he allowed them to call him Bob. He served as a consultant and friend to the Kootenays for the rest of his life.

Chapter 11

A Change in Momentum
(1892–93)

Chinese workers were highly prized because they were efficient, self-sustaining, and willing to work for lower wages than white navvies. Sections of the newly laid Canadian Pacific Railway were carved out by crews of Chinese workers. Baillie-Grohman brought in a large crew to hand-dig his canal. Once the projects were completed, however, the workers were dismissed. Those that mastered the English language found a niche as a storeowner, servant, market gardener, restaurateur, or laundry operator. Others followed the lure of gold, working placer claims with considerable success.

Indians and whites alike had very few short-term jobs during the early 1890s. There were guiding and packing jobs, and sometimes they might get road-building, messenger-service, or herding contracts. J.E. Humphreys at the Grange on Wolf Creek at Wasa had a succession of helpers, usually for one or two months at a time. In the fall he commissioned Indian herders to cut out his cattle from their stock and drive them back to Wasa from Bummer's Flats.[44]

The winter of 1891–92 was mild but sunless. There were many cases of influenza and pneumonia. Several students at the residential school succumbed. Seventy deaths were reported in the Kootenay agency. Those who overcame the illness were listless and vulnerable to "consumption" (tuberculosis). A large number of cattle had been lost the previous winter and the poorer Indian families had not been able to fill their meat requirement either by hunting or killing their own animals.

The town of Fort Steele continued to be a centre of business. In February of 1892 Norbury described Fort Steele as follows.

Fort Steele can scarcely be called a town as it consists of a Government building, gaol, hotel, saddlers shop, store, Customs House and Indian Offices with about three private cabins, all log buildings of course. Small as it is, there is a big business done for an up-country place. White and Indian trade concentrates here—I suppose that £7 to £10,000 circulates every year.[45]

When Baillie-Grohman arrived in the district nine years earlier, he noted there were eleven voters registered between Canal Flats and Tobacco Plains. By the 1892 election there were 25. Voters had to be land owners and British subjects, so this number does not include the dozens of drifters living in the hills, the seasonally employed sawmill or logging camp workers, or those living in a tent or squatter's shacks. It also does not account for the Chinese working mining claims or at menial jobs for white settlers. The white priests or nuns would not have a vote either.

In August of 1892 Norbury wrote about the arrival of the steamboat *The Annerly*.

The whole country was very much excited last week by the arrival of the steamboat *The Annerly* from the States. Everyone was doubtful whether the boat was even built (there had been a great deal of talk about her but no one had seen her) or still more whether she could make it up the river. Imagine our surprise when a beautiful steamer 93 feet long, 100 horsepower engine arrived three miles below Fort Steele, having come up from Jennings, 50 miles below Tobacco Plains, in two and a half days. The country is saved! At last we shall be able to live at a reasonable cost, instead of paying more for our supplies than any place on the American continent as we have done hitherto. Flour went down at once from $7 to $5 per 100 pounds, sugar from $15 to $9 and everything else in proportion.[46]

Captain Frank Armstrong of Golden had overcome the many challenges of riverboating on the Upper Columbia River. When he heard of *The Annerly* making its maiden voyage upriver from

F.S. 159 - 987

The Annerly, *the first sternwheeler to work the Kootenay River between Jennings, Montana, and Fort Steele. Note the cordwood stacked on deck for feeding the boilers.*

Jennings in August 1892, he decided to compete for the envisioned profits carrying freight on the Upper Kootenay River. He found willing workers at Wasa, who, with a master craftsman directing their use of lumber from Nils Hanson's sawmill, built the *Gwendoline* in Hanson Channel. The *Gwendoline*, launched by high water in June, steamed up to Canal Flats, where it was hoped she could use Grohman's canal and lock. The lock had been damaged by high water, so rather than wait for repairs, Captain Armstrong assembled crews to lay rollers so that the 63-foot vessel could be pulled across the flat to Columbia Lake.

In June of 1892, Dr. Charles MacLean had arrived in Fort Steele accompanied by his niece, Margaret (Mary) Bell. Miss Bell became the fourth white female residing in the community. Dr. MacLean was paid $500 by the provincial government to establish a practice in this remote area. The Department of Indian Affairs also offered a retainer fee equal to the provincial grant, plus would pay for Indian patients on a case-by-case fee.

Reports came in that smallpox cases were appearing on Vancouver Island. The Department of Indian Affairs arranged for vaccinations to be done on many of its charges in the Interior. The first shipment of "lymph" was given to Dr. MacLean who used it to vaccinate the pupils at the residential school at the mission. The acting Indian agent was given the responsibility of inoculating the Lower Kootenay band members near Creston. When he arrived there he discovered that the Indians were pulling up surveyors' stakes and generally hindering progress by Baillie-Grohman's workers. The main point of contention was a burial ground and a small garden. McLoughlin came to the rescue, and a meeting with the foreman of the dyking team quickly cleared away fears. There was never any threat to the graveyard, and a much larger plot, now safe from flooding, was cultivated for the band.

South of Fort Steele at Tobacco Plains there were many improvements to the land and opportunities for employment. The Indians chose to improve their cabins as well as expand their gardens. Renegades who used to cross the border were either employed with the new railway through the U.S. or were blocked by new fences on ranches on both sides of the border. The old Tobacco Plains Chief David had died in the fall of 1891. He was a disgruntled old man who never concealed his hatred and dislike of the whites. In his youth he had been the Buffalo Chief, leading the Kootenays on their annual buffalo hunt. David had also delighted in leading his people in their never-ending wars with the Bloods and Blackfoot. He sneered at those who herded cattle despite the need for beef to replace wild meat in the diets of his people. Indian Agent Michael Phillipps must have had some miserable moments with Chief David as a neighbour and his father-in-law.

David's eldest son Paul became chief. Paul was a very industrious farmer who had, on occasion, defied his father so that he could assist government personnel in solving local problems.

Michael Phillipps built an office and residence at Fort Steele to more conveniently carry out his duties as Indian agent. His family lived there for several months of each year. The older boys were able to care for the cattle and gardens at his Tobacco Plains farm. Phillipps took a leave from agency duties when he was obligated to return to England following the death of his mother. His father had died earlier, but now several aspects of the estate could not be settled until Michael was present. He arranged for F.P. Norbury to become acting Indian agent while he was away from July to early October 1892.

When Michael Phillipps had made his trip to England in 1885–86 nothing ran on schedule. By 1892 ships and trains were keeping reasonably predictable timetables. It was decided that Mrs. Phillipps could meet her husband in Golden when he returned. Rowena, who could speak little or no English, bravely set out along unfamiliar roads, walking or riding, leading two or three pack horses and packing her youngest daughter in a papoose carrier. The fire-breathing railway engines at Golden filled her with awe. She had kept her promise to meet Michael at that train station. Her trek became a family legend.[47]

In the winter of 1892–93, a crew of twenty men mined the ore at the North Star Mine. Joe Bourgeois had staked the claim of galena on what is now the Kimberley Ski Hill, and was doing all in his power to make it pay. He cleared a trail down to the Kootenay River so that teams could "rawhide" sacks of ore to a landing where *The Annerly* would load it for a trip downriver. The sacks of ore, each weighing 200 pounds, were carried on the steamer deck to Jennings, Montana—a town that sprang up to serve both railway and river traffic. The ore then went to a smelter in Great Falls, Montana, for processing.

Prospectors swarmed through the hills, looking for a find like Joe's. A group of four decided to hike over from Kootenay Lake and follow the St. Mary's River down to the Kootenay River. (Their route is now a "summer only" road.) They must have prospected every few miles, as it took them 37 days. They ran out of grub and were getting worried when they met some Kootenay Indians who fed them, then guided them to the mission. Their next move was to buy supplies at Fort Steele, then go back up the St. Mary's River as far as Mark Creek.

Walter Burchett, a farmer from Colbert, Washington; Ed Smith, an experienced miner; German immigrant John Cleaver; and Pat Sullivan, a red-headed Irishman, joined together for this prospecting trip. North Star Mountain was staked, so they scouted the hillside on the other side of Mark Creek. They found sufficient outcroppings to stake three claims: the Shylock, the Hope, and the Hamlet. By this time winter was approaching. It was agreed that at least one would remain at the discovery, working during the open season, while the others worked to gain funds for further development.[48]

An American, Tom Flowers, commissioned the Wasa boat builders who had built the *Gwendoline* for Captain Armstrong to create another hull for a future riverboat. The specifications given for the vessel, however, were incorrect, so when the steamer reached Jennings in 1894 the machinery from Bonner's Ferry proved too large to be installed. Flowers spent the next year having a second larger vessel, the *Libby*, built to use the engines. He optimistically tried a screw propeller, then found it could not be used on a river.

Surveys were commenced south of Fort Steele. More than one railway scheme was being considered. Americans considered sending spur lines to obtain Canadian coal, or to haul ore to their smelters. William Fernie's charter obtained in partnership with Colonel Baker was about to expire. Any company that actually laid the track would receive extensive land grants from the government. The East Kootenay businessmen attempted to connect with the CPR rail line at Fort Macleod, but at the same time wanted to avoid giving Canadian Pacific options on these new coal fields. The management of the big railway company knew they could wait and move when the time was right.

Following his stint as acting Indian agent, Norbury also left for a visit in England. He left his partner, Captain E.C. Parker, to care for the animals and general running of Fairfield Ranch at Fish Lake. He travelled via the Great Northern Railway from Jennings, Montana, to New York, sailed to "the old country," and had a good visit. When he returned he got off the train at Kalispell, where he purchased a team of horses and a camp outfit. He left Kalispell on the morning of March 29, 1893, and found he had to walk, leading the horses, in a foot of snow. After the first twelve miles of trudging he reached the first stopping house. The landlord warned Norbury that the snow was much deeper to the north. He made another twelve miles on crusted snow with the horses breaking through the crust and suffering from cuts on their legs. He decided not to make the horses suffer further indignities, so he took off the saddles and harness and carefully hung all in a tree off the trail. The horses were freed to return, on their own, to Kalispell. Luckily a rancher in Kalispell had agreed to care for them if they should show up there.

Norbury continued walking with a small backpack, holding a pound of cheese, three small loaves of bread, some tea, sugar, a kettle, axe, and one blanket. At dusk he found some men building a new house, who welcomed him. They were out of flour and out of bread so he shared what he had, leaving the next day with barely half a loaf. Twenty miles further on he was happy to reach a stopping house, but the owner growled, "You can't stay here, the missus is sick." The traveller asked if he could buy some bread. "Nope. There's no bread here. We've had no flour for over a fortnight. But there is another stopping house seven miles up the road." Weary and hungry, Norbury went on until he could go no more. He cut some branches for a bed and covering, and slumped into sleep for a few hours. When he awoke he found fresh snow on his shelter. He trudged on again, passing the desired stopping house before 6 a.m. Finally, at 10 a.m., he came to a ranch house where he was fed a good square meal. The following day he arrived at Tobacco Plains, where he knew all the citizens and felt sure that he could beg, buy, or borrow a horse. Any horse that was still alive was too weak to be ridden. Every report he heard was a lamentation about the number of cattle, calves, or horses lost thus far during the winter.

He faced more walking—hard walking—in deep snow. At Elk River Bridge he expected to find a party of surveyors, but they had left four days earlier. With no luck in finding companionship and a cooked meal, he was more than relieved to find their food cache. He found a tin of beef that served him well for the last two days of his journey. Eight days on the trail, camping outside following the first two nights, he had travelled 158 miles. No doubt he was most happy to get back to Fairfield Ranch, his home at Fish Lake.

Parker had been feeding their cattle for a shorter period than most of their neighbours. Already bare patches in their front meadow were promising fresh green growth. Parker reported that the winter loss was two yearlings and two two-year-olds, with eight spring calves either stillborn or only alive a few hours. Despite this being a loss to the partners at Fish Lakes, it was a much smaller percentage of the herd than that lost by Humphreys at Wasa, or Chief Isadore, or the Tobacco Plains herders.

Norbury had arrived home too late to be invited to an important wedding. Mary Rowena Phillipps, eldest daughter of the Indian agent, was wed April 4, 1893, to Colin James Sinclair, son of James and Elizabeth Sinclair of Fort Garry. Colin had a ranch south of the Phillipps property at Tobacco Plains and "had become pleasantly aware of P's part Indian daughter."[49] Father Nicolas Coccola married them at the agency. Charlie Edwards was best man. Other prominent citizens attended the ceremony. The official witnesses were Robert Galbraith and Dr. Charles MacLean. The Phillipps girls were beautifully dressed for the occasion.

> After the wedding, Charlie Edwards remembers, the bride went outside to the spot where the groom had been camping Indian fashion near the Phillipps' house, took down his teepee, packed everything in parfleches, helped to load the pack horses, mounted her saddle horse and the newlyweds were off to Colin's Ranch on Tobacco Plains. In 1900 Colin and his wife and family moved across the line to Canada where they took a ranch among Mary Rowena's people.[50]

Earlier that year, in March, the locals had drawn up a petition to have the trail to Tobacco Plains upgraded to a "waggon"[51] road.

Robert Galbraith mused on his role in the Fort Steele community. It was he who had requested the name change from Galbraith's Ferry to Fort Steele. He had asked for this change while the Mounties were still camped on his land, but Major Sam Steele had demurred. Perhaps Steele was modest. Perhaps he insisted that this was not a fort. It was a barracks, a camp, a post, but not a fort; however, a request sent to Ottawa after the troop had left allowed the name change. A new post office was established, and Galbraith arranged for his brother-in-law, Charles Clark, to become postmaster.

Galbraith was a businessman and a bachelor, and every bachelor appreciates a home-cooked meal. So when his sister, Catherine Clark, was kind enough to invite him for dinner, he accepted the invitation. On one such occasion he noticed his twelve-year-old nephew Herbert carefully practising his writing at the kitchen table. He looked up at his uncle and put his quill pen into the rim of the ink bottle. The nib broke. Herbert quickly assured everyone that he could whittle the feather to create a new nib. With careful strokes of his small penknife he tapered a point, and carefully split it. He dipped this into the ink and finished writing the page that his mother had assigned. Uncle Bob watched him, fascinated by his earnest concentration. When the lid was safely on the ink well, Robert reached for Herbert's slate. He set out three columns of numbers and asked the boy to add these up. Herbert passed this test efficiently.

They were called to the dinner table. Young Herbert said the grace, then ate quietly as the adults conversed. An amusing story was circulating about Colonel Baker's recent election campaign. Baker went to the small railway community of Field, B.C., where the community had turned out en masse to meet the politician. "We want a school," they emphatically informed him. "You shall have a school if you have fifteen pupils." The audience admitted there were only six children in Field. "But we expect you to find us the other nine."

At the end of this story Galbraith declared, "Fort Steele shall have a school soon!"

Chapter 12

The Flood, the Schools, and Optimism (1894)

Europeans and Americans were settling in both the East and West Kootenays, and soon the southeast of the province began to attract investor attention. Transportation links were slowly improving. Fear of an Indian uprising had been erased, and St. Eugene Mission School was operating to capacity (50 pupils). The dyking of the Creston Flats in the summer of 1893 yielded many more acres of arable land. Curious tourists who saw this mountainous area were delighted, finding the scenery beautiful despite scars left by forest fires.

The government had responded to the petition to upgrade the travel route south of Fort Steele. Norbury won the contract to build the Aberfeldie Bridge across the Bull River. This was a sturdy bridge wide enough for wagons. The work was done with a crew headed by a man named Kaufman, who was very skilful with axes, tools, and with handling the horses.

Another provincial election was held in 1894. Voters needed to be resident in the province of B.C. for twelve months, a resident of the district of East Kootenay for at least two months, and also be a British subject. Enumeration had to be done, so F.P. Norbury travelled the district from Rogers Pass, Donald, and Golden down to Tobacco Plains. Because the population was increasing, and the requirements for voting no longer included owning land, the revised Voters List allowed over 700 citizens to cast ballots in the July election. Colonel Baker was re-elected with scant opposition.

Spring planting went ahead slightly behind schedule. It was a pleasantly cool period in the valleys, but minimal melting was happening in the hills. During the first week in June the temperatures suddenly skyrocketed to near 37° Celsius (100°F). Water poured out of the mountains all over the province. Roads, bridges, and telegraph lines were washed out. The Fraser Valley became an inland sea. The Creston dykes were broken, and the reclamation project virtually nullified. To the north on Kootenay Lake, Kaslo's few buildings left in downtown following a fire in February were washed away by high water and high winds on June 3. The mainline of the Canadian Pacific Railway was unable to resume regular service for 41 days.

The commencement of river service up the Kootenay River was delayed. Captain Armstrong tied up his Columbia River steamers at Golden and prayed that the waterfront wharf would hold up under the bombardment of uprooted trees and other driftwood. Westport, across from Fort Steele, was flooded. By early August Armstrong had navigated the steamer *The Pert* across the flooded isthmus from Lake Windermere to Columbia Lake. *The Pert* carried passengers to Canal Flats, where the bridge across the Kootenay had been washed out. For months passengers were ferried across by canoe to catch the stage south to Fort Steele.

Meanwhile, Robert Galbraith hired T.T. McVittie to lay out streets and lots for the Fort Steele townsite. Michael Phillipps resigned as Indian agent and Robert Galbraith was appointed in his stead. When he took possession of the ample Indian agency office and home, he realized that he could designate one section as a classroom. He took it upon himself to advertise for a teacher.

The selected applicant was an experienced teacher, Miss Adelaide Bailey. This good lady instantly became a much-valued citizen of the burgeoning community of Fort Steele. She arrived in the summer of 1894 and arranged to board at a "nice" home. Within a few weeks, however, she raised eyebrows because she purchased a building lot and arranged to have her own house erected. Miss Bailey was welcomed to the community not only as the first teacher but also as an accomplished musician and a pioneer able to tell of her experiences in other parts of the province.

"Addie" was born in San Francisco on December 11, 1857. Her father went to Yale in 1859. Mrs. Bailey and two children sailed from San Francisco on the *Brother Jonathon* to Victoria, over to Vancouver, then upriver to Fort Hope. From Hope they were conveyed to Yale by Indian canoes. Adelaide was the eldest of thirteen children. She was given some instruction in music, French, and other niceties by the wife of the Minister at St. John's Anglican Church in Yale. In June 1875 the seventeen-year-old had studied enough to go to Victoria to write examinations to obtain Teacher Certification. In this era before there was a Teacher's College or Normal School, each candidate studied on her own and then had to recertify by taking tests each summer.

Young Miss Bailey was the first teacher at Hope. At the conclusion of her school year there, Superintendent Jessop, the provincial school inspector, observed her in action, then allowed her to accompany him upriver to Yale. The Fraser River was running so swiftly that the Indians resorted to towing the canoe as they walked along a footpath at the edge of the river. At one spot the tow rope broke and, as Adelaide later wrote, they "shot back with great velocity." The Indian crew then managed to take them to shore and ultimately deliver them safely to Yale, where Adelaide taught classes, including her young siblings, for the next three years.

From Yale she moved to Lytton, and during the move she experienced some thrilling trips with Steve Tingley of Barnard's Express. Before the railway bridge was constructed across the Fraser River near Lytton, passengers crossed the river in a basket large enough to carry a few passengers and a bale of hay, slung on a cable high above the river. There were other thrills in Miss Bailey's life. She was invited to walk across the railway bridge near Lytton and come back as a guest of Onderdonk in a decorated rail car, partaking of a champagne luncheon, on the first train travelling on that newly completed section of the Canadian Pacific Railway. Her job in Lytton ended abruptly because the school burned down. She was released from her contract and soon became the principal of Nanaimo's Girls' School.

In Fort Steele Miss Bailey very quickly became acquainted with the citizens, following the correct Victorian protocol of leaving a calling card and visiting at an approved "at home" time. The ladies—Miss Bell, Mrs. Clark, Mrs. Mather, Mrs.—

F.S. 14 - 02

The first schoolhouse in Fort Steele, built in 1894. In 1895, Miss Bailey and the school trustees stand in the doorway.

Back row (left to right): Trustee T.T. McVittie, Miss Adelaide Bailey, trustee Constable Hugh Barnes, R.L.T. Galbraith. Centre row (left to right): Hazel Galbraith, Esther Frizzell, Mabel Mather, Ethel Lewis, ? Forsyth, ? Underhill, Dave Emery, ? Glover, Herbert Clark, ? Forsyth. Front row (left to right): Mamey Lewis, Anne Downey, Mildred Mather, ? Forsyth, Hazel Mather, Pearl Mather, Elizabeth Neadig, Alberta Lewis, Maud Neadig, Unknown, Dan Lewis, Earl Mather, Percy Henry.

Levett, and the newly arrived mothers of other pupils—were delighted to have a new and very pleasant neighbour. The mainly male population accepted the advent of a school with a schoolmarm as a true sign that Fort Steele was becoming a civilized town.

Robert Galbraith recruited the surveyor T.T. McVittie, and the new Constable H. Barnes, to join him as official trustees for the Fort Steele School. There were initially ten students, but within a few months it was obvious that a proper school building was needed. Robert donated two lots, and the first schoolhouse—which stands today as the Anglican Church—was built.

During the summer of 1894 two new hotels were erected in Fort Steele. Robert Mather advertised in the *Golden Era* newspaper on March 10, 1894: "Dalgardno House. The largest and most commodious House in Fort Steele. Board by Day or Week."

A parallel advertisement claimed, "MOUNTAIN HOUSE. Edson & Co. EVERYTHING NEW. Board by the Day or Week. This house is under the management of E.J. Edson, better known as Johnny on the Spot."

These two establishments joined Charles Levett's Steele House, advertised as "The Oldest and Best Hotel in Fort Steele. First Class Table Board. Free Sample Room for Commercial Men. Strictly First Class."

In his role as Indian agent, Robert Galbraith visited the mission school once a month. He established a very good rapport with the Catholic sisters, frequently stating that while he was of a different denomination himself, he appreciated their teachings of the Indian children. The Indians, to all appearances, embraced Catholicism and worked very hard to observe the special rituals accompanying holy days. Those Indians who could arrange to travel gathered at the mission for Christmas and either Corpus Christi or Easter. Between religious obligations, the band chiefs assembled with Chief Isadore and his councillors. The chiefs, like Pierre Kinbasket of the Shuswap Reserve, each had a house at the mission to simplify their attendance at meetings. The gatherings of Kootenay leaders provided a forum at which successes could be reported, or requests made to the Indian agent for seeds or implements.

The following text is a condensation of Indian Agent Galbraith's report for 1894.

F.S. 5 - 71

A freight sled pulled by a four-horse team is shown here in front of Mrs. Levett's boarding-house. The rig may have come from Golden, 160 miles to the north, or from Kalispell, 165 miles to the south.

These Indians are gradually taking to farming, and their improvement is proportionately apparent. Some of those, however, who are located at long distances from the white settlements find much difficulty in disposing of the spare products of their farms. The spring freshets were extraordinarily high, doing much damage to the Indian gardens as well as those of white settlers.

The pupils at the industrial school are making good progress, and bid fair to be materially improved by the care and education bestowed upon them.

The statistics are given herewith:

Value of personal property	$ 76,000
Acres under cultivation	312
Acres of new land broken	79
Value of real and personal property	211,435
Ploughs	31
Harrows	11

Wagons	$ 14
Mowers	2
Horses	1,380
Cows	265
Oxen and bulls	77
Number of young stock	359
Value of furs taken	1,500
Wheat harvested bushels	310
Oats harvested bushels	2,050
Pease harvested bushels	165
Potatoes harvested bushels	1,240
Hay harvested tons	75

Kootenay Agency—1895
Canada Sessional Papers 1895 Vol. XXVIII

Meanwhile, the mission school was progressing very well. Father Coccola's official report talks of building an icehouse for storing meat, and about the fruit trees introduced two years in a row.

KOOTENAY INDUSTRIAL SCHOOL, B.C.,
8th July, 1895

The Honourable
The Superintendent General of Indian Affairs, Ottawa

SIR, I have the honour to transmit herewith my annual report for the year ended 30th June, 1895, with a list of government property under my charge.

The health of the pupils has been good, with the exception of a few cases of scrofula, a case of spinal meningitis and one of consumption. All possible attention has been paid to maintain a good sanitary condition among them, which is essential to their progress. They have all been vaccinated.

The conduct and general behaviour in both departments has been satisfactory.

The progress has been in accordance with the application, which indeed was most gratifying. Some of the pupils have considerably improved in writing and speaking the English language and can express themselves very clearly.

The new programme of studies has been followed, and the pupils have made very good progress in all the branches taught in the class room, especially in arithmetic and composition; they regularly correspond with pupils of other schools of the province.

A few of the children are endowed with good talents for learning; they excel in their class and perform every exercise with accuracy.

The following statement will show how the pupils stand in their studies:

1st standard	6	pupils
2nd "	17	"
3rd "	8	"
4th "	14	"
5th "	5	"

Our boys have at diverse times been called on as interpreters. On one occasion Gabriel had to interpret for the Indian chief and his people in the courthouse. The lad spoke well and audibly before the assembly of whites and Indians.

The whole of the work in the vegetable garden has been done by the boys. They take great interest in doing their work as perfectly as possible. They have also done the greater part of the ploughing and harrowing on the farm; the ground in cultivation covering this year more than forty acres. A specimen of the beautiful oats raised here was sent to the Indian office, where all who saw it said that it was the best oats in the district.

It being our aim to impart to the Indian boys under our control a practical knowledge of agriculture, as far as the means at our disposal will allow, we purchased last fall a thresher. The boys became greatly interested in running it, and threshed out one thousand, six hundred bushels of oats and one hundred and sixty-six bushels of wheat.

During the past winter the large boys have cut down and hauled logs to fence a piece of land bought at our expense for the purpose of affording them a sufficient practice in agriculture, as the school ground is rather limited.

They have practiced carpentry whenever the needs of the school required any work done.

With the assistance of the foreman they have altered certain partitions of their house to give better accommodation. A trench has been dug and pipes laid to let the water out from the laundry and from the kitchen.

In order to promote the health of the children who were accustomed before coming to school to live chiefly on meat, it became necessary to provide a place for keeping meat in summer, as it can be obtained only by getting a large supply; the boys have, therefore, built an icehouse which we find very serviceable.

They have supplied, sawed and corded the firewood for next winter. The smaller boys weed, take in the wood and do many useful things around the premises.

The boys' playground has been enlarged and attention is paid to their athletic training. As requested by the department, they are taught to sew on buttons and repair their clothes; one of them runs a sewing machine well.

The girls have been exercised in all domestic, laundry and dairy work. The large girls do the baking in turn; they make excellent bread and good pastry. All the cutting and fitting of their clothes have been done by them, also a considerable amount of sewing for the boys. They are also taught gardening. A portion of the garden attached to their playground has been set apart for that. They raise all kinds of vegetables and display great taste in the arranging of flowerbeds and walks.

We have done our utmost to succeed in having an orchard. Part of the trees planted last year are doing tolerably well, while those previously planted have failed. We are inclined to attribute this failure to the cold nights.

In January we were honoured by a visit from Mr. Vowell, Superintendent of Indian Affairs, who was agreeably surprised at the progress of the children and at the perfect order prevailing every where.

Mr. Galbraith, our agent, pays us a monthly visit.

The interest which he takes in the advancement of the children is a great inducement to urge them on in the performance of their duties.

On a few occasions entertainments have been given by our pupils, who acquitted themselves very creditably on their part.

This spring it had been decided that the Indians should clear, plough and level the streets leading through their village; not being accustomed to that kind of work, they went reluctantly at it; but I am pleased to state that our school boys went with scrapers and ploughs and began the work cheerfully and in good earnest; soon the Indians followed the example of their children.

The work performed gives a better appearance to the place.

I have the honour to be, sir,

Your obedient servant,

N. COCCOLA, Principal [52]

At that same time Norbury reported that 48 of his 50 apple trees, obtained from St. Catherines, Ontario, were budding very nicely. The flood of 1894 was the worst recorded to that date. But there were enough people in the East Kootenay to rebuild washed out roads and bridges quickly. The pace of life was picking up.

Chapter 13

Church, Concerts, and a Community Newspaper (1895)

In February of 1895 Norbury wrote, "Fort Steele is becoming horribly civilized." That may have been one man's opinion, but so much was happening that other local bachelors were being shaken out of their complacent, cozy routines. Stores and saloons now closed on Sundays. There were church services being conducted for various denominations. On February 22 there was a concert with one of the performers being "a witty man" (according to Norbury), getting off jokes with local overtones.

The biggest laugh came at the expense of Dr. MacLean and his niece. The physician was too penny-pinching to pay for someone to cut their firewood. He also realized that, according to the expectations for his respected vocation, he should not be seen harvesting his own wood supply. As a compromise he had on several occasions gone out with his niece after midnight to drag home a log or two. An operation like that, in moonlight, with him grunting commands at his horse, was bound to be observed and to become fuel for gossips.

A visitor in the audience that night also had firewood on his agenda. The *Gwendoline* and her sister sternwheelers were fuelled with firewood, so Captain Frank Armstrong came to Fort Steele to arrange for cordwood to be supplied at key places along the river. He rented a horse and—accompanied by the contractor—rode downriver. The flood of the previous summer had altered the river channel in some places, and high-water marking was very obvious. They chose sites where there was suitable beach access to a riverbank slightly higher than the high-water mark. The deck crew, plus "deck" passengers who paid the lowest fare, would throw down a gangplank at the landing and carry the cordwood on board as speedily as possible. Captain Armstrong then chartered the International Transportation Company, as the Upper Columbia Navigation and Tramway Company was not licensed to cross the border. He hired steamboat skipper James D. Miller (who had previously skippered *The Annerly* on the Kootenay River) to supervise the building of the new sternwheeler, the *Ruth*. The *Ruth*, 131 feet long, was to be readied for the 1896 shipping season. The *Gwendoline*, meanwhile, was enlarged to 98 feet for the 1895 season.[53]

The Fort Steele Mining Association was formed in 1895. It was a forerunner to the Board of Trade. A modern description of this new organization might be "The Fort Steele Booster Club." The directors were local businessmen such as Robert Galbraith, surveyor Tom McVittie, butcher Robert Sucksmith, hotelier and sawmill owner Robert Mather, carpenter John Grassick, storekeeper William Carlin, housepainter and newspaper owner A.B. Grace, and long-time miner Dave Griffiths.

Meanwhile, because Fort Steele now had 25—yes, 25 ladies!—niceties such as teas were happening. The ladies might compare magazines from "the old country," or comment on items in the Eaton's mail-order catalogue. Church services were being conducted in the schoolhouse, with the Anglicans at 2:30 p.m., and Presbyterians at 7 p.m., or vice versa. Miss Bailey quickly persuaded the Anglican women to raise money to buy an organ for the school, to be used for church services in that building. Miss Bailey was an accomplished pianist/organist. Mrs. Wallinger, a violinist, added sophistication to soirees and concerts. Dress and fashions also became important in their lives. Garments with flair were worn to social events and to church.

The village of Fort Steele was no longer a raw community, but had become a family place the instant the school was opened. Miss Bailey adapted quickly to each newcomer. There was firm discipline backed by compassion and understanding of each individual's level of understanding. New arrivals in the fall term included the Lewis family, who had evidently experienced discrimination in communities where they had lived previously. Hugh Barnes, a school trustee, was overheard when he asked the teacher whether coloured children were permitted to attend school in British Columbia. Miss Bailey replied, "Yes, all children are eligible." The father, Mr. Lewis, learned of this conversation and protested in a series of incensed letters. Government Agent James F. Armstrong was called upon to review the situation. His official response, written in his careful Spenserian hand, appears below.

Stipendiary Magistrate, Government Agent, Gold Commissioner, Assistant Commissioner of Lands and Works, Official Administrator &c., &c.

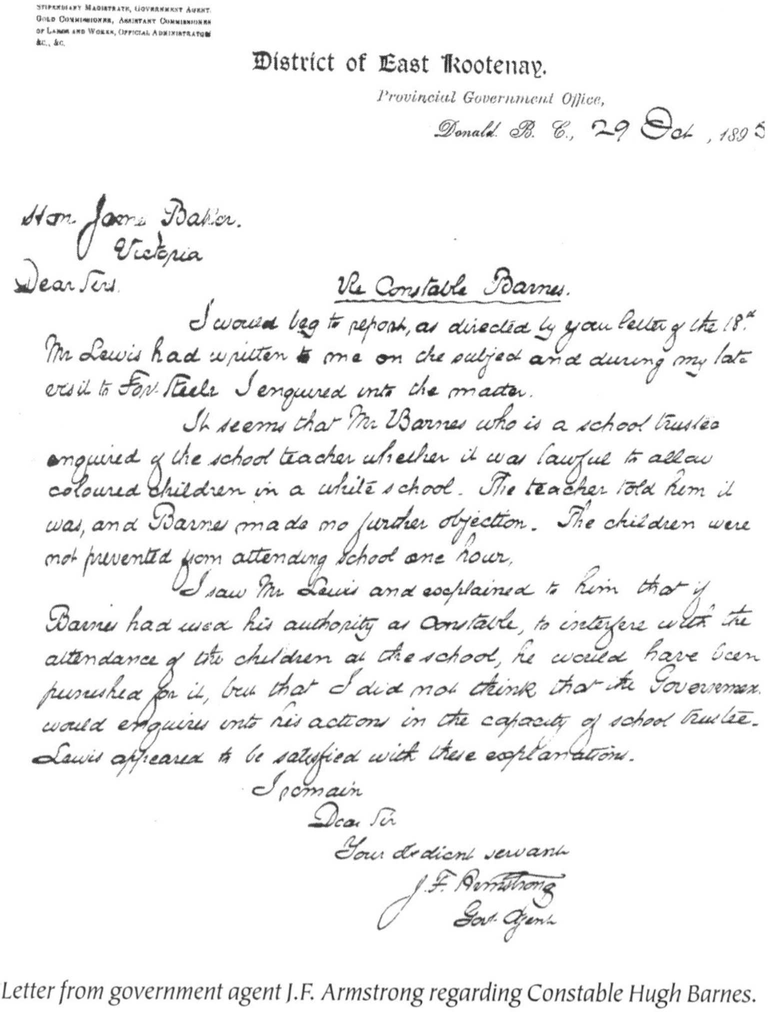

District of East Kootenay.

Provincial Government Office,

Donald B. C., 29 Oct, 1895

Hon. James Baker.
Victoria

Dear Sir.

Re Constable Barnes.

I would beg to report, as directed by your letter of the 18th Mr Lewis had written to me on the subject and during my late visit to Fort Steele I enquired into the matter.

It seems that Mr Barnes who is a school trustee enquired of the school teacher whether it was lawful to allow coloured children in a white school. The teacher told him it was, and Barnes made no further objection. The children were not prevented from attending School one hour.

I saw Mr Lewis and explained to him that if Barnes had used his authority as Constable, to interfere with the attendance of the children at the school, he would have been punished for it, but that I did not think that the Government would enquire into his actions in the capacity of school trustee. Lewis appeared to be satisfied with these explanations.

I remain
Dear Sir
Your obedient servant
J.F. Armstrong
Govt. Agent

Letter from government agent J.F. Armstrong regarding Constable Hugh Barnes.

Very severe winters had reduced the herds of deer and elk in the East Kootenay. At the same time, the population of both white and Native hunters had increased. Talks to create equitable boundaries for hunting during this hard time were convened at Windermere. The following document summarizes the agreement, and indicates the cooperation between many groups.

Memorandum of Agreement made in duplicate at Windermere,
District of East Kootenay, Province of British Columbia;
This 27th Day of September, 1895.
Between:
Abel, Chief of Columbia Lakes, Kootenay Indians
Pielle, Headman of the Kootenay Indians, St. Mary's.
Charlie Kinbasket, 2nd Chief of Shuswap Indians at Columbia Lake
Pierre Kinbasket, Shuswap Chief

One Part

John Cheneka, Chief of the Stonies, residing at Morley, in the N.W. Territories, and
George Crawler, Councillor of said Stoney Indians,

On the Other Part.

The said Chief and Headmen, Abel, Pielle, Pierre Kinbasket, John Cheneka, George Crawler, acting for themselves, and on behalf of the several Bands to which they respectively belong, because of the friendly relations hitherto existing between their several Bands,
    Do hereby agree as follows:
    That the Stonies shall have the privilege of hunting as far West as the Columbia and Kootenay Rivers, and that in return the Kootenay Indians, and the Shuswap Indians shall have the privilege of hunting as far East as the base of the Rocky Mountains, on the Eastern Slope thereof.

And that this mutual concession is made with the distinct understanding that the Game Laws of British Columbia, and the North West Territories, as the case may be shall be strictly observed, and that any infraction of the said Game Laws by the Stonies of British Columbia, or by the Kootenays or Shuswaps, in the North West Territories, shall be considered sufficient reason for withdrawing the concession above made, from the Band or Bands to which the Party, or Bodies Transgressing belong.

In witness whereof the Parties to this Agreement have set their hands hereto, this Day and Year above written: Signed in the presence of:

Abel X
   Chief Columbia Lake, Kootenay Indians (His mark)
A.K. Forget, Asst. Indian Commissioner
Pielle X Headman, St. Mary's Res. (His mark)
Charlie X Kinbasket,
   Second Chief of Shuswap Indians (His mark)
R.L.T. Galbraith, Indian Agent, Kootenay
John X Cheneka, Chief Stoney Indians (His mark)
George Golding, J.P.
George X Crawler, A Stoney Indian (His mark)
Pierre X Kinbasket, Shuswap Chief (His mark)
John McDougall, Missionary on Stoney Res.

I hereby certify that this Agreement, previous to its being signed, was carefully translated and explained to the Kootenays and Shuswap Indians, by Lewis Stowekin, Official Interpreter at the Kootenay Agency and by the Rev John McDougall, to the Stoney Indians.

Signed A.K. Forget[54]

In November *The Prospector* newspaper was launched. Starting a newspaper was a true vote of confidence in the future of Fort Steele. It was launched by Alexander Benjamin Grace, a veteran of the Union Army in the U.S. Civil War, who came to

Fort Steele as a house painter, decorator, and sign painter. He quickly became enamoured with the district and was a prime promoter for the rest of his life.

The first issues of *The Prospector* did not come off a press. Grace prepared a four-page two-column format, typing with a typewriter onto special waxed sheets. These sheets were duplicated on a mimeograph (or lithogram pad). He produced 175 copies each week. His efforts were noticed and praised by the *Vancouver World* and the *Vancouver Province* newspapers. "He turns out a capital little sheet, typed from A to Z, and Fort Steelites have every reason to be proud of the production."[55]

Fort Steele was on the threshold of becoming "The Capital of the Kootenays."

Chapter 14

A Thriving Community (1896)

Fort Steele school had put on its first Christmas concert in the Dalgardno Hotel. The newspaper noted that there were many social events during the 1895 holiday season. On the evening of Boxing Day, sleighs took two dozen "Steelites" to a dance hosted by Nils Hanson at Wasa. The party was treated to a sumptuous meal shortly after arriving. The floor was then cleared and dancing ensued with music by local fiddlers. Constable Hugh Barnes organized the transportation, emceed the activity on the dance floor, and delivered the revellers to their homes after daylight next morning.

Sadness, however, descended over the residents and visitors at the mission. Gabriel Benoit, a senior student at the Industrial School, became separated from his friends while on an outing. Searchers found his body the next day. The poor lad had frozen to death. Chief Isadore immediately cancelled the holiday dancing. The whole band honoured the young man with a funeral Mass on December 30, 1895.

During formal and informal meetings, the Fort Steele Mining Association (FSMA) had come up with a wish list of fourteen items. Several of their wants that they forwarded to the provincial government were for upgrading existing roads, trails, and bridges. To facilitate mining exploration, they asked for an improved trail with more bridges to the headwaters of St. Mary's River. Next they requested that the wagon road from Cranbrook to Moyie be rerouted by Palmer's Bar (present-day Lumberton), and for the bridges to be repaired across the Bull River and on other crossings leading to the Crow's Nest Trail. The hill on the wagon road to St. Eugene Mission was very eroded and needed grading. They requested a graded wagon road to the North Star and the Sullivan Mines, with spur roads to Cherry Creek (Mather's property) and Luke Creek. There had been mudslides up Wild Horse Creek, so that wagon road and trail needed servicing. The trunk road in the vicinity of Bummer's Flats had become a despised three-mile stretch of "heavy hilly road" and needed rerouting. One other recommendation was to "divert the road across from Fort Steele (in Westport) to coincide with streets surveyed." One might call that town planning! Last but not least, they wanted a continuous wagon road from Golden on the CPR to Kalispell on the Great Northern Railway.

Preparations for river transport from the south were underway. The federal government had granted a small amount to clear snags from the river and dredge the most obvious sandbars. The FSMA observed that the drawbridge to open the Fort Steele bridge for river traffic was too narrow to safely accommodate boat traffic going up to load ore at the North Star landing. Within a few months the span was increased to 40 feet. The leading citizens of "Steele" were achieving results.

An appeal was sent to the attorney general to request that a county court judge be sent to Fort Steele at least three times a year. It was noted that anyone presently engaged in a lawsuit had to go all the way to Donald, Kamloops, or Nelson—a very time-consuming as well as expensive undertaking.

The FSMA dreamed of one more facility that would fill the needs of district residents: a hospital. Letters from residents advocating the creation of a hospital appeared in *The Prospector*. It was pointed out that the sick or injured had nowhere to go. On a few occasions friends had installed a patient in a hotel room, but this was inconvenient for the hotel staff and barely satisfactory for a person needing extra rest. Therefore they created a committee to plan for a hospital, and F. P. Norbury was chosen to head it. An appeal was sent to the provincial government, but it was ignored. The local physician, Dr. Charles MacLean, was very quiet by nature, so he did not add his voice to the initial groundswell of planning.

Item number fourteen from the FSMA was acted upon before A.B. Grace published the list in his January 4, 1896, newspaper. Postal service had been minimal from the earliest inception. It had started as once-a-month delivery, then bi-weekly in good weather and monthly in winter. When Sam Steele arrived, the first mail delivery was incomplete because the mail carrier brought only as much as one pack horse could carry. The agent protested that he was paid for only one horse and he was not about to add a second animal unless he knew he'd be paid for it. Fuming, Steele arranged for constables to courier the mail from Golden to Kootenay Post (Fort Steele). Civilians continued with approximate service in subsequent years. The committee wrote a letter to J.A. Mara, MP, asking him to obtain weekly mail service year-round.

Meanwhile, on the river runs, Captain Armstrong found himself being hailed to landings for the sole purpose of sending out mail. Armstrong conceded that rural dwellers had virtually no alternative, but he decided to sell his own stamps. Each stamp was a mere five cents. The user was to also affix a Dominion stamp if it was forwarded from a Canadian post office, or an American stamp if it was deposited in the post office in Jennings. The American routing became very popular with the Fort Steele residents (very convenient and much speedier than the Golden stage service). River service, however, was subject to the whims of Mother Nature. Eighteen months after the co-existence of these Upper Columbia Navigation Company stamps with official postal stamps, someone tattled to Ottawa. Amused but kindly bureaucrats ordered Captain Armstrong to end the sale of his private stamps.

Columbia Laundry ran advertisements from the earliest printing of *The Prospector*. Mrs. Lewis took in washing. This was a service welcomed by bachelor businessmen as well as some of the working prospectors or woodworkers. Her husband dug a well on their property, reaching water at 86 feet. A friend agreed to supply a pump for this well. When the pump could be induced to work, it was a major blessing for Mrs. Lewis. Previously she had had to fetch water from the spring across the river. Mrs. Lewis also set a barrel at each corner of her house, hoping for the blessing of rainwater.

At that time laundry was still being done with muscle power. Each garment, rubbed with soap, was then pressed up and down on a corrugated washboard, wrung out, rinsed, and wrung out again. Whenever possible, laundry was hung on an outdoor clothesline to dry, but Mrs. Lewis had drying racks in her laundry room for use in bad weather. These she could lower to load easily, then raise to nearly ceiling height for drying. Her laundry, which was an annex to their family cottage, also had a small woodstove. The stove was used to heat water for washing, and later to heat flatirons for ironing. Mrs. Lewis worked very hard for the few pennies she earned serving her patrons.

In late January the community was shocked by the death of Miss Margaret Bell. Miss Bell was young and apparently in vigorous health. Whispering gossips tried to put the event in perspective. Miss Bell had arrived in Fort Steele in June of 1892, introduced as the niece and housekeeper of the newly appointed district physician, Dr. Charles MacLean. Dr. MacLean was a very quiet, self-effacing gentleman. At times observers had reason to doubt that Miss Bell was actually related to him. In the summer of 1895 another lady had arrived and moved into the household. She was introduced as the wife of Dr. MacLean. The doctor held a dispensary full of medical pills not available anywhere else. Was it possible that Miss Bell could have been poisoned? No magistrate could ask the coroner to investigate this possibility because the district coroner was none other than Dr. MacLean.

The community arranged for a respectful farewell service for Miss Bell. John Scott assumed the role of undertaker. The coffin was carried into the schoolroom, where Galbraith read the Anglican rites for the burial of the dead. Miss Bailey played appropriate hymns during the service, and as the body left the school her rendition of "The Dead March in Saul" boomed out from Fort Steele's new organ. Pallbearers were Messrs. Langley, Scott, Farquharson, Willmott, Little, and Clark.

Once the solemnity of the funeral and burial was passed, the citizens took advantage of smooth and solid ice on the river near town. Skating was an option for those who had blades to be strapped onto sturdy winter boots. Miss Bailey skated gracefully and was prepared to guide a few of her pupils who were learning to skate. Two leading citizens were pitted against each other to race on the nicest stretch of ice—upriver and back. William Carlin, the storekeeper, challenged Mrs. Levett, the boarding-house owner. Mr. Levett was the referee. Bystanders were gleeful, as the race was between the stoutest man and the fattest lady in town. Both skated well despite

F.S. 33-04

This view up Wild Horse Creek shows the Indian Agency and Robert Galbraith's house (centre left), and one of the earlier bridges on the road to Bull River.

their weightiness, and the referee declared a tie as they crossed the finish line; after all, he wanted to keep peace in the family!

Early that spring Robert Mather decided to move his family out to Dalgardno City, his dream community at Cherry Creek, about eight miles from Fort Steele. Mr. Morin became host and manager of the Dalgardno Hotel (later called the Windsor Hotel) and Mrs. Desrosier took charge of the dining room. The Mather family was very popular, so there were four official farewell parties—plus "Miss Hazel Galbraith gave a party for her little friend Mabel Mather who will move to Dalgardno City."[56]

Mather commenced operation of his sawmill, and promptly built a new ferryboat. No lots were sold at Dalgardno City, but many new residents were building in town. The Mather family reclaimed the Dalgardno Hotel of Fort Steele in October. Mabel was especially pleased to rejoin her playmates at school.

New houses were being built apace. Even the long-time patriarch of the community, Robert Galbraith, had a new home built close to the Agency Office. Out at Fish Lake Norbury built a sturdier house, and he purchased new furniture to fit it out.

Norbury had built a roothouse shortly after his move to Fish Lake. This stout log building, set into a hillside, provided a cool but frost-free atmosphere for storing bins of apples, potatoes, and other vegetables. A layer of dirt insulated the ceiling. A thick door, with panels about five inches apart, was filled with sawdust and was opened for as short a period as possible to keep the temperature uniform. The hillside shoulders of a further four to six feet kept the entranceway cool even in the hottest summer weather. This reliable storage area, cleaned out just before the new summer harvest, kept most varieties of apple firm for up to a year. Shelving on the walls held jars of any jams made during the berry season, as well as sealers of fruit, vegetables, or meat. The early "canning" jars had glass lids sealed in place under high temperature with a rubber ring and a metal clamp. This root cellar was one of three food-preservation methods learned by Norbury and his fellow settlers.

Freezing meat is a well-established mode of safekeeping. Before modern refrigeration, however, Mother Nature provided suitable temperatures for only three to four months each winter. A side of beef or venison could be hung on the porch or in a shed with no door, and roasts whacked off as needed. One February, following an extended thaw, Norbury reported that they had to throw away their meat as it was decomposing and definitely smelled "high."

Very early in his time in Canada, Norbury asked his mother for instructions on making bacon from the first pigs he fattened on his crop of small potatoes. She sent instructions for the Wiltshire Cure.

Take 1-1/2 lbs of coarse sugar, 1-1/2 lb bay-salt, 6 oz. of saltpeter and 1 lb. of common salt. Sprinkle each filch (side of a hog) with salt and let the blood drain off for 24 hours. Then pound and mix the above ingredients together and rub it well into the meat, which should be turned every day for one month. Hang it up to dry, and afterwards smoke at least 10 days.

The bacon, with the rind still on, was durable for months, and could be sliced for cooking with a sharp knife.

F.S. 59 - 01

F.P. Norbury's home at Fish Lake. "Tommy" Norbury, left, with Charlie Edwards, Captain Parker, Mr. Hannay, and his visiting sister, Mrs. Turner, with her dogs. For a later photograph, Mrs. Turner had her brother wrestle a dead bear and set it on a fallen tree to look "natural."

Later, Norbury's plea for help to make hams brought a comparable set of instructions with variations such as "leave in the salt pan, turning frequently for three days then pour over a quart of good vinegar. Turn them in this solution for one month, then drain well, rub with bran. Have them smoked over a wood fire. Be particular that the hams are hung as high as possible above the fire otherwise the fat will melt and they will become dry and hard. This recipe is sufficient to cure two hams of 16 to 18 lbs. Each—to be pickled one month and smoked one month."[57]

Butcher service was now available at Fort Steele. Robson and Sucksmith built a store, private residences, and a corral to hold cattle, many of which were purchased from local ranchers. The ranchers received up to seven cents a pound on their best animals, and buyers paid barely more than that just for a "joint" or roast of beef. Hogs were imported a few at a time, with each new shipment noted in *The Prospector*. The butcher shop had its own smokehouse to prepare these hams and the sides of bacon. The May 30, 1896, *Prospector* stated, "We now have three butcher shops going full blast and beef has dropped to eight cents." Bale Brothers were advertising butcher services, with large orders for camps a specialty. This would be a convenience for staff at the rapidly expanding North Star and Sullivan operations. As Fort Steele boomed, Malcolm McInnes, another butcher, arrived to compete for customers and become a valuable citizen of the district.

There was now a demand for fresh vegetables. Two suppliers were listed in *The Prospector*. Produce from Michael Phillipps at Tobacco Plains was available through the butcher shop—"Leave your order at Robson & Sucksmiths." Yee Lee had a market garden with good-quality vegetables in season.

The year 1896 saw an election for the dominion parliament. Member of Parliament John Mara had held the seat for the Conservative party. He was respected for the improvements he had sponsored in the huge riding, but there was discontent with what his party was doing in Ottawa. Visits from the candidates provided "entertainment" for local citizens. Hewitt Bostock, a rich entrepreneur from Monte Creek near Kamloops, leaped into the fray as a Liberal candidate even before he had been officially nominated. Bostock visited Fort Steele, addressing the hastily formed Liberal Association (F.P. Norbury, president, and Charles Levett, secretary). Bostock endeared himself to those present not only for his appealing words, but also because at the mention of funding for a hospital at Fort Steele, he reached into his pocket and handed a sizable donation to Norbury.

As the pre-election debates were waged, Norbury was temporarily estranged from his friend Hyde Baker. Hyde was campaign manager for John Mara. Norbury was doing all in his power to convince voters to support Hewitt Bostock. Arguments pointed out that the existing Conservative government was completely under the thumb of the Canadian Pacific Railway Company. It was hoped that the Liberals would make life a bit easier with freer trade. Bostock handily won the huge Yale-Cariboo-Okanagan-Kootenay riding. Liberals also formed the federal government. In Fort Steele, however, it was an exact tie between the candidates!

Election returns were published in *The Prospector*, June 27, 1896.

The voters' list appeared in the May 16, 1896, issue of *The Prospector*. Editor A.B. Grace amended it, claiming that not all were able to vote: "The editor has dropped names from the

Voters List for Fort Steele District

Baillie, Wm. H.
Baker, James
Baker, V.H.
Bale, David
Bale, F.A.
Blatchford, Wm.
Bloomburg, J.B.
Bornais, J.B.
Bossee, Wm.
Bott, W.J.
Boyle, Peter
Bradford, W.H.
Branchand, S.A.
Brown, J.J.
Burns, Wm. V.
Campbell, Glen
Carlin, Wm.
Clarke, Chas.
Cleman, C.B.
Cochrane, T.H.
Davidson, Walter
Dawson, Wm.
Dean, W.A.
Dempsey, Robert
Dewer, Robert
Dodd, John
Dole, Lemuel
Doull, Wm.
Edwards, C.M.
Fenwick, AB.
Fenwick, T.H.L.
Freeman, F.L.
French, Wm.
Hanson, Nils
Hoggarth, Geo.

Galbraith, R.L.T.
Goldie, George
Goodridge, Wm.
Griffiths, Dave
Grassick, John
Langley, J.B.
Leighton, Thos.
Levett, John
Levett, Charles
Lockwood, Harry
Mather, R.D.
McGee, W.S.
McKay, J.G.
McKinlay, Jas.
McNeil, John
McTavish, A.
McLeod, Angus
McVittie, Thos.
Moore, Roger
Norbury, F.P.
Parker, E.C.
Parry, Edward
Phillipps, M.
Pugh, Ben
Quirk, Pat
Roberts, T.L.
Robson, Thos
Sucksmith, John
Sullivan, Jere
Sundin, Eric
Wallinger, N.A.
Willmot, Percy
Woods, F.W.A.
White, E.M.

official list (total 72) of those who have died or moved away. We will venture to guess that possibly 55 on this list will cast their ballot (in the Federal Election). And dear readers, the editor Mr. Grace, an American vitally interested in politics, was not eligible to vote!"

Riverboat traffic commenced at the end of May. The first boat of the season, *The Annerly*, was greeted by a 21-gun salute (or, at least, a volley of rifle shots!) when it arrived on Monday, May 25. It brought in hay, oats, flour, and eleven passengers, then left Tuesday with 21 tons of ore from North Star Landing. The new vessel, the *Ruth*, with 275 tons register, came in next. She took 70 tons of ore bound for U.S. smelters. *The Annerly* returned on Thursday, May 28, leaving with 25 tons of ore the next morning.

The following week the *Ruth, Annerly, Gwendoline*, and *Rustler* all docked at Fort Steele. The *Gwendoline* was sent upriver to Canal Flats, where she took on 30 tons of supplies for Fort Steele. The steamers were working the river as quickly as possible between loading and unloading, then moving the short distance to the waterfront warehouse to take on several tons of ore. The ore in bulk was packed in little sacks only eighteen inches high and about eight inches in diameter. Each sack weighed at least 90 pounds, but some of the silver lead concentrate was up to 200 pounds for the same volume.

Early in June the public school pupils bid good-bye to their teacher, Miss Bailey, when she left to visit Victoria. At St. Eugene Mission School it was now decreed that the students should have summer holidays with their families. The teaching sisters made plans to go away to visit their mother house, and to see family and friends. Sister Cassilda and Sister Joseph of Angels started by stage for Golden, but they turned back when they were informed that an accident had halted train service. Sister Joseph became ill and declined to travel. It was decided that a senior student, Cecilia, would travel with Sister Cassilda. They boarded the *Rustler* to travel to Jennings, Montana, where they could catch a train to Portland, Oregon. The *Rustler* piled into the rocks in the canyon. Sister Cassilda prayed loudly, "Lord save us. At least save Cecilia. Her parents would never forgive themselves for having allowed her to come with me."[58] Another boat appeared and rescued the passengers. One record claims it was the *Ruth,* but *The Prospector* noted, "*The Annerly* rescued the passengers and crew and towed the *Rustler* to a sandbar. Nothing will be saved but the machinery."[59]

Sister Cassilda and Cecilia returned safely six weeks later, accompanied by the Mother Provincial. The staff at St. Eugene's Mission was quick to report that its fervent prayers had assisted the safe conclusion of Sister Cassilda's travels.[60]

Editor A.B. Grace had a new building erected on Riverside Avenue, and imported a printing press. *The Prospector* of July 18, 1896, appeared in five-column large-page format. *The Prospector* kept readers informed about new arrivals in town, weddings, town improvements, news from around the world, and social gatherings.

Charles Levett, owner of the Steele House hotel, had a large two-storey edifice built close by. Mrs. Levett intended to operate a high-class boarding house, and Charles was watching for a buyer for the hotel. They were in no hurry to sell, and planned to watch for the right successor, who would pay optimum price and carry on their hospitable style of management.

A.B. Grace and Tom McVittie were chosen to represent the Fort Steele Mining Association at a Mineral Exposition in Spokane. The exhibit of ore specimens was augmented by 1,100 copies of *The Prospector* to be given away. When the delegates arrived at the Spokane Fruit Fair, they were thrilled to observe a demonstration mine at work.

> The tunnel was 70 feet long, five feet wide, seven feet high, walls of basaltic rock, with a shaft 35 feet deep to allow workers to haul up LeRoi ore from two carloads positioned on railroad tracks under the building. There were demonstration drilling contests held in the main building, and additional display of a working placer hydraulic mine set with trees, shrubs and even moss gave viewers an accurate representation of actual workings.[61]

Building contractors McLeod and Boeson arrived in Fort Steele in August, commissioned to build a store and residence for A.W. Bleasdell, the druggist. Bleasdell took possession in October. By then the carpenters were constructing a new

Courtesy Jean Ann Debrecini

Costumed summer interpreters posing in front of The Prospector *office on Riverside Avenue, Fort Steele Heritage Town. Historic street scenes are well-researched before being "staged" for summer tourists. The photographer was Brian Clarkson of Cranbrook.*

restaurant. Bale and Scott, similarly employed, were building a fine new residence for Nils Hanson at Wasa. Dempsey and Grassick had been working at the mission, adding new buildings to the school. Lumber was being used as fast as it came out of the sawmills at Wasa and Cherry Creek.

The mining camp adjacent to the North Star Mine and Sullivan explorations was originally called Mark Creek Crossing. Colonel Ridpath and a group of American investors took over operations in the summer of 1896. Ridpath, aware of the phenomenal success of the diamond mines in Kimberley,

South Africa, chose to rename the infant community Kimberley, British Columbia. The name was not adopted immediately; familiar terminology persisted, as reported in *The Prospector*: "A party visited the North Star mine last week. Miss Bailey, Mrs. John T. Galbraith, Mr. & Mrs. Binmore, Mr. & Mrs. Bleasdell and John Grassick were hospitably entertained by Mrs. Desrosier who did everything possible to make their visit an enjoyable one. The group is indebted to Messrs. Williams and Brown for the many courtesies extended while visiting the workings of this wonderful mine. The party returned on Sunday much pleased with their visit to the largest silver-lead mine on the continent."[62]

Williams was a very tall, very skinny man who found work in the office of North Star Mine. It was rudely rumoured that he had at one time travelled with a circus, being shown as a "Living Skeleton." Williams was frequently dispatched from the mine to do errands in Fort Steele and was well known in town. A visiting salesman, who had been demonstrating a very early phonograph, was having a drink with a local in the Dalgardno when the lofty messenger glided up to the bar. "What is that?" stammered the salesman. "Oh," shrugged the local, "that's Williams from the North Star." "From the North Star, you say? I presume they keep him to trim the wicks of the Northern Lights."

The opening of the Pioneer Drug Store was one more milestone in the citification of Fort Steele. Bleasdell advertised: "Only purest drugs ordered. I aim to keep a complete stock of Drugs, Patent Medicines, Stationery, Spectacles and Drug Sundries." Further, he offered free delivery within the city limits. He also had a wooden sidewalk built in front of his store.

A.W. Bleasdell was a graduate of the Ontario College of Pharmacy, with diplomas from Manitoba and the North-West Territories. He moved his family from Fort Macleod, North-West Territories, to Fort Steele in October of 1896. His inventory soon expanded to include Havana cigars, popular magazines, Castile soap, perfume, playing cards, toilet paper, machine oil, gun oil, sweet oil, raw oil, and Christmas cards. Later he added fishing tackle, pocket compasses, mineral glasses, and magnets.

Bleasdell wrote fresh advertisements almost every week and created a welcoming atmosphere within his store. Soon he was talking the jargon of miners and going prospecting to stake his own claims. Mrs. Bleasdell and their son Willie quickly adapted to Fort Steele, making an expanding circle of friends.

The first of several barbershops in Fort Steele was owned and operated by James Highwarden. His advertisement described him as "Tonsorial Artist—Shaving and Haircutting." He was a musically gifted gentleman who played for dances and other community functions, and despite the fact that he was "Negro," Highwarden was one of the most popular individuals in Fort Steele.

He became school janitor for a time, and his wife operated a millinery and dressmaking shop in an extension of Highwarden's Barber Shop. In 1898, when there was competition from four other barbers, they built a room where they could offer hot or cold baths to men in from their work in the hills. Later, surprisingly, certain hours were set aside for female patrons. *The Prospector* noted, "Highwarden's bath rooms open for ladies Tuesdays and Wednesdays from 2 p.m. to 5 p.m. in charge of Mrs. Highwarden."

Livery stables were built adjacent to two of the hotels to accommodate the teams and riding horses of the travelling public. Robert Mather had the first one for the benefit of the patrons of his Dalgardno Hotel, and William Forsyth of Mountain House followed suit. A new independent then advertised, "FREEMAN & LESSARD, Livery Feed and Sale Stable, Fort Steele, B.C. SADDLE AND PACK HORSES. TEAMING OF ALL KINDS A SPECIALTY." The stables went through a series of partnerships, but the care and rental of horses was a thriving business for all the years that Fort Steele flourished.

Chapter 15

Home and Garden—1890s Style

A man may work from sun to sun
But a woman's work is never done.

A homemaker in early Fort Steele was faced with numerous challenges. She had to keep home and family clean when there was no running water indoors or out. The streets were alternately dusty or muddy, so dirt was regularly blown or tracked indoors. The quality and quantity of firewood in the woodshed assisted or hindered the fires in her cookstove and heater. This was an era when cooking porridge took many hours, and doing the family laundry took all day, with Monday used for washing and most of Tuesday for ironing. Bread had to be kneaded, and raised at the right temperature, and then baked. Meals were prepared from the basics with no quick alternatives available at the stores. Shoes and boots for all members of the family were kept polished. It was a busy life, but her successes brought comfort to members of the family and thereby to the community also.

Families wishing to gather their own firewood had to go with a horse well beyond the "city limits" to cut trees. The trees had to be limbed, bucked (sawn) into suitable lengths, and then dragged home. Each log was set on a sawhorse and cut into blocks. A preferred length was sixteen inches. Each block had to be set on the chopping block and split into sections with an axe or a wedge and maul. Then the wood had to be stacked carefully to dry.

Newcomers could purchase a few cords[63] of wood from W.L. Schagel. A cord was delivered in four-foot lengths, so the homeowner had much cutting and splitting to do before filling his woodshed.

Southern Sunshine Cook Stove specifications

Size	Size of Covers	Length of Fire Box	Size of Oven Oven	Shipping	Weight Price
7	7 in.	18 in.	16x17x12in.	138 lbs.	$5.97
8	8 in.	20 in.	18x18x12in.	175 lbs.	$7.35
88	8 in.	22 in.	20x20x12-1/2in.	191 lbs.	$8.88
9	9 in.	22 in.	20x20x12-1/2in.	197 lbs.	$9.00
888	8 in.	24 in.	22x22x13-1/2in.	225 lbs.	$10.38
19	9 in.	24 in.	22x22x13-1/2in.	230 lbs.	$10.58

The kitchen stove was central to life in the home. This cast-iron fixture was alternately slave and slave driver. There was wood and kindling to be cut and carried in. When ashes built up inside the stove, the front door would be opened and the wrench applied to rotate the grates. The ashes tumbled into the ash box, and the airflow improved. Ashes eventually had to be taken out. Periodically the stovepipe would have to be taken down and cleaned. There were draft controls and dampers, which, if in the wrong position when the fire was lit, would flood the house with smoke.

Patience and perseverance were prerequisites to learning to cook using a wood stove. Green or punk wood did not raise oven temperatures to the desired level for baking bread or pastry, but dry resinous logs were likely to scorch a cake in the oven or burn a pot of stew if it were left unstirred. Stovetop cooking also depended on the quality of the fire in the firebox. For a quick fry, the stove lid was lifted and the frypan set above the flame.

The wives of American immigrants to Fort Steele had an advantage over English women. Those from the U.S. had grown up with a similar stove, learning step by step from their mothers. The English women had used gas or coal stoves, if they had cooked at all, for they often lived in a home where there was at least one servant. One of the most pitied was Mrs. Cowell, the wife of an ex-army engineer, who had been recently posted in India. After years of being waited on hand and foot, she arrived in Fort Steele, where no servants were available. She found that reading instructions from *Mrs. Beeton's Household Management* or *Mrs. Beeton's Everyday Cookery* were somewhat helpful, but many things frustrated her to the point where she would collapse in a near faint. She confided in Mrs. Mather, one of the most energetic, best-adapted women in Fort Steele. Mrs. Mather's advice was succinct. "There is a laundress now in Fort Steele. Dinna be so proud that you cannot hand over your washing to Mrs. Lewis. And as for the rest, loosen your stays and keep your chin up."

Mrs. Cowell wanted to learn how to prepare a "bird" for Sunday dinner. She found it difficult to visualize what *Mrs. Beeton's* directions meant, so she appealed to her neighbour for a demonstration. It is not recorded whether she was able to overcome her fear of handling poultry, even if someone "murdered" the creature before handing it to her. Mrs. Cowell kept trying to function in her new environment, but when the Mathers moved out of town a few months later, she and her husband, a civil engineer and assayer for Noel Wallinger, decided to leave Fort Steele.

Mary Jane Mather served good meals to her family and kept her home sparkling clean. She directed the day-to-day operations of the dining room in the Dalgardno Hotel, and on special occasions planned and produced multi-coursed banquets for over a hundred guests.

An advertisement for a home cobbler's set. Pioneers living in small towns like Fort Steele found these sets to be indispensable.

Catherine Clark had learned many survival techniques in her years as one of the only white women in the district. She did the planning—coaxing her husband to help with the heaviest jobs—to make sure everything was done in season. Charles Clark was paid as postmaster, but report after report in *The Prospector* mentioned, "Mrs. Clark worked sorting the mail until midnight." She kept her husband's hair neatly clipped when there was no barber in the district. When Charles shot a deer, he'd sling the animal across his horse and bring it home for his wife to skin, clean, and butcher. Mrs. Clark learned how to tan the deer hide and made several useful items, starting with a footstool, using the leather as the seat. She then searched for suitable curved branches of maple to make an armchair with hide on the back and the seat. She made a leather apron of deerskin, but as this tore easily she sought out cowhide, and wore this to protect her clothing while sawing and carrying wood or doing repair jobs. One job she became familiar with was shoe repair. With a *Home Cobbler* set, one could handle the discomfort of a protruding nail or anchor a loosened heel. She even managed to put new soles on her favourite boots when the mail-order house failed to supply suitable replacements for several months. Her son was groomed and schooled by his mother until he was a teenager. Herbert saw his mother as the competent manager that she was,

Kerosene lamps, used during the boom years, needed refilling about once a week, but their light was much brighter than candlelight.

and he never found a woman to measure up to her standards. He remained a bachelor.

Thankfully, candles had been replaced by kerosene lamps. These lamps, when properly cared for, gave a reasonably good light for working in the kitchen or reading in the front room. They required refilling about once a week. Each homemaker kept a small funnel with her can of kerosene (sometimes called coal oil or paraffin oil.) If weather permitted this job was done outside on the porch. The wick would be trimmed with a pair of scissors. The fragile glass chimney usually needed to be cleaned, and this was accomplished by rubbing inside it with a rumpled-up newspaper. The newspaper was easier to handle than a rag inserted by hand, even if the woman's hand made a dainty fist within the curvature of the glass. When the lamp was lit, one aimed for optimum light with the wick tall enough to burn without smoking.

Lanterns, which could be carried outdoors, were windproof adaptations of the oil lamp. A trip to the outhouse after dark, even with a lantern, could be a thrilling undertaking. (This is why a chamber pot was a standard piece of equipment in every household. Women and children used it as an alternative site to empty their bladders at bedtime or in the dark early morning hours.) The other uses for lanterns were as carriage lights on a wagon or sleigh if it happened to be operated outside daylight hours. It could also be hung up when working in a barn or root cellar.

Once a year the biggest cleaning job of all was undertaken: spring cleaning. When the bright sunshine of springtime flooded over the district, and the winter-weary citizens changed their heavy coats for regular suit jackets or mackinaw shirts, the women became increasingly aware of dirty windows, and smoke-stained walls and curtains. As soon as it was warm enough that the door could be left open, and no fire was needed in the stove for a few hours, they would decide to freshen their places up. This job involved taking the wood box, the stovepipes, and the ash box outside to be emptied of splinters, soot, and ash, and then reassembling the stove and stovepipes. Scatter rugs were hung on the clothesline to be beaten, brushed, and pounded on both sides. Wooden floors were not only swept and mopped, but also oiled. Curtains were taken down and either beaten like the rugs or washed, rinsed, and hung on the line. Windows were washed, and stoves were polished, as was the silverware. Finally, the rugs and curtains would be put back, more clean and fresh than before.

Small gardens were cultivated in many yards. Preparing the plot entailed digging and picking rocks, then digging again and picking more rocks out. Picking the rocks was a job that the children could do, but an adult would have to dump the wheelbarrow at a site where the rocks would not reoffend. Children were also handed a trowel or coal shovel and a pail to collect manure off the street. The manure was worked into the dusty soil. All the dishwater was carried from the back door and flung over the plot. Most of the bathwater or floor-washing water was dedicated to the garden plot. During the growing season there was weeding to be done, chickens to chase away, and, finally, harvesting as each crop ripened. Popular items in these early gardens were scarlet runner beans, peas, carrots, beets, parsnips, and a variety of squashes or gourds. Once those had been grown successfully perhaps another small patch would be prepared—with lots more rocks to be removed—for strawberry plants, raspberry canes, or rhubarb.

The main crop in the market gardens was cabbage. These were seeded in a "hot bed" in March and transplanted to the regular garden in May. The hot frame was a box set upon a deep pile of fresh manure. The south edge was lower than the backboard, and the top was covered with a glass window. The decomposing manure provided heat to counteract frost. Sometimes April sunshine added to the spontaneous heat, and the windows were raised for a few hours to avoid cooking the seedlings. The Chinese market gardeners found ways to discourage slugs, cutworms, and insects. The garden area was treated with lime in the fall, and a circle of wood ash was put around each cabbage plant once it was set in the open.[64]

Proud and ambitious housewives found a place to plant a few flowers. The plot for flowers needed water, so the contents of the family washbasin was carefully directed to this area. Many times, too, the chamber pot was emptied on the flower garden. Favourite flowers that managed to bloom in the East Kootenay's hot and dusty season and also survive the winters were hollyhocks, pinks (a small carnation), clarkias, gypsophilla (baby's breath), pansies, California poppies, and daisies.

Chapter 16

Exciting Times
(1897)

The community of Fort Steele was anticipating many great things in 1897, such as expansion and rapid development of the town, neighbouring townsites, working mines, and sawmills springing up nearby. But it was not expecting a mail robbery.

Alf Doyle, the mail-stage driver, stopped overnight at Hanson's Wasa Hotel in Wasa. He checked his wagon just before going to bed at midnight. The mail was all right at that time. The next morning at about seven, he returned to the wagon to see that the load had been tampered with: The Fort Steele sack was gone. Hanson and his guests at the Wasa Hotel searched around the parked wagon and found the mail sack, as well as a few parcels spread around. The mail sack was cut open and the letter sack was missing. There was fresh snow on the ground, so the nearby tracks were carefully examined. An overshoe track led from the wagon to the discarded mail sack. Eric Sundstrom carefully measured the shoe prints. Hoof prints coming and going showed that the robber had mounted a horse. The tracks were easily traced, and all present noted that the horse had only half a shoe on his right hind foot.

Doyle hitched up his horses and followed the tracks all the way to Fort Steele. Once at the town he delivered the mail to the postmaster, then sought out Constable Barnes. Barnes quickly obtained a search warrant, vowing to search every house in town should that be necessary. Meanwhile, a passenger on the stage had followed the tracks of the robber's horse to Levett's stable. The horse, which had been stolen complete with saddle from Charles Levett at approximately one o'clock that morning, looked as if it had been driven hard.

Percy Wilmott, the liveryman, co-operated by removing the partial shoe from the horse's right hind foot so it could be taken to court for evidence. Doyle accompanied Constable Barnes, C.M. Edwards, Hyde Baker, and Eric Sundstrom to the home of Alexander Leitch.

The first items noted were the overshoes that matched exactly the measurements and pattern of the tracks near the Wasa Hotel. The next observation was that the stove was very hot. Not a trace of the letter sack or the hundreds of missing letters was seen. Alf Doyle poked into the stove, where he found rivets, staples, a hasp, and a metal label where the name goes on a mail sack, plus a watch. These were cooled, then wrapped up to be taken for evidence. There was a false shelf near the stovepipe. Sundstrom tried to punch that shelf loose. When he failed, Leitch took the stick, poked hard, and a roll of bills fell down. Constable Barnes caught the roll and quipped, "That's a nice little roll!" to which Leitch said, "Yes! It is the last dollar on earth that I have. Take care of it!" Constable Barnes arrested Leitch and searched him, finding $100 on his person. Both rolls of money were handed to Edwards, who counted them. Leitch claimed the first roll was $990, but Edwards found $1,000. The robber was taken to jail, and the house was searched again. They found a new hunting knife, presumed to be one made specially for Hyde Baker, and a pair of men's hairbrushes with their monogram plates removed. Wrapping paper marked "Miss Jessie Lewis" was also collected as suspicious.

The following morning, Monday, January 25, 1897, Alexander Leitch was brought before Messrs. Galbraith, Norbury, and MacLean, Justices of the Peace, for a preliminary examination on a charge of robbing Her Majesty's mails. He was committed for trial to the first court of proper jurisdiction either at Donald or Kamloops. (It was a common practice to have two justices of the peace sit on serious crimes, and this startling crime drew forth all available justices.)

By the time The Prospector appeared on January 30 with a triple headline on its second page, every tongue in town was wagging. The mail robber had lived in Fort Steele for several months. He was suspected of forgeries, and of robbing a store till. He had been in Wasa the two previous mail days, observing the way mail was handled. It was fortunate for the investigators that the fresh snow gave only one set of tracks to observe. This issue of the paper featured official notices that "all Fort Steele mail after January 1st had been lost, so communications should be duplicated to insure prompt attention." This was a time when money was usually sent in cash form or cheques. (Postal money orders were introduced later that year.)

C.M. Edwards, Charles Clark—who identified the metal fittings from the letter sack—and Miss Jessie Lewis, who was unsure why wrapping paper with her name on it was in Leitch's house, all gave testimonies. The prisoner reminded Miss Lewis that shirts from her mother's laundry were wrapped in that paper. Then Alfred Doyle gave a detailed recounting, including identifying the overshoes as those making the footprints between the mail wagon and the large cut mail bag discarded at Wasa. Constable Barnes testified at length, after which a recess was called for one hour. Eric Sundstrom was sworn in and neatly recounted what he saw at Wasa, in Fort Steele, and at the home of the accused. C.M. Edwards, a government clerk and mining recorder, presented the final evidence. *The Prospector* crowed that the robber was "Caught Inside of Six Hours from the Time He Done the Job."[65]

Leitch was escorted to Kamloops, where he languished in jail until a trial in June. All the witnesses had to travel to Kamloops to testify. In the Kamloops court Leitch was represented by R.L. Reid, a lawyer from New Westminster, and prosecuted by Deputy Attorney General Smith. He was charged with robbing the Fort Steele mail stage, and he pleaded "not guilty." This was a trial with a jury of twelve local citizens, with J.F. Smith chosen as foreman.

The Kamloops *Inland Sentinel* described the courtroom scene.

The witnesses examined were Eric Lundin, C.M. Edwards, C. Clarke, H.W. Barnes, A.W. Blaisdell, P. Willmot, G.E. Parke, W. Dorman and Chas. Warren. Briefly told, the facts of the case are that on the night of January 23rd last Leitch removed from the Fort Steele mail stage three mail bags, carried them to his cabin, removed all that was valuable, including a package of $1000 from the Bank of B.C. and burned the bags and the contents of no value to him. The several witnesses made a pretty strong case against the accused, but it was not until the teller of the Victoria branch of the Bank of B.C. gave his evidence that the prisoner realized the hopelessness of his defence. Mr. Parke, the teller, identified one of the notes found in Leitch's possession by marks in red ink on the back, and brought out the significant fact that the package of notes was made up of 100–$10 Bank of B.C. bills, exactly the same denomination and amount of the package belonging to the bank stolen from the mail bag. When Mr. Parke concluded his evidence Leitch conferred with his lawyer, and as a result Mr. Reid withdrew the plea of not guilty. The jury, upon instructions of the judge, then entered a general verdict of guilty.

Mr. Justice McColl said the prisoner's case had been a hopeless one from the start. It was most important that public mails should be absolutely safe, particularly in a mining country where so much depends on the safe transit of letters containing documents relating to mining transactions and remittance for renewal of miner's licenses or recording of claims. He sentenced Leitch to ten years penal servitude.

The Judge ordered that the $1,000 be handed over to C.W. Ward who appeared for the Bank of B.C.[66]

The prisoner was transferred to jail in New Westminster and from there to Stoney Mountain Penitentiary in Manitoba.

The winter was soon over. Riverboats began bringing freight and passengers in, unloading all, then as quickly as possible taking on a shipment of ore sacks before sailing away, southbound again. On May 7, 1897, the steamer *Ruth*, with sixteen passengers and 120 tons of ore, got a drifting log caught in the paddlewheel. The mishap occurred about 75 yards below the elbow in the canyon between Fort Steele and Jennings. Captain Sanburn was powerless to control the vessel. The *Ruth* crashed into some rocks and split open, but the deck hands managed to transfer passengers, baggage, and mail to safety.

Unfortunately, Captain Armstrong in the *Gwendoline* was close behind. The *Ruth* blocked the narrow waterway, and despite Armstrong's efforts, the *Gwendoline* hit the *Ruth* broadside. Light was fading. The *Gwendoline* was unloaded. All the crew and passengers huddled together overnight, and at daylight the next morning they hit the trail, and reached Jennings on foot.

Two vessels wrecked! When the news arrived at Fort Steele on Tuesday evening, May 11, intense excitement was created, and knots of men discussed the implications until a late hour.[67]

The *Ruth* was a total loss, but Armstrong had the *Gwendoline* patched and sailing again by June 5. American officials ordered the *Gwendoline* tied up until she was inspected and certified. Frank Armstrong grumbled but could find no way to defy the ruling. He paid $400 for the certification and was cleared to work the *Gwendoline* by June 12. Meanwhile, the captain ordered that an extra shift be set to work on his *North Star*, which was nearing completion in the Jennings shipyard. The International Navigation Company was going to profit from the 1897 shipping season despite the accident on May 7!

While the steamers were out of service, a stage company, the Kalispell Stage, tried to fulfil the locals' needs. John Weightman had been complaining of deteriorating road conditions, especially near the Elk River. But on his May 25 run he was horrified when the Elk River Bridge collapsed, dropping the stage into the water below.

> Fortunately, a number of people were on shore who succeeded in getting the passengers out, then the horses and stage. Nothing was lost and the entire outfit escaped with a large-sized ducking.[68]

John Weightman's stage accident emphasized the need for improving the wagon road south from Fort Steele. The citizens advocated a prompt replacement of that bridge, including upgrading the approaches and grading the rutted sections near the Elk River. Freighters and stage drivers alike hated a long, steep, sandy hill at Sand Creek that at times required them to winch the wagons to the top. Part of the 1897 road budget was put to clear a new route with better grades.

The streets of Fort Steele echoed with the sound of hammers and saws. Hotel bars were filled in the evenings. Two of the restaurants were open 24 hours a day. Homes, businesses, and civic amenities were being constructed.

The pace of life at Fort Steele was becoming more and more hectic. The citizens worked hard and played hard. The Americans traditionally arranged great festivities for the Fourth of July. Canada's own July 1 holiday was barely acknowledged, but the Queen's birthday on May 24 was a very special observance here and throughout the British Empire. On June 22, 1897, a special anniversary was celebrated: Queen Victoria's Diamond Jubilee. Ten eager volunteers sat down to plan an extra-special program to celebrate the 60th anniversary of Victoria's accession to the throne.

The town was decorated with evergreens and flags. People came from miles around. There were horses at every hitching post, and the livery stables were full. The community that had until recently been populated by bachelors became aware of the many ladies and children in town. The crowd enjoyed the glorious sunshine and the holiday atmosphere. They watched two horse races that had to be run by heats down Rocky Mountain Avenue. The winner of the 600-yard race was Homely Hank, with Nigger coming in second. The saddle horse 400-yard race was won by Little Dick, with Roaney in second place. The horses had their names in the paper, but no mention was given to the owners or riders.

Wrestling on horseback was a dramatic display of strength, skill, and timing practised by Indian athletes. The crowd fell silent watching, fascinated, voicing a collective "ooh" when each participant stayed seated on his horse following an extended clutch. The horses paced apart. The combatants circled and re-engaged. Finally one would succeed in lifting his opponent off his steed. A cheer went up. Another pair took their place in the ring. After numerous well-executed, hard-fought matches, Baptise won the first prize, and Eusta the purse for second.

Next there was a bicycle race. Bikes had suddenly become very popular in the district. C.M. Tulloch came first, and Dan McNeish of Steele House second.

The other competitions were variations of track-and-field events with adult male entries except for a boys' 100-yard foot race. Dan Lewis, C. Quinliven, and H. Richardson won the boys' winnings. Ladies and girls could only be bystanders.

Tom Fenwick topped the running long jump, and A.I. Robinson won the shot-put competetion. The 100-yard dash was won by Henry Broulette, and the 300-yard foot race saw C.M. Tulloch in first, McIntosh second, and Eusta (the athletic competitor from wrestling on horseback) in third position. There was a cigar race in which the gentlemen dashed 100 yards, retrieved a cigar that they lit, and returned to the start line, puffing on the cigar. Quinliven, the blacksmith, won that race, and a visitor, Bannister, came second. The final race was a semi-comic "Fat Man's Race" that was won by John McMahon of Moyie, with Steele's own storekeeper William Carlin close behind.

The afternoon was given to a football (soccer) match between the Indians and the whites. Charlie Edwards attempted to illustrate the finer points of the game for the Indian boys. The Indian athletes kicked and kicked and kept the ball in motion. Wilmshurst sustained a kick in the shin by a moccasined foot and swore that the fellow had an iron toe. The game concluded with a scoreless tie despite the efforts of Myles Beale and A.I. Robinson. The audience, having no bleachers, moved around, mingling with the crowd, meeting old friends, and being introduced to newcomers. The sound of the football match enhanced the holiday atmosphere.

The Jubilee celebrations carried on with dinner and a dance at Dalgardno Hotel. After supper Joseph Laidlaw, co-convenor of the Jubilee Committee, presented prizes to the winners of the morning's races. Colonel Baker was introduced to say a few appropriate words, then the dancing began.

It was an exciting time in the East Kootenay.

Chapter 17

Building
(1897)

The Prospector newspaper listed all incoming passengers arriving in Fort Steele during the first few weeks of the shipping season in 1897. Many of these same names appeared in subsequent issues with an announcement that a store, a residence, or a hotel was being built by them.

Robert Mather sensed the need for more hotel rooms, and added a 50-foot annex onto the Dalgardno. Dan McNeish upgraded Steele House, and George Watson outfitted the new Grand Central Hotel. In June the Big Tent Lodgings were advertised. It was a hotel under canvas, containing separate rooms with "new beds and new bedding" at $2.50 per week.

C.F. Venosta, the chief real estate agent for all the Robert Galbraith holdings in town, built the Hotel Venosta, which he set Harry Rhineman to manage, with Rutherford in charge of the dining room. The International Hotel was also opened for business that same week.[69]

By July 17 the St. Mary's Inn Annex was ready for occupancy, and the triangular-shaped main building, two storeys high, was completed two weeks later. It stood across Riverside Avenue from the Dalgardno. An Oriental Hotel under W.A. Steward was also opened in midsummer. Mountain House opened in August, and the Coeur d'Alene Hotel was ready in September. Fort Steele now had ten hotels and Mrs. Levett's lodging house. The average price of hotel construction was about $1,500.

In a comprehensive list of recent buildings, or improvements to existing buildings, *The Prospector* gave costs in the October 2, 1897, edition; they ranged from $250 for a very simple dwelling to $2,500 for the new Government Building.

Courtesy Naomi Miller

The Government Building, built in 1897, was the proof that Fort Steele was the most important town in the East Kootenay until the staff was transferred to Cranbrook in May 1904.

The Government Building attracted a lot of attention. Firstly, it meant that Fort Steele was the most important centre in the East Kootenay. Secondly, government agent Armstrong ordered that the building be constructed at an angle—"slantindicular" to the street. The explanation for the positioning was "to keep the prisoner's exercise yard out of view from the children." The new building had several offices upstairs, three jail cells and a courtroom on the main floor, and the jailer's living quarters in an annex. The jailer's quarters were occupied for the first few weeks by Armstrong, transferred from Golden before his private dwelling was completed.

Robert Galbraith donated two acres of land, overlooking a bend in Wild Horse Creek, as the site of Fort Steele's Diamond Jubilee Hospital. The initial building was erected for $850. Galbraith also donated the furnishings for one ward, stating it was in memory of his brother John, the pioneer of the original town on the site, Galbraith's Ferry.

Another public building that added a new dimension to the town was Coventry's Opera House. A grand ball was held in

September to celebrate its opening. H.J. Coventry advertised a firm "No alcohol on the premises" prior to the opening as well as the second dance in his new hall. The dances were voted a success, but Coventry realized that the gentlemen were stepping outside into the shadows and returning with liquor on their breath. He sold the building to Colonel Hugh Henderson, who quickly fitted out the upstairs to become the Kootenay Men's Club.

Courtesy Martin Ross

Coventry's Opera House, built in 1897. Many meetings and performances were held here. The Kootenay Men's Club, housed on the upper floor, was replaced by the Masonic Lodge, which owned the building until Fort Steele became a Heritage Town.

Across the river at Westport there was a soda bottling works, warehouses for the CPR, and the shipping company. Plans were laid for a brewery over there. Also in Westport was the Wallinger/Fenwick dairy and Emma William's "Tin House."

The Roman Catholic congregation erected a church in Fort Steele for its growing number. Again, landowner Robert Galbraith kindly donated two lots for this purpose, and shortly thereafter he allocated four lots for the new two-roomed schoolhouse. A much larger schoolhouse was needed because new families had increased the number of school-aged children to almost 80.

Outside town, Finch and Jones built a new sawmill and the established lumberman, Schagel, added a planermill.

There were 27 new residences given on *The Prospector's* list. Three of those new homes were priced at $2,000. Mrs. Dimmick had a two-storey building in which she proposed to offer nursing home care to the sick and enfeebled. Robert Galbraith, still a bachelor, had an elegant $2,000 home built close to the Indian Agency office. He was able to heat that big house with cordwood paid for by the Indian Affairs Department. Galbraith was the richest man in Fort Steele, owning most of the unsold lots in town, and holding the mortgage on many others. He was also paid $1,200 a year plus expenses to serve as Indian agent. The third expensive home was built for George Watson, a hotelier and mining promoter.

Nils Hanson of Wasa, who was already profiting from the boom with lumber sales, ordered two railcar loads of furniture. The contents were sold directly off each freight wagon when it arrived in Fort Steele. A small furniture store owned and operated by J.D. McIntyre started later that summer, with the stock arriving by riverboat.

The telegraph office was built and the wires connected to Spokane and the American railway systems. The first message was received on September 3, 1897, and P.O. Rooke promptly dispatched a reply. Shortly after the office opened it was discovered that Fort Steele's clocks were half an hour off by standard time. Canada was the first country in the world to be divided into time zones. Sanford Fleming insisted that railways must have definite consistent clocks to make for safe scheduling and convenience. The U.S. railroads promptly followed his example. In October 1884 a conference was held in Washington, D.C., for the purpose of fixing a prime meridian and a universal day. Greenwich, England, was given zero longitude with the globe divided into 24 time zones, each covering 15 degrees longitude. To assist the town to switch to the correct time, A.B. Grace purchased a large clock that was set in the window of *The Prospector* office. The editor commissioned Rooke to regularly check the time in Missoula. Should *The Prospector* clock be off, he was to rush across the street to arrange its correction.

The Roman Catholic Church was built and opened with fanfare on October 31. Shortly thereafter, notices in *The Prospector* stated, "Mass will begin at 9 a.m. sharp. Now we have Standard Time there is no excuse for tardiness.–Fr. J. Welsh."

Other buildings included a new office for Dr. Watt, a tin shop for T.C. Armstrong, an assay office for W. Leete, a butcher shop for Malcolm McInnes, workshops for various carpenters, a hardware store for F.H. McBride, an office building for C.F. Venosta, a tobacco store for J. Kaufmann, an addition on the drugstore for A.W. Bleasdell, and similar improvements to stores, barbershops, and restaurants. That fall visitors were astounded by the changes that had occurred within a five- or six-month period. Fort Steele had changed almost beyond recognition.

The Fort Steele Mining Association (FSMA) furthered the interests of those with mineral claims. It had acted as a voice for citizens across the district when it appealed for better roads and improved mail service, but it was not readily recognized by those in other communities.

Dr. Watt announced that a Board of Trade was needed to present this bustling community to the outside world. Other newcomers added their voices, endorsing the proposal. On September 1, 1897, the inaugural meeting was held to establish the Fort Steele Board of Trade. Thirty-six gentlemen became charter members. These men, listed in the next issue of *The Prospector*, were Dr. Hugh Watt, T.T. McVittie, A.W. Bleasdell, Wm. R. Ross, H.W. Herchmer, Wm. M. Titus, W.E. Johnson, A.C. Roberson, L.R. VanDecar, T. Ede, A.W. McVittie, C.M. Keep, F.A. McBride, J.R. Goff, A.B. Grace, John Fitzgerald, A.C. Nelson, C.F. Venosta, F.H. Shepherd, O.S. Frizzell, H.D. Henderson, G.H. Gilpin, Guy Lindsay, Wm. Carlin, D. McIntosh, R.L.T. Galbraith, H.E. King, E.J. Cann, W. VanArsdalen, H.D. Stewart, W. Wade, Frank E. Leach, George B. Watson, Jno J. Lamont, with J.A. Harvey as president and Wm. Baillie as secretary.[70]

Fort Steele now had a rudimentary building to serve as a hospital. The FSMA had appealed to the provincial government for funding to assist with the erection and operation of it. They were denied their request, and rumour prevailed that Colonel Baker had pleaded that any hospital money for the East Kootenay should be assigned to Cranbrook. On an official visit to Fort Steele, this member of the legislature was confronted. He claimed that he had not voted against the grant for Fort Steele. (He was absent from the house when the vote was taken.) But he was shamed into making a personal donation of $25 to a hospital canvasser, Miss Adelaide Bailey.

The community was pleased to contribute to the building and fitting out of the Diamond Jubilee Hospital. This was a project in which ladies could participate. The committee assigned to canvass for funds included Mrs. Levett, Mrs. Binmore, Miss Bailey, Mrs. Bleasdell, and Miss Frizzell Further to supplying

F.S. 5 -63

The symbolic laying of the foundation for Fort Steele Diamond Jubilee Hospital. Dr. Hugh Watt (white beard and frock coat) is next to Robert Galbraith. The ladies, left to right, are Mrs. Levett, Mrs. Bleasdell, Miss Bailey, and unknown.

monetary needs, this committee accepted donations of sheets, pillowcases, towels, blankets, cutlery, soap, dishtowels, dishes, salt and pepper shakers, lamps, and a broom and dustpan. Once the painting and finishing was completed the hospital committee, headed by Robert Galbraith, advertised for a matron. The wages of this live-in nurse would be paid from subscriptions, the earliest form of medical insurance.

The Board of Trade promptly put four items on its agenda. Creating a fire brigade was high on the priority list. It was thought that a brigade might add impetus to the building of a waterworks. Three fire wardens were appointed and given the authority to inspect premises to look for fire hazards. Archie McVittie and Constable Barnes commenced these duties immediately, but fire warden and carpenter John Grassick was working at the mission and was home only on Saturday nights. *The Prospector* later carried a memo that "Fire Inspections will resume when A.W. McVittie returns." The very dry climate in summer months accentuated danger from grass fires, while in the winter uncleaned stovepipes often led to chimney fires. An overturned kerosene lamp had started a fire that wiped out Barkerville's main street. Mercifully, when a drowsy (or intoxicated) guest in the Venosta Hotel knocked over a lamp the fire was confined to one room, thanks to an alert staff. Fort Steelites wanted fire protection, and it became a reality by March 1898. Finally merchants and homeowners could buy fire insurance.

The waterworks obtained water from a 25-foot well beside Wild Horse Creek. A large Worthington steam pump capable of lifting 1,000 gallons a minute lifted the water into the new water tower. The cylindrical wooden tank held 20,000 gallons and sat inside a 50-foot tower. (The replicated water tower today has no water tank; it serves as an observation point at the opposite end of town from the original.) The water mains were laid and fire hydrants connected. Very few households obtained direct access to water. Hotels, the school, businesses, and homes continued to use outhouses for the next 20 to 60 years. Nonetheless, a fire brigade was formed, and volunteer firemen trained in the use of big hoses and the new hydrants. Small fires were quickly contained. On September 1, 1898, the first major fire destroyed T.C. Armstrong's Tin Shop, but the nearby buildings were saved.

A very internal challenge for the new Board of Trade was sidewalks. In this town where streets were either muddy or dusty, pedestrian traffic needed continuous walks of uniform height. It was a proud day when the sidewalk stretched from the Dalgardno to Dr. Watt's home on Riverside Avenue. Merchants on Main Street had each laid a few feet of sidewalk in front of their respective doors. Gradually additions were made until Main Street also had a continuous boardwalk.

Item number three on the Board of Trade's agenda was incorporation. Members felt that they were capable of conducting civic duties in their own boomtown. Further investigation into the requirements of incorporation showed them they could work towards preparing for the future, as was discussed in the article from *The Prospector*, shown at right.

While these requirements were being read Robert Galbraith seized on the last and muttered, "You cannot go a single step further until I agree to sign. I own half of Fort Steele." Members tabled the topic of incorporation for the next few months, but murmurs of disappointment mentioned the towns in the West Kootenay. Rossland, Grand Forks, and Nelson had received

MUNICIPAL INCORPORATION

Many of our most prominent citizens are in favour of Fort Steele becoming incorporated as a city municipality. There are many advantages, in our opinion, that would flow from such incorporation, but under the provisions of the Municipal Incorporation Act of this Province, though so far as population and other requirements are concerned Fort Steele is amply qualified to take on the dignities and responsibilities of a city municipality, it is impossible that this place can become incorporated before the 1st of January, 1899, some sixteen months hence. Applications for incorporation must be in the hands of the Lieutenant-Governor at Victoria on or before the 30th day of June in any year, and the letters patent of incorporation are issued to take effect at the beginning of the following year. In order to become incorporated at least 100 British subjects of the full age of 21 years, must have been residents of the place seeking incorporation for at least six months previous to the signing of the application. Persons owning in the aggregate more than one half in value of the real estate within the area sought to be incorporated must sign this application and the values will be indicated in the register of Absolute Ownership in the Land Registry of the District within which the proposed municipality is situated.[71]

special dispensation from the provincial legislature to shorten the waiting period. Each of these communities had received its Charter of Incorporation in April, signed by Lieutenant-Governor Edgar Dewdney (Edgar Dewdney, who directed the building of the Dewdney Trail in 1865, was back in Victoria, holding this prestigious office after several years as a Member of Parliament in Ottawa, followed by the top post in the federal Indian Affairs Department, and a term as lieutenant-governor of Manitoba and the North-West Territories.)

The fourth item on the Board of Trade's agenda was to improve customs services. Citizens and merchants were frequently frustrated because shipments were delayed. Norbury described waiting several weeks for his new boots, mailed from England but held at the customs office in Donald, despite an arrangement made to guarantee duty payment at Fort Steele. The riverboats had been stopped at Tobacco Plains for customs inspections, hindering travel timetables. There was a Customs House built at Cranbrook. At that time it was a very impractical location. Finally they were able to have a customs officer at Fort Steele, so inspection and duty collection were just a few steps away from the new stores and residences in Fort Steele. Charles Clark, brother-in-law to Robert Galbraith, was customs officer and postmaster at Fort Steele. The June 5, 1897, *Prospector* noted that Clark fell off the gangplank while doing a customs inspection of cargo on the incoming *Gwendoline*. Clark resigned as postmaster at the end of October. He and his wife were given a party with numerous expressions of appreciation. E.J. Cann undertook postmaster duties and created a post office within his store so that Charles Clark could concentrate on his customs duties.

The Board of Trade continued to have a finger on the pulse of its boom town. Members of the organization were pleased that their initial efforts were improving the quality of life for fellow citizens. So much was happening in this year of 1897 that *The Prospector* twice increased in size. There were many activities presented under the headlines of its pages.

Chapter 18

Other Headlines (1897)

In January 1897 the population of Fort Steele was 300. By mid-summer it was ten times that, and still growing.

The Anglicans had regular Sunday services in the schoolhouse, conducted by lay reader Robert Galbraith. The Presbyterians commenced Sunday worship under L.W. Patmore, also in the one-room school. The congregations agreed to alternate afternoons and evenings. Miss Bailey played the organ for weddings, funerals, and regular services for the Anglicans and also—when requested—for the Presbyterians.

Across the river at the mission, Mr. Haney and Dr. Milburn, Crow's Nest Railway construction contractors, had pressured Father Coccola to build and staff a hospital. Father Coccola and Sister Conrad visited Seattle, Portland, and Montreal to recruit nursing sisters. A hospital with 40 beds was built on the bank of St. Mary's River. The earliest patients were handled in an old building, and then transferred when the new building was ready. They were kept busy during the fall of 1897 with sick or injured workers. The following summer the construction camps were hit by mountain fever (typhoid), which was fatal if untreated. The sisters handled huge numbers of patients. At one point a large tent was set up to handle convalescents. When the epidemic subsided, a railway commissioner visited. He was surprised by the small percentage of deaths and asked the sisters their secret. "Cleanliness, fresh milk and good whiskey."[72]

Right Reverend Paul Durien came from New Westminster to visit at the mission. The bishop travelled by railway to Golden, and was conveyed up the Columbia Valley in a carriage from the mission. He had first come to St. Eugene Mission on horseback via the Dewdney Trail from Hope, and made a later inspection by coming inland on the American railway as far as Bonner's Ferry.

The object of this visit was to bless his flock of Kootenay Indians, and to lay the cornerstone of the new church at St. Eugene Mission. The ceremony was carefully planned. "Dignitaries attending included Lieutenant-Governor Edgar Dewdney; Colonel James Baker, M.P.P.; A.W. Vowell, superintendent of Indian Affairs for the province; R.L.T. Galbraith, Indian agent; and each of the band chiefs from the East Kootenay district. Father Nicolas Coccola, Father Norbert Oulette, Brother John Burns, Reverend Sister Conrad, and the other teaching Sisters were also present for this joyous, yet solemn, occasion."[73]

On Dominion Day, Canada's 30th birthday was celebrated at Moyie. A number of Fort Steele residents went to the town, 53 kilometres away, to join in the fun. Public transportation between Moyie and Fort Steele was offered by White-Fraser's stage line until late 1898, when the Crow's Nest Railway was completed. Hardy citizens wishing to compete or participate in events were quite prepared to travel all day and stay overnight in the host community. Moyie had lake frontage, so a few swimming races were scheduled in the competitions. *The Prospector* noted that J. Wilmshurst and M.L. Poland won their respective races in the water. A great deal of fun was generated by a raft race that Frank McMahon won, with Wilmshurst coming in second. Dry-land competition included foot races, bucking competition (sawing race), and climbing the greasy pole. It became a district tradition for neighbouring communities to rotate the hosting of celebrations of major holidays.

Another indication of the impending importance of Fort Steele was an influx of barristers and solicitors. The first to arrive was W.R. Ross of Manitoba on May 1, and John Campbell of Victoria on May 22. Campbell was permitted to practise by virtue of his membership in the British Columbia Bar Association. Ross was not allowed to practise until he passed examinations set by the governing body in Victoria. So, a few weeks later, Ross and another lawyer, H.W. Herchmer, were advertising as "Agents for Phoenix Insurance Company and the Hamilton Powder Company."

J.A. Harvey arrived from Ontario with his family, built a house, set up a small office as a mining broker, and became involved with prospecting and working on various claims. The three new residents were shocked when the lawyer, John Campbell, passed away very suddenly. The whole community voiced deep sympathy for the Campbell family, which had been preparing to move to Fort Steele from Victoria. It was known that Campbell was a Mason. Although there was no lodge in the East Kootenay at that time, 40 Masonic Brethren undertook to give him a Masonic funeral.[74]

By midsummer the three out-of-province lawyers had filed the initial applications to take the British Columbia law examinations. Each quietly resented the legacy left by Judge Baillie Begbie that "admitted any barrister from Great Britain to practice law in the colony/province of British Columbia. Permanent membership in the Law Society was automatically granted to British barristers. For one year (1858–59) barristers from other British possessions and men qualified to plead before the U.S. Supreme Court could be enrolled temporarily."[75]

George Anthony Walkem, trained in McGill University and articled under Sir John Rose in Montreal, applied for admission to the B.C. Bar in September 1862, and was refused. John Robson petitioned on behalf of Walkem. Governor Douglas passed the appeal on to the Secretary of State in London, England. In June 1863 the Legal Professions Act allowed any barrister properly enrolled in the Empire to apply for admission to the British Columbia Bar and to expect to be admitted. Begbie still rejected Walkem's application. Finally, in November 1863, Begbie received communication from London that forced him to enrol Walkem. In February 1874 George Anthony Walkem became premier of the province prepared to admit Canadian lawyers, after a six-month residency, to the British Columbia Law Society.

Messrs. J.A. Harvey, W.R. Ross, and H.W. Herchmer submitted a petition to the B.C. Law Society on August 18, 1897. It noted that the three men were new residents of the province, but recognized lawyers elsewhere, and wished to write their examinations for admission to the B.C. Law Society in November. They also pointed out that taking the examination in Victoria would necessitate five days' journey in each direction, so they requested that they be able to write it in Fort Steele before a Stipendiary Magistrate.

They received the official reply from Victoria in October. The decision from the bencher's meeting, October 4, 1897, declared, "Such a course cannot be pursued." The date set for writing was the second Monday in December.

W.R. Ross left Fort Steele early in November to visit his wife and family in Victoria, and prepare for them to move once he was called to the bar. After the stage had left Fort Steele on Saturday, November 27, telegrapher Rooke received a telegram for H.W. Herchmer. The telegram announced that the date for writing the bar examination had been moved ahead by one week, to Monday, December 6. Herchmer ran to find James Harvey. The two of them hurriedly packed their valises and arranged for private transportation. The liveryman drove his team at a good clip and delivered Herchmer and Harvey to the overnight stopping place of the mail stage. The last-minute change in examination dates could have excluded these men for another twelve months. In retrospect, it is a classic example of frustrating yet comical "remote control" leadership from the capital city.

All three men easily passed their examinations and were officially called to the bar. The dignified old Sir Henry Pellew Crease presented W.R. Ross, H.W. Herchmer, and C.S. McCarter of Golden, while Hubert Robertson introduced James A. Harvey. They could now freely practise law in the province, attending court when necessary.

Concerts, minstrel shows, weddings, dances, church services, political meetings, and even "balls" became regular activities at Fort Steele. Reports in the expanding newspaper *The Prospector* indicate a very busy, lively community. The Christmas concert combined children's presentations with performances by adults. An Indian Boys' Band was formed at the mission school and brought to town to raise funds for St. Anthony's Church. The Fort Steele Band was organized in October 1897. The Mathers hosted a magnificent St. Andrew's Day supper and ball. The year climaxed with the inauguration of the Men's Club.

The Kootenay Men's Club was organized shortly after Colonel Hugh Henderson purchased the Opera House from Coventry. *The Prospector* described the clubrooms upstairs for its readers.

[They] are very handsomely fitted and furnished throughout. The reception room is immediately to the left of the entrance. At one end of it writing tables have been placed with receptacles for Club stationery. Opening off the reception room is the reading room, a spacious, airy well lighted room, in the centre of which runs a long table on which is placed a large assortment of home and foreign periodical literature embracing most of the favorite publications of the day. The nucleus of the club library is also in place, and this will be added to from time to time. To the rear of the reading room is an apartment devoted to those who care to play chess, checkers, cards etc. and where it is intended to introduce a billiard table. Bathroom, lavatory, etc. have been provided for and when all is completed the Kootenay Club will have quarters as convenient and complete as any similar organization in the interior.[76]

Invitations were sent out to ladies and gentlemen for the official opening on the afternoon of Monday, December 13. The wives of future members and single ladies such as Miss Bailey were delighted to attend, as they knew it would be a male bastion. Light refreshment was served to those attending the afternoon opening. Altogether it was a most enjoyable occasion. There was, however, an unexpected backlash: Constable Barnes inferred that liquor laws were violated.

On Tuesday last Messrs. H.D. Henderson, F.P. Norbury and M.A. Beale, respectively the President, Vice-President and Secretary of the Kootenay Club, appeared before Stipendiary Magistrate Armstrong charged by Constable Barnes with infraction of the liquor law by the sale of liquor to members of the club.

Constable Barnes gave evidence to the effect that liquor was being kept in the Kootenay Club and that it was being sold to members, who gave their IOU for the amount charged for the liquor, and at the end of the month those IOUs would be settled for cash.

Mr. Henderson admitted that the evidence of the Constable was correct, but he was not aware that the

Club in supplying liquor in this manner was breaking any law of the country. Similar Clubs existed in nearly all the cities and towns of any size in the province, and they had not been interfered with. He could not see why an exception should be made of the Kootenay Club. However, the Club did not desire to break any law of the country, and, if the course they were pursuing was illegal he would immediately take out a license and in all respects conform to the law. But he would ask that the magistrate adjourn the case so that the opinion of the Attorney General could be had on the legal aspect of the matter.

The magistrate accordingly adjourned the case for one month.[77]

Information sent from the attorney general's office allowed Magistrate Armstrong to state that the Kootenay Men's Club was not violating any regulations because the liquor was not sold for profit. The Club installed the promised billiard table, with considerable difficulty negotiating the staircase on the side of the building. The members added two significant bylaws a few weeks later:

1. No gentleman residing within a twelve-mile radius of Fort Steele shall be permitted to enter as a guest.

2. Wives and lady friends may be entertained at the Club on Thursday afternoons only—3 p.m. to 7 p.m.

The Kootenay Men's Club was indeed a major social centre for the men in the district. By February 1898 the club had 60 paid-up members and was open from noon to midnight with a steward and assistant steward on duty, serving sandwiches and snacks and liquid refreshments. The club's success provided citizens with one more reason to proclaim that Fort Steele was the capital of the Kootenays.

Chapter 19

Mining

More mining was done in the bars in Fort Steele than in the hills. These hours of mining talk were the pulse of the district. Statements appeared in *The Prospector* claiming that for every 1,000 people in town, 2,000 more were in the mountains, grubbing for gold or hoping to find an exposed vein of galena. Editor A.B. Grace had become an enthusiastic participant in the exploration and excavation as well as a speculator of the mineral wealth in the district. Each issue of the newspaper presented up-to-date reports of specific activity or lists of newly registered claims.

The names given to claims were quite imaginative. The mining registrar had to be alert to these names to not allow duplication, at least within the East Kootenay. A sample of these names is quoted from *The Prospector*, February 27, 1897.

These claims have been sold or bonded in the Fort Steele district, since January 1st, 1897:

Quantrell	Orphan Boy	Contact
Big-three	Orphan Girl	Almadon
Helping Hand	Caustic	Rams Horn
Lone Star	Utopia	Gem
Colorado Boy	Whale	Stoney
Carbonate Hill	Eureka	Mystic
Bachelor	Golden Fleece	Woodstock
Twilight	Elk-horn	Duke
Big Horn	Pearl	Lottie
Gold Horn	Alberta	

Every man, woman, and child heard talk of workings, findings, and current speculations. They would be aware of mining vocabulary, including the following:

Free gold–easily separated from the surrounding sand and gravel
Placer claim—a site on a creek, bar, or hillside where the miner is working to recover gold
Quartz gold—requires crushing to obtain the gold
Giant—a water cannon used for hydraulic mining
Rocker—a small wooden device used to screen and catch gold
Sluice Box—a wooden flume with cross ribs, which is used to wash gravel and catch gold
Tunnel—a horizontal passageway dug into the mountain
Timbering—building a wooden framework in a tunnel
Vein—a deposit of ore or coal having a more or less regular length, width, and depth
Shaft—a vertical tunnel
Stope—a step-like tunnel at an angle

Some novice prospectors might have read *Minerals and How to Study Them,* written by a Yale professor, Edward Salisbury Dana, and published in 1896 by John Wiley and Sons of New York or Chapman and Hall, London, England. Other newcomers would trudge through the hills with an old-timer, trying to learn what to look for.

Many a find was virtually accidental. The man or his horse slipped, peeling moss off a rock face. The prospector used his pick to check behind the dull surface. If he was rewarded with a chunk of heavy ore with sparkles he took a sample or two to be tested at the assay office. He had to devise a marker, and to blaze a route to be able to return several miles from an established trail. (There was no neon-coloured surveyor's tape in the 1890s.)

When the assay report was encouraging, "Joe Prospector" would return to the site equipped with metal tags for marking the corners of his claim. A mineral claim—at least four times the 100-foot square allowed for a new placer claim—was to be marked off in as neat a rectangle as the land formation would permit. Joe set up camp on or near his claim and dug around the outcropping to learn the extent of the mineral deposit. He had several options. To renew his claim he had to perform yearly assessment work for a prescribed number of man-hours or dollars paid to a helper. A certificate of improvement would be allowed if, after basic spring cleanup, work was undertaken to build a trail or improve a trail to a wagon road. Mr. Prospector would likely take on partners in this venture, or sell to a conglomerate, or at the very least arrange for some moneylender to bond the property. A bond indicated a willingness to finance development work, or when circumstances permitted, to purchase equipment to be brought in so that ore could be taken out to a smelter.

Fort Steele was the business centre for miners in the East Kootenay. The stores did their best to supply individuals as well as camps with groceries and basic equipment. Mining brokers eagerly sought the opportunity to buy and sell claims. Some brokers blissfully accepted the word of a prospector about the claims up for sale. The more conscientious brokers personally inspected each property before selling to investors here and abroad. The mining recorder had an office in Fort Steele from 1887 onward, and all miners' licences, claim registrations, and declarations of work done were handled here. The annual report of the minister of mines included statistics and details collected here. From 1898 to 1911 the reports from South-East Kootenay District, Fort Steele Mining Division, were prepared by gold commissioner and government agent James F. Armstrong.

The Fort Steele Mining Division extended from the headwater of the Kootenay River and Finlay Creek south to the American border, and west from the Alberta Territory approximately 80 miles, to include a total of almost 7,000 square miles. J.F. Armstrong endeavoured to visit the active operations. The busiest galena extractors were the North Star group, above the mining camp later known as Kimberley, with "2,700 feet of drift, shaft and raises," and St. Eugene Mine, with "2,700 feet of tunnelling and 270 feet of shafting and sloping: cost $35,000.00," as described in agent Armstrong's 1902 report. Another galena body that was worked inter-mittently to the 1950s was the Estella group behind Wasa.

Perry Creek was the leading gold producer, with Bull River yielding rich returns when low water permitted. Wild Horse Creek was fully staked, but there was little more than certification work done on most claims.

The Dardanelles mineral claim about ten miles from Fort Steele, almost opposite Victoria Ditch on the southeast bank of the Wild Horse Creek, had been worked by an arrastra. There was quartz, from which they hoped to extract gold, and galena with grey copper and iron pyrites. A full-fledged stamp mill was too heavy and too expensive to bring to this site, so the Banks brothers constructed an arrastra with timber cut right on their claim.

The arrastra itself is a tight, wooden, circular tank 9 feet in diameter and 30 inches deep, bound with iron bands. The wooden bottom is paved over with large stones tightly wedged in. In the centre of the tank is a vertical 12 by 12 inches wooden shaft set in a suitable step—bearing and provided with four wooden arms, to each of which is attached by chains, two stone drags, making eight in all. These drags weigh from 200 to 500 pounds each.

Motion was conveyed to this shaft through a horizontal wooden gear wheel 5 feet in diameter, with wooden teeth, which in turn, connected with a similar but vertical wheel on the main horizontal shaft of 12 by 12 inch timber, on which was hung an overshot waterwheel, 20 feet in diameter, with a 24 inch face and buckets 9 inches deep. The water for driving the wheel was carried from higher up the creek by a 12 by 12 inch overhead box flume.[78]

The ore was brought down the steep hillside on a "go-devil"—a sled with spikes on it. The empty sled was turned spikes up for the return haul of a mile and a half. Each trip saw one-half ton of ore in sacks delivered to the arrastra. The lone horse on the job brought down 30 tons of ore for grinding. The screen of #20 mesh caught sufficient gold and silver to pay for the year's operation, but yielded scant profit.

The B.C. government introduced frequent changes to the mining laws. The local provincial Member of Parliament,

Colonel James Baker, occasionally consulted Fort Steele mining men. If they were against a proposed clause of new legislation he actually voted against it! Baker was developing the new community of Cranbrook, to the dismay and disgust of Fort Steelites. When it came to mining, his interests were in the developing coal fields around the infant community of Fernie. Coal mining was included in reports of the minister of mines after 1899.

Fort Steele enjoyed visits by the federal Member of Parliament more than the controversial provincial representative. Hewitt Bostock was a jovial fellow with a cattle ranch in Monte Creek, near Kamloops, and a part owner in the *Vancouver Province* newspaper. During his visit in September 1897 he was taken up Wild Horse Creek to view the hydraulic workings of the Invicta Company. The stage, driven by Alf Doyle, held Liberal faithfuls Dr. Watt, F.P. Norbury, James Durick, A.C. Nelson, T. McNaught, and William Baillie, besides Bostock. Mine manager Young prepared some lunch for them before conducting a tour of the operation. A five-inch monitor was throwing its deluge of water into the steep gravel banks. Gravel and boulders roared and rattled as they tumbled down, and the run-off streams were directed through sluice boxes. The work of gathering gold was wet, but very effective and profitable.

On the other side of the Wild Horse another hydraulic crew—all Chinese—were working the Nip and Tuck Mine. These hydraulic workings continued night and day as long as the water supply held out. Night operations were supplied with electric light from a pelton wheel in the river. Bostock was surprised and delighted by the extent of the workings he had seen.

"Bostock was then escorted down a trail to visit Dave and Mrs. Griffiths. The group was presented with fresh plums off the Griffiths' trees. Mr. Griffiths eagerly talked of his earlier days on the Wild Horse, and gloated that he had sold the Invicta claims for $100,000: half in cash, half in stock in the company. The visitors hated to leave the hospitable Griffiths but had to get back to the 'city' before dark."[79]

Mine developers had to contend with many variables, such as the market price for their product and the government regulations. The operations at North Star Mine shut down for a few months in 1898 because of a stockpile of ore and a drop in the price of silver. In 1899 the government dropped a bombshell: "No miner shall work underground for more than eight hours at one time." Miners had been working ten-hour shifts for $3.50 a day. Mine owners complied with the eight-hour law by dropping the pay to $3.00. Many miners, especially those in isolated camp bunkhouses, wanted to work the extra two hours and refused to accept the pay cuts. Miners across British Columbia went on strike. Each mine owner bargained with his crew. Some operations in the West Kootenay never reopened after the strike.

Fort Steele held the registration centre for mining claims for a brief period after the government office moved into Cranbrook. The communities directly affected by mining grew in the early 1900s. Fernie became a creditable town supported by coal mining; the St. Eugene mine was the chief employer of citizens of Moyie until 1913; and the North Star and Sullivan mines startled the world by producing past the year 2000 from the mountains behind Kimberley. There were several gold rushes in British Columbia, but never much of a "galena rush."

Chapter 20

Busy Times
(1898)

The year of 1898 dawned clear and very cold. The railway was coming to the area. The new school was opened. Gold fever attracted some Kootenay citizens to join the Klondike gold rush. Congregations were preparing for services with an ordained minister to replace the lay readers. And the ice harvest began in January.

Ice harvesting was done on nearby small lakes and occasionally on a quiet lagoon beside the Kootenay River. The crew watched as the ice formed, measuring the depth and clearing the surface of snow whenever necessary. Snow acts as insulation, and if not removed, the ice would not freeze to the required depth.

The ice was pierced by an auger to permit the ice saw or saws to start the cut. The ice saw had much larger teeth than the regular crosscut for tree falling or bucking. A cut was made straight across the pond, then a cut parallel to that was made. The strip was then cut into blocks. Blocks were cut approximately 20 by 20 inches. The blocks were lifted out with large ice tongs and loaded onto a sleigh parked on the ice. One man stood on the ice and another on the sleigh deck to slide the blocks into place. The loaded sleigh was driven to the icehouse, a building with extra space between walls, insulated with sawdust. A ramp was set in place to slide the ice blocks onto a bed of sawdust, and then the blocks were stacked almost the height of the building. Fresh snow was packed between the blocks with irregular surfaces. New clean sawdust was poured between the ice and the walls. A thick layer of sawdust over all insulated the top layer of ice.

Courtesy Martin Ross

The Fort Steele two-room school (right) opened in January 1898. St. Anthony's Roman Catholic Church (left) was built for $700 and was served by a priest from nearby St. Eugene Mission.

The sleigh returned to the pond for load after load. As the area of open water increased, men and horses moved cautiously, as no one wanted to swim in January. Drifting ice blocks were gingerly retrieved with a pike pole. George Geary had helpers that came back year after year, but a newcomer who had misstepped on the last day vowed, "Never again." The ice harvesters definitely earned their pay.

School opened on January 10, 1898, with Miss Bailey and her 72 pupils settling into the new building. Even though the students were respectful and hard working, and the teacher experienced and efficient, another adult was obviously required for the Fort Steele School. Mrs. James Clark came in as a classroom monitor for two terms. The students did their assignments by writing with a slate pencil on a slate. The teacher had to check the work before the slate could be cleaned for the next day's lessons. Boys delighted in spitting on the slate, then rubbing off the writing with a rag. The girls, each with a rag neatly pinked around the edges, kept a small bottle of water in their desk to wash the slate. When the slate rags

Courtesy Martin Ross

The Presbyterian Church had the largest congregation during the boom years. It was lit by fancy acetylene lamps.

became stinky the teacher pleaded for clean rags to be brought to replace them.

The curriculum during Miss Bailey's days "embraced reading, spelling, writing, arithmetic, grammar, composition, history (English and Canadian), geography, and physiology (anatomy, physiology, hygiene, and agriculture). In addition to the above the following subjects may [have been] taught: book-keeping, mensuration, geometry, drawing, algebra, temperance, music, needlework and calisthenics."[80]

The school served pupils from Grades One to Eight. Visiting superintendent Dr. Pope, and later inspector William Burns, praised the results achieved by Adelaide Bailey's classes. In 1897 Herbert Clark won a medal upon completing Grade Eight with high marks. Four years later, after being privately coached by Miss Bailey, Clark passed entrance examinations for the University of Toronto. This teacher read widely and was one of the first to take advantage of library books loaned from Victoria, a boxful at a time. She felt that the children had plenty of exercise doing their chores at home. On cold days, however, students stood beside their desks and did calisthenics to overcome the chill in the classroom. On the iciest days Miss Bailey heated a flat rock on the heater, wrapped it in a towel, then sat with her feet on it to achieve a degree of comfort. Children were allowed to drape wet clothing over the screen beside the heater to dry. An older student was often assigned to turn the garments to prevent scorching. Boys routinely wore wool or fleecy long underwear. Many girls and women also adopted "long johns" in the coldest season. Schoolwork had to be done even if the floor was cold. The pupils alternately roasted or shivered, depending on the whims of the big heater in the back of the room.

The Presbyterian minister Reverend John Glass Duncan arrived in Fort Steele on January 13 on the stage from Golden, transferred there from Kamloops. He promptly arranged that services would be held in the Opera House on Sundays at 7:30 p.m.

Within a month the Presbyterian congregation had commenced fund-raising to build a church, established a choir led by Mrs. Frizzell, conducted Sunday school each week, and petitioned the Church and Manse Building Fund for a loan. Trustees elected to direct the building were Messrs. Henry Kershaw, Malcolm McInnes, Robert Duncan Mather, and Dr. Hugh Watt.

The adopted financial plan was based on the assumption that the cost of the building would be $800. Half of that sum was requested from the Presbyterian Church of Canada for Manitoba and the North-West Territories, $150 was sought as a grant, and $250 as a loan to be repaid over three years—$50 the first year and $100 for each of the next two. The congregation was expected to raise the other $400.

The whole community rallied behind the Presbyterian fund-raisers. The Ladies' Aid Society under president Mary Jane Mather, vice-president Mrs. Goodenough, and secretary-treasurer Mrs. McInnes, assisted by Mrs. Underhill, organized soirees, socials, pie sales, Christmas parties, and more. Their enthusiasm and energy buoyed the minister and the rest of the congregation through good times and bad.

By July the congregation was ready to call for tenders, and by September it welcomed a visiting Reverend Charles W. Gordon, the secretary of British Columbia Northwest Missions, to preach the first sermon in the church.

Only months later—by the end of 1898—the railway bypassed Fort Steele in favour of Cranbrook, and citizens began to move away. The building and equipping of the church had gone over budget, despite an outright donation of an organ worth $300. By 1900 the remaining congregation had to apply for a further loan of $400 to retire the mortgage. The full-time minister was transferred, and students were supplied to serve the district each summer.[81]

The 1898 Presbyterian Church still serves the public from its new site within Fort Steele Heritage Town.

Meanwhile, the Anglicans discovered that their meeting place, the one-room schoolhouse, was available for full-time possession. They organized as a congregation, choosing the name "St. John the Divine" for their church. They appealed to the bishop of British Columbia for a minister, appointed T.T. McVittie and Noel Wallinger as wardens, A.W. Bleasdell and G.H. Gilpin as vestrymen, Charles Edwards and C.M. Tulloch as sidesmen, Harry McVittie as choirmaster, and Miss Bailey as organist. Robert Galbraith and James Armstrong continued their roles as lay readers, conducting regular services or funerals.

Galbraith, a school trustee, announced that there was $80 unpaid on the former schoolhouse. He requested that the newly formed congregation retire this debt as soon as possible. At the same time he donated four lots to the Anglicans, two for a vicarage and two for when (and if) they should build a larger church.

In August *The Prospector* announced, "Anglican Bishop Dart has appointed Charles Ault Procunier, MA to St. John's Church. He is one of the best speakers in the Kootenays, having been a Methodist minister for twelve years." Procunier arrived and commenced services promptly. Mrs. Procunier and their three small children came from Kaslo to Fort Steele a few weeks later, as soon as they were able to arrange transportation on the Crow's Nest Railway. On October 29, 1898, *The Prospector* ran a notice stating, "All ladies and gentlemen who are interested in Shakespearean study and literature and who are anxious to organize a reading club are cordially invited to the home of the Rev. C.A. Procunier on Thursday evening, Nov. 3rd at 8 p.m."

A ladies' guild for St. John's Church was formed in February. The ladies present chose officers for the ensuing year: Mrs. Armstrong as president, Mrs. Bleasdell as vice-president, and

Miss Bailey as secretary. The other members attending that first meeting were Mesdames Charles Clark, Charles Edwards, Ben Huckle, George Gilpin, Charles Levett, John Galbraith, James Clark, James Durick, W. Ross, A.C. Nelson, and N.A. Wallinger; Miss Watson also attended.[82]

The Shakespearean Club and the euchre games were interdenominational social events. There were dances, concerts, sports days, and meetings. Fort Steele was no longer a sleepy backwater. It was *the centre* of the East Kootenay, where the "Fire Laddies Ball" in March was outshone by the "Masquerade Ball for Hospital Benefit" in April. There were celebrations in Fort Steele for the Queen's birthday and the fourth of July.

Lots were still selling in Fort Steele, but the personable agent C.F. Venosta suddenly left the district. Robert Galbraith posted this notice in *The Prospector* on April 9, 1898.

Today I have appointed T.T. McVittie agent for the Fort Steele Townsite in place of C.F. Venosta.

All persons having business in connection with the Townsite are directed to transact same with T.T. McVittie and make all payments due or accruing on lots already sold to him.

R.L.T. Galbraith

Later that summer town lots were offered for sale, with the bonus of 10,000 feet of lumber included.

Talk of gold finds in the Klondike spurred some of the restless prospectors to try their luck in the north. No one raised an eyebrow on hearing that Bob Dore or Patrick Quirk, Wild Horse pioneers, were provisioning up in Victoria, but Captain Frank Armstrong? Armstrong vowed to build a steamboat to run between Lake Teslin and Dawson City. He took a crew of 40 men, all necessary machinery with specialists to install them, and a portable sawmill to cut the lumber. Armstrong built the *Mono* in Alaska and worked her on the Stikine River the first summer, wrecked it, collected the insurance on it, bought the wreck back "for a song," patched it, re-floated it, and went on to the Yukon River. The following season he piloted the steamer *Gleaner* on Lake Bennett and a steamer on Lake Tagish; however, he retained his interests in the International Navigation Company and the Upper Columbia Navigation and Tramway Company, returning to the East Kootenay in 1900.

Two riverboat companies now served the Jennings–Fort Steele run. Considerable excitement was created with the arrival of the first boat of the season earlier than usual on April 29, *but* it had taken twelve days to make it upriver instead of the usual three in ideal conditions. *The Prospector* told the residents all about it.

> The brand new *J.D. Farrell*, 126 feet long, 26 ft. beam, 266 tons was fitted with elegant staterooms, bathrooms, dining room, and illuminated with electric lights including a powerful search light for night travel. The arrival was signalized by a salute of dynamite strikes. The Fort Steele Brass Band played on the bridge and afterwards on the deck of the steamer.
>
> Sixteen passengers arrived on the *Farrell*, including the owner Mr. Farrell of Moyie, founder of the Kootenay Navigation Company. The crew were M.L. McCormack— Captain; Geo. H. McMasters—pilot; Jno [sic] Smith— mate; first engineer, 2nd engineer, two firemen, steward and stewardess, cook, 2nd cook, waiter, watchman and ten deckhands.[83]

The following week three boats tied up at Fort Steele in quick succession. The *North Star, Gwendoline,* and *J.D. Farrell* collectively delivered 117 tons of freight. On the downriver trip the *North Star* had an accident at the same site as the *Ruth* had foundered. Luckily the damage was light and the ship quickly repaired. A crew member, however, lost his life when a lifeboat that had safely delivered passengers to the shore fouled on a cable, snagging the man into the rushing current. Meanwhile Captain Sanborn, formerly of the *Ruth,* went to the Klondike to supervise D.D. Mann's boats on Teslin Lake.

The 1898 river freighting season was one of the busiest times on the upper Kootenay River, primarily to ship ore out from North Star Landing. By late fall, however, the Crow's Nest to Kootenay Lake rail line was completed. Captain Miller had orders to sell the *Gwendoline.* The little ship was purchased to serve on the Duncan Lake run above the north end of Kootenay Lake. She was loaded on three flatcars near Libby to be transported past the waterfalls, unloaded, and then re-launched at Bonner's Ferry. Other riverboats had been safely transported in this manner. The *Gwendoline*, however, toppled off the flatcars and landed upside down in a canyon, smashed to smithereens.

The Jubilee Hospital was struggling financially. A determined hospital board arranged fund-raisers, and politely appealed to the provincial government for justifiable maintenance costs. It was also discovered that when Dr. Watt succeeded Dr. MacLean as the district physician, the appointment omitted the annual financial allotment previously awarded. After May 1 the new hospital at the mission was the preferred destination of sick or injured men. Dr. Watt used the St. Eugene Hospital operating room to treat patients such as "Thomas Edwards who has been seriously ill with lung trouble. An incision was made and a couple of quarts of watery matter removed. The patient has experienced a remarkable improvement in health."[84] Dr. Watt had the assistance of an experienced nursing sister.

The Fort Steele hospital did not cater to maternity cases. Mrs. Dimmick nursed confinements and deliveries in her home. "New arrivals" were noted among the general items in *The Prospector,* and these early birth announcements were numerous in this booming community.

Dr. Watt, and a newly arrived Dr. Brodie, formed a partnership in Fort Steele. They were contracted by the railway to deal with medical emergencies in the various construction camps along the new right-of-way. Dr. Brodie looked after the western section while Dr. Watt was in charge of the eastern part.

The Kootenay Men's Club was a favourite gathering place for its members and guests from out of town. Colonel Baker enjoyed dropping in and relaxing. He found a ready audience for tales from other parts of the province such as the following one.

As you know the Canadian Pacific Railway is attracting well-to-do tourists to Banff and points west. This is an account of one of the citizens of Field, in the northeast corner of our riding.

Three Oxford professors booked a trip in Yoho Park. They were met by a bearded, burly fellow in rough clothing who quickly had their belongings lashed onto pack horses, put the three onto saddle horses and led them off. The guide gave accurate commentary on the geology, flora and fauna as they went along. But he frequently digressed to ask the visitors about political happenings and current events in England. The professors considered his questions impertinent chatter so they started private conversations in French. The guide chatted easily. They switched to German. The guide continued, using German. The miffed professors fell silent. Their host cheerfully sang out—"anyone for Greek, gentlemen?"

They made camp and were served a good meal. Before settling in for the night one of the professors let his curiosity overcome his dignity. "Who are you?" he challenged the guide. "Oh, I'm a Cambridge man myself. I'm here because I'm the black sheep of my family. My old man is the Archbishop of Canterbury![85]

Frederick Paget Norbury came to the district as a greenhorn, but he paid very close attention to how things were done in pioneer settings. He ranted about young Englishmen who "don't know how to use any tools, which they break or spoil. They don't know how to cook, wash clothes or mend, yet in a few days they'll be trying to tell you how to run the show." Norbury not only survived—he prospered, while working on physical tasks such as bridge building, or mental tasks when called as a justice. When he was the president of the local Liberal Association, he was sent as a delegate to a convention in New Westminster. From there he went to Victoria to attend "some mining business," and was a guest of Lieutenant-Governor Dewdney. At the end of 1898 his friends threw a farewell party at Hanson's Wasa Hotel. Norbury rented his ranch to his friend Charlie Edwards, feeling optimistic that his obligations in England would let him return. The years went by. Norbury inherited the family estate in Worcestershire, married in 1907, fathered two sons and a daughter, and died in 1931 at the age of 64. The Kootenays had lost a pioneer citizen, whose letters now held in the B.C. Archives provide an eyewitness view of the area during the early years.

Chapter 21

Building the B.C. Southern Railway
(1897–1899)

The future of the Kootenay mines was dependent upon a suitable transportation system. East Kootenay coal fields lay waiting to be tapped. West Kootenay smelters awaited coal or coke from the Elk Valley. A railway was the most obvious answer, but building a railway was costly.

The builder of each new section of rail line bargained with local, provincial, and federal governments for land allowance. To protect his own interests in the Fernie coal fields, Colonel Baker obtained a charter for the "Crow's Nest and Kootenay Lake Railway." Baker was unable to raise sufficient funds within the three years of his charter, so in 1891 a consortium took over, gaining a new charter for what was then called the "B.C. Southern Railway." The Canadian Pacific Railway (CPR) was not yet prepared to co-operate; general manager William Van Horne stated that a railway through the Crow's Nest was not needed for at least ten to fifteen years.

By 1893 the Canadian Pacific Railway had purchased a private narrow-gauge rail line between Medicine Hat and Lethbridge and began converting it to standard gauge. With this connection to Lethbridge the CPR was poised to push westward. The B. C. government had been pressuring the federal government to provide subsidies to make the Crow's Nest Railway possible. Van Horne, too, made proposals to Ottawa, seeking a subsidy to build a railway through the Crow's Nest Pass. An economic slump around the globe, with the deepest depression occurring in 1894, rendered further appeals useless.

The Laurier government, elected in 1896, had to counteract the stagnation left by the recent depression. It planned to open up the west, to bring settlers onto the prairies, and to bargain with the management of the CPR. Early in 1897 it was agreed that the CPR would be given a subsidy for building a line through the Crow's Nest Pass *on condition* that freight rates be cut on grain from the prairies to Fort William and on the inbound settlers' effects. The government relinquished the clause on settlers' effects by 1922, but the "Crow Rate" was extended to westbound grain shipments. The Crow Rate (applied to wheat that never was transported by the Crow's Nest Railway) was in effect for 100 years.

The Laurier government resolved to avoid giving the CPR a virtual monopoly on lands adjacent to new lines. It ruled that the CPR could have only one coal mine in the Elk Valley, and that mine was not to come into production for at least one year after satisfactory service had been established for the nearby working coal mines at Coal Creek and Michel. The CPR opted for its six sections of land at what became Hosmer.

Several tentative surveys had been done. All of these routes had Fort Steele as the point where a spur could go up to the North Star Mine, and then continue westward through Moyie (where the St. Eugene Mine needed service), beside Goat River to Kootenay Lake. The grades, with the exception of one stretch west of the Crow's Nest summit, were amazingly gentle for such mountainous country. Contracts were let for clearing, grading, tie making, and building a water tower every eighteen miles. Subcontractors for each section created campsites with the least expensive buildings possible. It was said that the barns for the horses were better than the bunkhouses for the workers.

Agents in eastern Canada hired crews. The advertised rate of pay was $1.75 a day less 70 cents a day for board. The recruits were given a ticket to the end of line near Fort Macleod, and had to walk carrying their few possessions, 30 or 40 miles to the camp for which they were hired. A goodly number of the workers were European immigrants who spoke little or no English. Even if workdays were lost due to accident, illness, or extremely bad weather, the charge for room and board continued. Many times a worker was declared to owe the contractor money rather than receive a pay slip. The subcontractors themselves were pushed by Canadian Pacific Railway officers to hurry, hurry, hurry. There were times when they could not meet their payroll because they had not been paid.

During that first winter a bunkhouse at Sand Creek collapsed. Dr. Watt was called to treat a worker whose legs had been crushed and broken in several places. Dr. Watt volunteered to bring the man to the Fort Steele hospital. The camp manager would not allow this, as he had no authorization to pay the fee of one dollar per day for the injured man. The contractor claimed that if hospitalization was indeed necessary, the patient must be taken to Fort Macleod. Dr. Watt did what he could at the campsite, envisioned the agony that would be created by a long bumpy trip, and prayed that the injured man would survive and regain the use of his legs.

The Christmas season gave further frustration to workers who were told that they owed the contractor money rather than receiving a pay cheque.

> Four husky men came into Fort Steele from Egan's camp and made application to the Government Agent for food and lodging. They stated they were destitute. They had been working on the railway for some months but found from month to month that they were deeper in debt to the contractor, who charged for necessary articles of wearing apparel as well as the $4.50 per week for board. With the number of days they were idle during the month they could not get square with their employer on their $1.50 per day.
>
> The men were fed and lodged overnight in the jail. The following morning they were given breakfast and took the road for Goat River from where they hoped to obtain work in the West Kootenay.[86]

By the end of the month a commission was appointed by the Dominion government to investigate the ill treatment of labourers. Charges against contractors had been voiced by workers all along the line of work on the Crow's Nest Railway. Judge Dugas, Frank Pedley, and Appleton commenced taking evidence along the line westward from Fort Macleod.

The CPR anticipated unrest among the thousands of workers building the B.C. Southern Railway. They requested that a few members of the North West Mounted Police be stationed at points along the way to act as security guards. Corporal McNair, aged 33, a smart veteran of the NWMP who had been part of the troop of Mounties representing Canada at the Diamond Jubilee celebrations in London, died suddenly at Wardner. He had been ill with fever, nursed by Engineer MacKenzie and others, but appeared to be regaining good health. At 9 p.m. he wrote a letter to Sergeant Cole at Crow's Nest Lake, requesting that a replacement be sent out for him. MacKenzie went out briefly, and returned to find the corporal lying in one of the cells adjacent to his sleeping quarters, shot through the head, still clutching the revolver responsible.

His remains were brought to Fort Steele. The burial took place Friday morning from the Episcopal Church. A cortege paraded along Riverside Avenue, preceded by the Fort Steele Brass Band, playing the sorrowful strains of the "Dead March in Saul." The coffin was shrouded with the Union Jack. Pallbearers were Captain White-Fraser, Sergeant Lott, J. Doyle, H.W. Herchmer, G.H. Richardson, and F.C. Rankin. Upon arrival at the Mounted Police burial site, Government Agent Armstrong and Robert Galbraith gave a graveside service.[87]

Workers went on strike at many of the camps along the line. Managers such as Egan presented their excuses to Stipendiary Magistrate Armstrong. Egan began paying wages in March "after a brief misunderstanding." Other contractors, or their bookkeepers, were charging their men for non-existent "mail service." Some demanded repayment of rail fare from the eastern city where hiring was done and the agent had supplied "a *complimentary* ticket to the end of line." A group of Italians was hired with the offer of $1.75 a day and deductions of $3.50 per week for board. They were paid the going rate of $1.50 per day and charged $4.50 per week for the poor-quality food served to them. When their leader—the only fellow with a modest understanding of the English language—complained, he was repeatedly told that he had heard the agent's offer incorrectly.

It was not surprising that there were strikes and walkouts. It is surprising that the work was completed within a year and a half.

Several tentative surveys had been done. On much of the route beside the Kootenay River there were narrow benches with little alternative terrain nearby. Most of the way was through Crown land. The CPR agents sat down behind closed doors to bargain with individual landowners on their proposed route. Although Robert Galbraith was anxious to have the railway come through Fort Steele, he was not prepared to donate his property to the corporation. He offered to sell the station site for less money than he'd charge an incoming businessman. Colonel Baker, however, having secured or sold his interests in the coal fields, was prepared to grant free right-of-way through his Cranbrook estate.

Naturally, when the CPR head office learned these facts their plans quickly changed. Fort Steele would be bypassed. Wardner was chosen as the logical place to build a bridge across the Kootenay River. The survey chose a route through the smallish gully known as Isadore Canyon. A camp was built south of the canyon. The kitchen crew built stone ovens for baking and preparing camp meals. The barns and blacksmith shop were built first for the care of the horses. Labourers lived and dined in tents well into the snowy season.

Behind the surveyors came the axemen, clearing trees and brush. The good timber would be set aside for building. The branches and scrub were collected and burned. Hillocks were broken with picks or grubhoes, then the loosened dirt collected in scrapers pulled by a horse or team. Wherever possible, the dirt was dumped into a nearby hollow. When the roadway was levelled and compacted, ties were laid. Last but not least, the steel was laid. A train engine pushing a flatcar loaded with rails came to the end of track. The crew lifted a rail, marched forward, set the rail down, and spiked it in place. The partner rail was lifted, moved forward, laid the correct distance from the first, and spiked. The train advanced 32 to 39 feet; the next pair of rails was handled and installed. The crew soon moved in rhythm, and 1.5 to 3 miles of track were laid on a good day.

Tie cutting was a specialized task assigned to individual axemen. Each man would have a quota to fill from an assigned block of timber. His equipment was a short one-man crosscut saw, a heavy double-bitted axe, a broad axe, and a pickaroon. The tie hacker felled a tree with his saw, trimmed the branches off to where the trunk was too small to make a tie, and then stood on the trunk, trusting the top tree limbs to hold the trunk steady. Ties were flattened on two sides. First the hacker scored the cut lines with the thin blade of his double-bitted axe; this scoring was to keep chips from splintering along the natural, spiral grain around the trunk, as well as to define the parallel edges. Then the carefully sharpened broadaxe was swung into action. The master tie hacker could produce a surface that looked like it had been planed. Next the hewn tree would be bucked into eight-foot lengths. The pickaroon was then hooked into each tie to drag it to the nearest road. Bark was left on the rounded sides of the ties, but most of that rubbed off during transportation to the collection point.[88]

Harvesting ties became a major source of income for ranchers during the winter because the railroad needed 2,800 ties per mile during construction, as well as a steady supply of replacements. A tie hack would be paid 12 to 25 cents per tie depending on the time and circumstances. Tie camps operated at Bull River, near Fort Steele, from 1897 into the 1930s.

During the height of construction activity two new graduates of medical school were brought in. Dr. King was on the section east of Wardner, and Dr. Frank William Green was responsible for the Goat River to Kuskanook section. Each was provided with a horse, an extensive kit of surgical instruments, and a small variety of medicines, and told to "go to work." In retrospect these two doctors later recalled that their method of treatment was crude. In their right-hand pocket they carried a quantity of lead and opium pills, and in their left-hand pocket compound cathartics. They would administer either one kind of pill or the other according to the patient's condition. These young doctors were very popular, so evidently their system was successful.

Dr. F.W. Green arrived at Goat River Crossing at the height of a typhoid epidemic. One of the bunkhouses was designated as a hospital, with a cook and three male nurses. These staff members were exhausted and left en masse. Dr. Green had to attend the patients, cook for them, and bury the dead. The unfortunate doctor had to make all funeral arrangements and conduct gravesite rites. In one case the able-bodied men refused to carry a coffin, and Dr. Green had to pay each man two dollars to carry it just a few hundred feet.

When the Goat River patients were able to return to work, Dr. Green was able to patrol his section of the right-of-way. He arrived in Kuskanook to find a few drunks harassing a newly arrived white nurse. With the help of another nurse, a "Negro," he put the terrified lady in a rowboat and gallantly rowed her to another landing where she could leave by the steamer for Nelson.

Dr. Green and Dr. King arrived in the Kootenays as penniless new graduates, and neither could afford to pay their dues to the B.C. College of Physicians. They happened to meet in the Cranbrook Hotel late in 1899 just as their contracts with the CPR were about to expire. King suggested they become partners and set up in Cranbrook. "And we will have to register with the B.C. College. I have avoided talking to you these last few months because I was afraid you'd turn me in for practicing without a licence." Dr. Green roared with laughter. "I had the same fear about you." The two set up a clinic that was carried on by Dr. W.O. Green, F.W.'s son, and is still serving citizens of Cranbrook a hundred years later. The two young doctors were able to send their patients to the brand-new St. Eugene's Hospital in Cranbrook.[89]

The east-west railway missed Fort Steele by seven miles. A jitney service ran between Eager Station and Steele. The trains running through included a mail-sorting car. As schedules were being created *The Prospector* noted, "The Fort Steele Board of Trade asked Hewitt Bostock, MP to arrange that Fort Steele mail be left at the junction, rather than go into Cranbrook. THIS WOULD SAVE 24 HOURS."[90]

The Canadian Pacific Railway's connection with the West Kootenay was hailed as a satisfactory marking of British territory north of the 49th parallel. Passengers and freight travelling along the new line from Fort Macleod were transferred to the SS *Moyie* or another CPR lake steamer at Kuskanook (Kootenay Landing), near present-day Creston. These boats served Kaslo, Ainsworth, Nelson, and some private landings on Kootenay Lake. From Nelson there was a short railway to Robson, meant to connect with Arrow Lake boats coming south from Revelstoke on the CPR mainline. Within a year the CPR had built the Columbia and Western Railway from Robson to Grand Forks, and surveyed for the future Kettle Valley Railway through Princeton and the Coquihalla Pass to Hope.

Within three years the steamer ride from Kuskanook to Nelson was supplemented by a railway connection from Nelson to Proctor. At low water the West Arm of Kootenay Lake was very challenging for the captains or pilots of the sternwheelers, and heavy freight would definitely be transferred to train at Proctor. The railway connection along the isolated rocky southwest shore of Kootenay Lake, between Creston and Proctor, was finally built in 1930. By that time Fort Steele had a railway station; the Kootenay Central Railway had connected Colvalli on the B.C. Southern Railway line to Golden on the CPR mainline in 1915.

Chapter 22

Chins Up
(1899)

Fort Steele promoters tried to carry on the boom activities that made them so proud. For two years they had dreamed of being a city served by the new Crow's Nest Railway, but the railway had bypassed them and made tiny Cranbrook a division point. *The Prospector* kept pointing out the good things to the town's folk with such assessments as this one on January 14, 1899.

Assessed valuation of Cranbrook
1,088 lots of which 160 have improved value of $55,815.
908 lots with total value of $16,315.
Personal taxes assessed–$12,500.
Electoral voters last election–31
Total population–200

Assessed valuation of Fort Steele
Originally plotted 27 acres subdivided into 240 lots
Lately plotted 509 lots
Valuation of Fort Steele–$134,310.
Voters–179
Total population–800

Fort Steele had previously benefitted from the influx of the families of the developers of new communities nearby. Kimberley, Moyie, and Wardner each started as camps for the miners and sawmill workers. Now Fernie was in its infancy as coal mines were brought into operation. The migration of people and businesses to these four new towns was quietly accepted.

F.S. 163 - 01

The William Langley residence, Fort Steele. Note that the walls are vertically erected logs. The adjacent barn has a traditional log structure; the fence's pickets are unpeeled sticks.

Any loss by Fort Steele to the upstart community of Cranbrook was noted with jealousy and increased resentment of Cranbrook's founder, Colonel Baker!

The Opera House was the site for many performances. There were many talented locals who teamed together for fun and fund-raising. The Comedy Company earned enough for more fire hoses. The Band Boys raised enough to build their own Band Hall. The Fort Steele Orchestra held a concert to support the Jubilee Hospital. Then came the Minstrel Club, the Orpheus Quartet, and the Quadrille Club. When the school bell cracked and its ringing offended the ears of all who heard it, the constable, school trustee and band captain Hugh Barnes and Mrs. Huckle quickly devised fund-raisers to replace it. The Kootenay Club decided they would prefer to have their own building rather than continue on the upper floor of the Opera House. The newly constituted North Star Masonic Lodge fitted out the former Kootenay Club premises to meet their needs, while the Club met on the main floor for several months. And each December the Opera House was used for the school's Christmas concert.

The Opera House still attracted many travelling entertainers. The New York Metropolitan Opera Company visited here and performed *La Bohème*. Pauline Johnson, the Indian poetess, gave an elegant performance here. Touring companies such as the Harry Lindley Company and the Cosgroves returned every few months. An advertisement of their performance appeared in *The Prospector*.

At the Opera House   Jan. 26 & 27

COSGROVE CO. MERRY MAKERS
Edison Kinetoscope, The Wonder of the Age
Artistic, Refined and Delightful Amusements

COMIC SONGS, MUSIC,
ELOCUTION AND DANCING.

KUM ONE   KUM ALL
And We Will Entertain You

Dances were well attended by the social leaders of the district. Mather's Dalgardno Hotel, now renamed the Windsor, frequently hosted celebrations, although the Opera House became a preferred venue. Reports typically concluded, "They danced till the sun came up." Shortly after the Kootenay Club was formed, the gentlemen spruced up their rooms with potted plants and artwork. The Club hosted a dance on the main floor with refreshments to be served upstairs, reached by an outdoor staircase; however, "some joker applied axle grease to the stair rail which resulted in a number of spoiled white gloves and considerable unnecessary profanity."[91]

Another banquet and dancing hall was created when George Shier merged the International and Venosta Hotels. "Downstairs the bar was enlarged, a card room created, plus a commodious

The Windsor Hotel, built by Robert Mather as the Dalgardno, continued to serve the public until 1958. It still stands today in its original location.

room for commercial travellers. The new well-lighted office was in front of the dining room. The newly refinished rooms, 23 sleeping rooms in all, are on the second floor."[92]

Unhappily, three months later the International Hotel burned to the ground. The fire also claimed three other buildings and tested the new Fort Steele fire brigade to the utmost. Tinsmith and volunteer fireman T.C. Armstrong lost his business, but the crew was repeatedly praised for containing the fire to the small section of Riverside Avenue.

Attendance at the school averaged 85 students. Miss Bailey and Maria Clark, the monitor, managed to accomplish all the necessary instruction and inspection of work. School inspector William Burns praised Miss Bailey for her efficiency. At his spring visit he quietly mentioned that he was surprised to find only one certified teacher. In his October report he forcefully recommended that a second teacher be employed. Advertisements were circulated: "Male teacher wanted. Must hold B.C. certification. Apply to R.L.T. Galbraith, Fort Steele."

John Fingal Smith, a Scot born in Prince Edward Island, was hired to teach in the senior room. Smith had come to B.C. in 1875 to teach in Bishop Cridge's Boys' School. He later went the Cariboo and taught in Clinton for six years. In 1886 he was the first teacher in Ashcroft. Two of Miss Bailey's brothers were prominent business-men in Ashcroft; it was there that John F. Smith was introduced to Ade-laide. Miss Bailey had taught in Clinton prior to moving to Fort Steele. Both teachers regularly renewed their certifica-tion in Victoria each summer. It is distinctly possible that Smith re-sponded to a personal invitation from Fort Steele as well as the official advertisement. Miss Bailey had her salary cut to $60 per month. The

Courtesy Martin Ross

The interior of Fort Steeele's Presbyterian Church. Weddings, funerals, and Sunday services are still conducted in this 1898 church.

new principal, Smith, started working for $70 a month. Smith made a point of escorting Miss Bailey to every dance or entertainment in Fort Steele. He dutifully joined "Addie" in volunteer duties for the Jubilee Hospital. They may have attended church together, but not regularly, for he was Presbyterian and she a staunch Anglican. Even so, they played music together at church functions.

> The Presbyterian Church Social on Tuesday 7th began with a collection of airs on the bagpipes by Mr. Smith. Greetings by Reverend Duncan were followed by a quartet singing, a duet, a playlet, a violin solo, guitar and mandolin pieces. Miss Bailey acted as accompanist. The church was nicely decorated and lit by acetylene gas. The crowd were supplied with coffee, sandwiches and cakes supplied by the audience—eaten whilst strains of the bagpipe infused new life into the meeting.

Rev. Duncan announced profits of $65 to be used to reduce debt on the church building. A vote of thanks by Dr. Watt brought loud cheering. The Ladies Aid received valuable assistance from members of other churches.[93]

Miss Bailey responded to the new pressures in her life by resigning as organist in her church. The congregation responded by putting together a purse for her, and reading her an address in which they expressed their "thorough appreciation of the faithful and painstaking manner" that characterized her "performance of those voluntary duties." She was also recognized as "the one who took the initiative in organizing this parish." The letter was signed by lay readers Robert Galbraith and J.F. Armstrong, Vicar C.A. Procunier, and church wardens Thomas T. McVittie and N.A. Wallinger.[94]

John Fingal Smith and Adelaide Bailey were friendly neighbours, but apparently there was some disagreement between the two in adjacent classrooms. *The Prospector* on October 14, 1899, stated, "Mr. John Fingal Smith has sent in his resignation as teacher in the public school and the trustees have accepted same. Mr. Smith has been appointed to a clerkship in the office of Gold Commissioner Armstrong. The trustees have telegraphed Victoria to have a new teacher appointed."

Reverend Charles Procunier became the substitute teacher until a Mr. William Tompkins arrived to assume the position.

The Fort Steele hospital was described as "comfortable and well appointed." A resident matron had charge of patients for 24 hours every day. Miss Hearle, the first "matron," became known in town as the lady who walked up to the Invicta Mine unescorted. Miss Hearle opted to create a private nursing home in Cranbrook and was succeeded by Miss Thomas. Miss Thomas had trained in London, England, and had previously worked in the Lethbridge Hospital.

Local merchants donated a great deal of the food served in the hospital. Mrs. John Galbraith regularly supplied milk, and when Galbraith's cow was dry, she thoughtfully arranged for Mrs. Levett to take milk to the hospital. The hospital committee received some money from the provincial government—less than originally requested but sufficient to add a new room that served as an operating room.

The three churches were catering to the families of all possible parishioners. In 1898, Sunday, the day of worship, briefly became more solemn because all businesses shut down. Gradually, however, stores found it to their advantage to be open when miners and sawmill workers came into town on their only day off work. The Roman Catholics ran fewer notices in the newspaper than the other churches, but on September 23, 1899, *The Prospector* printed this notice: "Rt. Rev. Donteville, Roman Catholic Bishop, arrived at St. Eugene Mission on Saturday last. He held a confirmation service at St. Anthony's on Wednesday at which a large number of candidates were confirmed." Sunday School at St. John's was at 2:30 p.m., and Sabbath school at the Presbyterian Church was at 2 p.m. For one afternoon each week children were shown that religious denominations were different.

Many a well-dressed couple strolled along the wooden sidewalks of Fort Steele. All the social events and regular church services kept fashion in focus. The tailor Leon Cohn advertised that he was an "importer of fine woolens" or "seasonable and fashionable suitings." Gentlemen could now arrange for made-to-measure garments. At that time trousers, held up by suspenders, were not creased down the front. Most suits included a waistcoat. In the waistcoat was a watch pocket, and a parallel pocket in which the watch fob or chain was anchored. The suit jacket was fashionably closed by only the top button. The "correct" gentleman buttoned all buttons only when chilly weather made this preferable. Dress shirts were white, with detachable, stiffly starched collars. Broad, patterned cravats were still being worn, but slimmer ties were becoming an option. Footwear varied somewhat, with highly polished boots or oxfords being favoured for special occasions. And there was always a hat to suit every mood from the many styles made during that era.

Footwear, fashion accessories, and even ready-made suits were now being sold in local establishments. The Fort Steele Mercantile Company, Gilpin and Lindsay's Store, and Washburn and Purveyance all advertised men's clothing for sale.

There were several dressmakers prepared to serve the ladies of the district. The barber's wife, Mrs. Highwarden, was an early asset. Then Miss Durick took an apprenticeship in

Courtesy Dover Publications

Typical men's and ladies' fashions for fine occasions in 1901.

the east and came back claiming to know the very latest fashions. Mrs. Goodenough, Miss Fletcher, Miss A. McNeish, and Mrs. Harwood were all seamstresses. These gifted ladies also made children's clothing. For the housewife who sewed, several stores offered fabric and accessories such as braid, collars, lace and ribbons, buttons, and hooks and eyes—but no zippers.

By 1899 ladies' fashions were changing. The skirt was slimmed from the nine-panel, back-opening, voluminous garment to five panels, with a side or front opening. Blouses remained bosomy with high collars, in a single coloured material. But brighter colours such as peacock blue, cherry red, or bright green were now used to dye good material for suits, dresses, or skirts. Milady always wore a hat when away from her own house. Hats became smaller, decorated proportionate to their size, and younger women usually chose to have shorter hairstyles.

Through the ages hair styling has long been an indulgence for women of all ages. Hair, the crowning glory for women and girls, took a lot of care in that era before bathrooms, or permanent waves. Basic to shiny, tangle-free hair was "100 brushes per day." As soon as a little girl could count that high, she would sit brushing her own hair for this time-consuming ritual. If little Emma or Maude was a tree-climbing tomboy her mother would have to prepare for the process by combing out tangles—and perhaps leaves—before a brush could be used effectively. Then on hairwashing day, when the hairbrush and comb were also washed, the child's hair was fixed in cotton rag strips to create ringlets or curls.

The adult female sought to have a fashionable head of hair with a similar brushing regime. The utilitarian style swept the hair up top or centre back, rolled, and pinned into a bun. Braided hair did not rate as a fashion option, possibly because it reminded viewers of the Chinese man's queue or the braids of both male and female Kootenay and Shuswap peoples. Curls could be induced by certain time-consuming routines, usually following the shampoo/hair washing done in conjunction with the weekly tub bath. Rinsing was ideally accomplished with a bucketful of warm water from the rain barrel. The methods of curling ranged from rags similar to those used in children's hair to pin curls tightly twisted around a finger and pinned flat against the scalp. There were small wooden rollers that grasped the hair like a clothespin (and would be uncomfortable to wear while sleeping). And curls could be made, or refreshed, with a heated curling iron. This instrument had to be carefully heated in hot coals, removed before the handles were damaged, and carefully and quickly wiped with a scrap of clean towelling to remove any ashes or soot. In pioneer times it took considerable dedication and ingenuity to transform locks into ringlets or curls, but most women did careful preparations, if not regularly, at least for special occasions.

A report of some social event or other was in virtually every issue of *The Prospector*. Wives of prominent citizens made it known which date or days they would be "at home." Whenever possible, other ladies would attend an "at home" for a few minutes, perhaps longer. Each hostess was prepared to follow the protocol learned in her youth, and expected her guests to do likewise. The *Home and Farm Manual* provided a detailed list of "Philosophy and Precepts of Etiquette":

- A formal call shall not exceed fifteen or twenty minutes.
- The gentleman retains his hat and gloves during his call, which must be brief.
- Ladies making a morning call generally keep on their gloves and retain their parasol.
- When callers retire, the hostess rings for a servant to see that they are attended to the door.
- Modern fashion declares a call is made between noon and five o'clock.
- Every caller should provide a calling card.

The style of these "calling cards" ranged from severely plain to those with ornate borders. A single lady should have only her name on her card: Miss L. Kershaw, for example. A married lady was permitted to have her street address plus the day of the week when she was "at home." The card would never give her Christian name. It was "Mrs. [husband's initials or full name]." Gentlemen were expected to have a card, too. Married couples might share a card—for example, "Mr. and Mrs. A.W. Bleasdell."

There were definite rules for making introductions. An unmarried lady extended a handshake to another lady or to a married gentleman whose name was well known. The single lady, however, merely nodded when being introduced to a single man.

Many of the rules infer that a servant was likely to answer the door. The caller would tend his or her card, which the servant would convey to the mistress. On a designated "at home" day the hostess would decide whether to personally greet the visitor at the door, or have the servant conduct him or her into the drawing room. On an undesignated day, the mistress was privileged to say "not at home" if she did not feel like talking to a visitor.

For the most part "at homes" were just that—a time set aside to quickly catch up with the neighbours' news in the front parlour of private homes. But in April 1899 Mesdames Ross and Edwards arranged something more: "A Delightful Social Event." *The Prospector* reported this event as an "at home given in the rooms of the Kootenay Club. The reception was on the lower floor. Dancing followed. Refreshments were served upstairs in the Reading Room."[95]

Whether the record was made up by the calling cards or the hosts had guests sign a register, the guests' names were carefully listed and published in the newspaper. Heading the list was Colonel Baker, Mrs. Baker, and V. Hyde Baker. There were 33 mesdames, sixteen misses, and 94 gents, some from Moyie, Fernie, Wasa, Spokane, Wardner, and Cranbrook.[96]

There were many birth announcements during the boom years at Fort Steele. For the latter part of her pregnancy, the mother-to-be abandoned her corset and wore a flowing robe. She could no longer go out socially, but she could invite a handful of her closest lady friends to visit her in the privacy of her own home. Once, when schoolteacher Miss Bailey made a visit to one of her pregnant Anglican friends, she confided that she did not plan to marry until she was past childbearing years.

When a new child was born, or when there was a death in the family, citizens arrived to offer congratulations or condolences. The visitor, whether an intimate friend or an acquaintance following an obligatory courtesy, would hand his or her calling card to whomever answered the door. The resident could then note how many thoughtful people had come to the door.

The Durick family must have had frequent visitations when first a son was born, then three weeks later the father James Durick (partner of William Carlin in the oldest general store in Fort Steele) died, followed by the mother becoming very ill, and the infant dying the following month. A year later, when the estate had been settled under the hand of James F. Armstrong as administrator, Mrs. Durick moved to Victoria. She sent a message to A.B. Grace, who published the following announcement: "Mrs. Durick is pleasantly domiciled at 19 Rae Street in Victoria where she will be glad to see her Fort Steele friends when they visit the city."[97]

The Kershaw family, of three generations totalling sixteen people, arrived in July 1897. They built a large home called "Sunnyside" on the corner of Mountain Avenue and Hazel Street. The house was large enough to accommodate roomers or lodgers, and had one of the earliest bathrooms at the back of the house "where hot or cold water baths [could] be taken at a moderate charge." Henry Kershaw bought various mining claims, and after carefully considering the options, he opened what was described as "a bright and cozy lunchroom on Riverside Avenue." It was in a strategic location, in St. Mary's Inn near the stagecoach office. When the stage arrived from Golden with the mail, there were often people lined up for several blocks. *The Prospector* also noted, "It is a place that will be appreciated by citizens generally when they want a light and tasty meal. The finest tea, coffee and cocoa will always be found there, freshly made and daintily served. There will be homemade bread, cakes, pastry, honey and confectionery of all kinds."[98]

In June 1898 he opened a store and ice cream parlour, with a billiard room at the back. The ice cream parlour was open daily except Sunday. The ice cream was made by hand in special tubs ranging from two- to fourteen-quart capacity. Cream, eggs, sugar, and flavouring went in the metal tub, which was set in a larger wooden container. Crushed ice was poured into the space between inner and outer chamber. The lid was clamped in place and stirring was done by turning the handle that relayed, by gears, to the paddles within the mix. The tasty result was stored amid blocks of ice in the cold room behind the parlour.

Also advertised at Kershaw's Store were the "best quality California fruit, choice Havana and Mexican cigars, 'Tanglefoot' fly paper, cider, California wines, candies, chocolates, mincemeat, marmalade, nuts, eggs, a full line of Patent Medicines, and ladies dry goods." All of that, and also "Half hour billiard lessons given at moderate cost."

The eldest son, Henry Kershaw Jr., was married to his fiancée Clara Tabiner on January 3, 1898. In September 1899 Henry Sr., his wife, and some of the younger Kershaws left Sunnyside for the young couple. They had built a new building on Riverside Avenue that had the store, lunchroom, billiard parlour, and family sitting room on the lower floor. On the second floor were six good-sized bedrooms, a bathroom and washroom. In an annex were the dining room, kitchen, and bakeshop. Henry Sr. managed this complex until his health started to fail. He and his wife then moved to San Francisco, where he died in 1906. Henry Jr. operated the big store until he lost it in the big fire of 1906. Following that he moved into the recently vacated Canadian Bank of Commerce building. Henry Jr. became the postmaster about the time of this move. He set the post office (with an ornate counter and wicket) in the rear of the building that still bears the Kershaw name in Fort Steele Heritage Town.

On September 23, 1899, the following advertisement appeared in *The Prospector:* "W.A. Prest, well known photographer, will open up a studio in Fort Steele next Tuesday, where he will be prepared to take portraits and (commissions for) views."

A travelling photographer needed a lot of equipment to do his work. First there was a fairly heavy camera, framed in mahogany or cherry wood, with polished, lacquered brass fittings. This unit was set on a tripod. The more sophisticated cameras could be clamped upright or sideways, depending on whether a vertical or horizontal shot was desired. The bellows could be set at alternate focal lengths. The separate lenses, mounted in brass, were changed to accommodate to the distance. Glass plates dipped in a silver emulsion were the film. The size of the plate, specific to each camera, ranged from 3-1/4 by 4-1/4 inches to a whopping 20 by 24 inches. When the sitter or sitters were in place, an assistant stood by to fire the flash. The photographer crouched under a canvas canopy and counted, aiming to open the shutter at the exact instant that the fired magnesium flared to illuminate the room. The photographer then created a tent by dropping part of the canvas so he could remove the exposed plate from the camera to its safe, dark carrying case. A replacement glass film was inserted into the camera in the almost dark of the tent. Those being photographed would be posed again, and as the camera had no viewfinder, the cameraman had to sight his subject(s) again, peering from behind the camera. Then the assistant would prepare the prescribed amount of magnesium in his metal saucer, strike a match, and ignite the "flash powder" at the correct instant.

Following the picture taking, the films were taken to a darkroom—perhaps a closet with only a "ruby" light, which was a small lamp with a red glass window. The exposed plate was developed by laying it in a chemical bath for a prescribed brief period. The plate was transferred to a tub for "fixing,"

F.S. 31 -145

A portrait of Charles and Mrs. Levett, who pioneered as hotel owners of Steele House, then changed to operating a first-class boarding house.

then set into a rack to dry. Once dry it became the negative. The negative was laid over prepared film paper, inserted while in the darkroom, then carried out to a bright light, briefly exposed, then covered again. This paper was taken back to the darkroom, immersed in developer, then in a second bath to neutralize the developer, and finally dried.

W.A. Prest set up a studio in a hotel "commercial room," but was willing to take his camera and his assistant to a private home. The Levett portrait was taken in their parlour. Mrs. Levett is rolling her eyes as if frustrated by the long time created by faulty moves by Prest or his assistant. Prest was also commissioned to take pictures at the St. Eugene Mission School. These were used in the Indian Agency report published the following year. Prest's scenes at the village surrounding St. Eugene Church may be the ones that appeared in *The Golden Jubilee Of The Oblates* 1860-1910, a commemorative look at the Roman Catholic order and its work within British Columbia.

Fort Steele Fire Brigade sought to prevent its fire hydrants from freezing by covering them with boxes filled with hay. Much to their consternation neighbourhood cows learned to tip over the boxes and consume the insulation! The Water Works Company arranged for Riverside Avenue to be raised to provide extra dirt cover for the waterlines. Freshly graded, with continuous sidewalk fronting prospering businesses, Riverside Avenue took on very creditable significance.

Chapter 23

Patriotic Fervor—1900 Style

The citizens of Fort Steele had been able to keep abreast of the unrest and skirmishes in South Africa by reports published in their weekly newspaper. When Britain formally declared war against the Boers in October 1899, the editor of *The Prospector* made arrangements with the Canadian Pacific Telegraph Company to receive daily reports from the Transvaal. These telegrams were promptly affixed to the bulletin board in front of the office. Those with errands on Riverside Avenue soon made it a habit to pause to read the latest bulletins. The war became as much a component of daily conversations as the shenanigans in the legislature or the optimistic speculations about developing the many local mines.

Young men contemplated volunteering for the British army. Some made tentative inquiries early in December, but all stayed to celebrate Christmas before making the move. The first four locals to be accepted were Alistair Irvine Robertson, Ben W. Huckle, Oliver S. Rooke, and Frank E. Leach. (Leach was a graduate of the Kingston Military School.) Mesdames Ross and Nelson succeeded in collecting $100 for these volunteers leaving for South Africa.

Rumours circulated that a Canadian contingent would be formed under Colonel Sam Steele. The prospect of serving under the former leader of the Mounted Police attracted even the hesitant. A recruiting depot was set up in Fort Steele on February 5, 1900. Captain Parker, an old army officer who had lived in the district for some time, came out of retirement and was promptly appointed recruiting officer. His personal popularity added much to the enthusiasm. Recruits poured in all day Monday and Tuesday until the complement was filled;

in fact, the applications were in excess of the 40 members required. There were recruits from Fernie, Wardner, Cranbrook, Kimberley, and Fort Steele; all were experienced horsemen and good shots. A number of the men were ex-members of the North West Mounted Police. Two recruits were appointed sergeants and eight named as corporals during the movement of "C" squadron to the mustering point.

The recruits from out of town were billetted at the Windsor Hotel. The men were given a smoking concert at the Windsor on the Tuesday evening. An even more rousing send-off was arranged for Thursday evening at the brand-new hall of the Fort Steele Brass Band. The program was lengthy, with music, songs, and speeches followed by supper and dancing.

Departure was on Saturday. Captain Parker assembled his troops and arranged for them to meet the Nelson company in Cranbrook. Fort Steele citizens turned out en masse to see them off, and many drove all the way with the lads. The Fort Steele Band furnished the music along the way until their instruments froze up. At Elko, Wardner, and other places along the line, people assembled to cheer the boys on their way to war. The grand finale was at Fernie, where the whole town turned out; stores were closed and much mine work was stopped to assist in bidding good-bye to the contingent. Fernie residents raised one thousand dollars for the Patriotic Fund.

The special train pulled into Winnipeg on Monday, where a big crowd met the recruits, marched them to the drill hall, and provided them with a fine feed. After a few patriotic speeches the men lined up and roll was called; then they marched back to their specially decorated coaches. Harry Melton, a popular citizen of Fort Steele, carried the Union Jack while wearing a hatband of stars and stripes (he had recently renounced American citizenship). A larger streamer proclaimed, "East Kootenay, B.C. Troop: From Steele to Pretoria." The next coach was embellished with flags and "From Nelson to Pretoria or Bust; Strathcona Horse." The crowd assembled at the time of their departure was far larger than that which greeted them. The citizens were very warm-hearted despite the frigid winter temperature.

Other propaganda claimed that the Boers were confident that they could beat the British ... *if the Canadians would not*

F.S. 106 - 07

Riverside Avenue viewed from the roof of the Carlin and Durick store, c.1901. Windsor Hotel is in left foreground.

interfere. Furthermore, the Boers were offering a reward for a Canadian, dead or alive.

While travelling eastward a few members of the East Kootenay contingent composed some verses that could be sung or spoken to keep enthusiasm high. The words appeared in several local newspapers, sent by telegraph.

The Strathconas were temporarily quartered in the exhibition building in Ottawa, where they occupied cattle sheds labelled with the names of various breeds of cattle such as Durhams, Herefords, Shorthorns, Holsteins, and so on, which caused "no end of chaff and amusements."[99] There the unit was drilled and issued clothing and equipment. They were issued horses collected from farmers or the herds of wild horses from the prairies. Lord Strathcona, the former Donald Smith of the Canadian Pacific Railway, financed the unit.

They left Ottawa by train for Halifax and sailed on the SS *Monterey* on March 17. The ship was very crowded. Men slept in hammocks below decks until they crossed the equator, then many went onto the deck with their blankets. About one third of the horses died on the voyage. "Dead horse fatigue" was the nastiest duty assigned, involving removing the carcass from its tiny stall and heaving it overboard.[100]

The unit disembarked at Cape Town, where they were drilled to regain their land legs, and awaited replacement horses from Argentina. They were transferred to Durban on the SS *Mohawk*, and then sent by train to the front between Natal and Zululand. The Boers were skilled snipers. The advancing British troops soon learned that "three on a match" could be fatal. When those on night duty lit a cigarette, the Boer sniper followed the lighted match, sighting accurately by the time the third smoker started puffing. The warning was relayed to the Canadians, and "C" squadron lost no night watchmen.

The Strathconas, led by Colonel Samuel Benfield Steele, accomplished the various duties efficiently, advancing across the veldt and hill country. Fort Steele residents were saddened to learn of the death of Captain (now Sergeant) Parker in an incident on July 30, 1900; however, he was the only casualty in this unit.

The troops were recruited for one year of service. In February 1901 the Strathconas were transported to England (no horses were on board this ship) and given three weeks' leave. The regiment was given a farewell banquet by Lord Strathcona, then sent by train to Liverpool. From there they sailed on one of the Allan Line ships nicknamed the "Rolling Polly," which took three stomach-churning weeks to cross the Atlantic. The unit was paid off in Halifax. They had been promised 25 cents a day, but Lord Strathcona added another 25 cents a day, and gave each man his Lee Enfield rifle, 45 Colt revolver, bandolier, and a train ticket to his point of enlistment.

Sam Steele returned to Canada with his troops, visited family briefly, then returned to South Africa, where he joined the newly created South African Constabulary as a senior officer under Robert Baden-Powell.

Despite having some members overseas during the Boer War, the Kootenay Men's Club flourished and decided to build its own clubhouse. Tenders were called in February, and by April 28, 1900, The Prospector made this announcement: "The Kootenay Club took possession of their new clubhouse on Wednesday evening. There was no formal opening of the club, although there was the informal opening of several small bottles."

The Opera House became the Masonic Lodge, with the former Kootenay Club premises fitted out to serve as the meeting place for North Star Lodge #30. The Masons had been meeting in H.G. Parson's warehouse, first to arrange for a charter, then to become properly constituted under the

Grand Lodge of British Columbia. The assembled gentlemen had family roots across the continent. Indeed, Albert Grez produced transfer records from his mother lodge in Chile. The group that undertook to sponsor this new group was the Kaslo Masonic Lodge. Reverend Charles Ault Procunier had come from Kaslo to Fort Steele. The officers elected were reported in *The Prospector* on March 11, 1899, as Worshipful Master William Roderick Ross, Senior Warden C.A. Procunier, Junior Warden H. McVittie, and secretary-treasurer A.W. Bleasdell. The affiliates who made up a quorum to validate a new lodge included Robert Galbraith, Dr. Hugh Watt, John Grassick, Edmond Elton, Robert Mather, George Shier, John Goff, H.W. Herchmer, Neil Curran, J.R. Goff, and G.H. Gilpin. The Lodge was now in a position to admit new applicants who had not had the opportunity to join in their earlier years. Instantly, Constable Hugh Barnes, government agent J.F. Armstrong, editor A.B. Grace, lawyer J.A. Harvey, the McBride brothers, lumber mogul J.H. King from Cranbrook, government clerk A.C. Nelson, and Windsor Hotel barman Harry Mather entered the lodge and quickly passed to full membership. The inaugural meeting with installation of new officers was followed by a "splendid banquet at the International Hotel hosted by George Shier."

The Masons elected new officers at the end of each calendar year. Charles Ault Procunier became their Worshipful Master. In June he attended the Grand Lodge meeting in Vancouver. His tenure in St. John's Anglican Church, Fort Steele, suddenly ended when he accepted an appointment to St. Peter's in Revelstoke. Procunier had entered the Masonic order in the Revelstoke Lodge while he was the Methodist minister in that community. He had barely settled his family into the vicarage near his new church when he was informed of a forthcoming visit to the North Star Lodge by the Grand Master of B.C. He hastily dispatched a letter to Secretary Bleasdell, "Please call a meeting for October 9th or 10th, either before or after Chapter Institution." He described his travel plans: "By leaving Revelstoke Monday a.m. I can reach Steele by Tuesday p.m. and leaving Steele Friday can reach home Saturday eve." This route entailed a train to Arrowhead, sternwheeler down the Arrow Lakes to Robson, train to Nelson, boat to Kuskanook, train to Eager Station, and finally the stage to Fort Steele. In subsequent years Procunier returned as a provincial officer of the Royal Arch Masons, or as chaplain of the Grand Lodge.

At the school the new principal, W.L. Tompkins, had arranged for repairs and renovations for the building. New blackboards were installed in the primary room, and new seats were acquired for the senior room to accommodate the 38 older students. It was requested that donations of cash be made to cover the $50 shortfall on school improvements.

T.T. McVittie, a long-time resident and the earliest registered surveyor in the East Kootenay, travelled east to wed Anna Galbraith, niece of Robert Galbraith. This must have been a courtship by correspondence, but the ensuing marriage was a very happy one. The newlyweds arrived at his newly renovated home on Riverside Avenue about New Year's Day. Anna eagerly joined the Anglican congregation at Fort Steele, and on June 10 she was confirmed with Mrs. Procunier, Mrs. Levett, and two teenaged boys, Herbert Clark and Walter Taenhauser. McVittie and his wife had one child, a son, who unfortunately died in infancy. Mrs. McVittie was a charming hostess, and in later years competed with her sister-in-law, Mrs. Archie McVittie, by entering garden produce and cut flowers in the Cranbrook Flower Show and Fall Fair.

Revised Voter List: May 12, 1900	
Fernie	471
Michel	88
Empire	16
Cranbrook	416
Kimberley	39
Elko	13
Fort Steele	335
Wardner	26
Tobacco Plains	8
Moyie	185
Wasa	16
Tracy	6
Total in East Kootenay	1,614

In May 1900 a provincial election loomed again, the first in many years in which Colonel Baker was not running for legislative office. A variety of names was bandied about. William Fernie seemed to be a favourite and a logical successor to James Baker. The riding population had shifted surprisingly since *The Prospector* employee William Baillie had challenged Colonel Baker.

J.C. Costigan of Cranbrook decided to run against William Fernie, simply because he was incensed by the recent political actions of Premier Joe Martin. An audience in Moyie nominated Fort Steele lawyer J.A. Harvey, but Harvey emphatically declined. Suddenly a group recruited Edwin Cleghorn Smith, despite A.B.

F.S. 5 -430

Edwin Cleghorn Smith, MPP, 1900-1904. Smith was one of the discoverers and part owner of the Sullivan Mine at Kimberley. Portrait by Skene-Lowe photographers, Victoria.

Grace's opinion that the candidate was a "quiet and unobtrusive gentleman but not a politician."

E.C. Smith was one of the founders of the Sullivan Mine, and now ran a small ranch. He won the election, as a supporter of Premier Martin. Martin lost his majority, and 48-year-old James Dunsmuir was sworn in as premier. Victoria was in a bit of turmoil with many recent political shifts and upheavals. Prime Minister Laurier appointed Sir Henri Joly de Lotbiniere as lieutenant-governor, assigning the Protestant Québecer to be a stabilizing force in a western province.

The Prospector reported the unusual appointment with the comment that their former MP, Hewitt Bostock, had been suggested for the position, so "his nose was out-of joint." Bostock's service to the Laurier Liberals within British Columbia and for one term in the House of Commons was rewarded, however, when he was appointed to the Senate in 1904.

At this time Elk Valley coal mines were being brought into production. For a few days in September Fernie hosted

Setziburo Shimizu, the Japanese consul at Vancouver. Shimizu examined Crow's Nest coal and arranged for a quantity to be forwarded to him in Vancouver. The ships of the Japanese navy currently used coal from Wales, but if Crow's Nest could be secured more cheaply and expeditiously, a portion of the supply would be purchased at a West Coast port. (Lack of transportation followed by two World Wars precluded sales for some time, but now Japan is the prime customer for Crow's Nest coal.)

Fort Steele residents followed news from the Boer War from a more personal point of view now that sons or neighbours were overseas. They found the daily bulletins rather discouraging, and suggested that Grace condense the reports to items once a week.

Increasingly, the families of Fort Steele were facing the choice of whether or not to leave the town for better opportunities, and, if they moved, deciding which of the new communities nearby offered schooling for the children plus long-term prospects for the father.

Chapter 24

Fort Steele Starts to Fade
(1901–03)

The lads returning from the war in South Africa found a community in mourning because Queen Victoria was dead. It was politically correct to quietly contemplate the Empire's glory during more than 63 years of her reign.

But Fort Steele citizens were facing up to their own losses. The Fort Steele Mercantile Store had closed and moved into Cranbrook. J.D. McBride had set up his brother in a hardware store in Cranbrook, and once that was well established, McBride closed the store on Riverside Avenue and joined his brother. The Pioneer Drug Store moved from Fort Steele to Fernie. A.W. Bleasdell went alone to Fernie until a new home was built. Mrs. Bleasdell packed their son Willie off to McGill University, and then cheerfully transferred to Fernie. Constable Barnes was transferred to Fernie. Harry Drew and O.S. Frizzell were now in business in Kimberley.

The town's most vocal advocate, A.B. Grace, had to admit that a slowdown was happening. He reduced the size of *The Prospector* from eight pages, eight columns wide, to six pages, six columns wide. Grace still found newsworthy items to report, but he had far fewer advertisements than before. When waxing philosophical he inserted this whimsical observation.

How An Editor Makes Money:
A child is born: the doctor in attendance gets $10, the editor gets 0. It is christened and the minister gets $5 and the editor gets 00. When it marries the minister gets $10 and a piece of cake, and the editor gets 000. In course of time, it dies, the doctor gets from $5 to $100,

the minister perhaps gets another $5, and an undertaker gets from $25 to $50. The editor prints a notice of death and an obituary two columns long and gets 0000 beside lodge and society resolutions, a free card of thanks, and a lot of poetry. No wonder an editor gets rich.

The Prospector continued to report on the comings and goings of locals. It also noted events that truly affected everyone, such as an early ice harvest when over 1,000 tons had been installed in storage by February 9, 1901.

Two local bridges had made headlines that year. Nils Hanson of Wasa paid for a bridge across the Kootenay River. He employed Dave Bale of Fort Steele and a crew of nineteen men to build one of the best and most substantial bridges in the district. The bridge's pilings were driven in in January, and it was all completed in early March. The Wasa bridge was nine feet above high-water mark, 560 feet long with a draw of 38 feet to allow passage of steamer traffic. Over 80,000 feet of timber and two tons of iron were used. It was rated capable of carrying a load of 30 tons. This bridge served Wasa travellers until 1946.

As soon as Dave Bale returned to Fort Steele, he commenced building some cribbing to hold the pilings on the Wild Horse Bridge. Less than two months later, however, an exceptionally intense run-off destroyed the central foundation and the bridge was washed away. Bale won the contract to replace that bridge across Wild Horse Creek, commencing in August.

The melodramatic headline in 1901 was "Frank J. Lascelles Shoots His Chinese Servant." This English aristocrat lived just north of Canal Flats. He was having a new, larger home built. The carpenter, J. Lambert, sleeping in an adjacent bedroom, was roused several times by the sound of Lascelles pacing around, talking to himself. At dawn the house shook when Lascelles slammed the door as he stormed outside, wearing only pajamas. Lambert pulled on some clothes so he could follow. The Chinese servant also decided to investigate and stepped outside, getting his head blasted off by shots from both barrels of a shotgun. Lascelles calmly stepped inside, ignoring the trembling witness, donned an overcoat, loaded his pockets with cartridges, and strode off into the bush.[101]

F.S. 8 -01

The Fort Steele Mercantile Store, c.1898, offered a wide range of goods for sale. When the owner later transferred to Cranbrook, the new store retained the same name.

The Prospector failed to print a follow-up of the story, partly because a lawyer claimed privilege of privacy. Two days later the murderer gave himself up to a Windermere police posse. An influential friend from Golden took custody of Lascelles until his brother arrived from England to escort him home. A justice of the British Columbia court accepted the plea of "temporary insanity," and closed the case. Frank J. Lascelles left behind a nicely developed estate beside Columbia Lake, but continued to enjoy luxurious living on various family properties in England. In 1922 he was a guest at the wedding of his Yorkshire cousin, Lord Lascelles, to Princess Mary, daughter of King George V and Queen Mary.

Another real shocker kept Steelites worried for several weeks. Charles Clark, the collector of customs duty and former postmaster, had gone missing, suffering from a condition of "nervous prostration accompanied by some neurasthenia symptoms and insomnia. He left his house on Wednesday morning (July 17) and it [was] feared that he may have slipped into the river and drowned. There was nothing in Mr. Clark's domestic financial or official business that should justify him doing injury to himself."[102]

The following week *The Prospector* reported that Messrs. Mather, Watson, and Dimick were in a canoe searching for any trace of Clark. While attempting to run a swift piece of water the canoe capsized, throwing the men into the river. Dimick and Watson managed to reach the shore with difficulty. Mather clung to the upturned craft until it hit a logjam; the boat was sucked under the logs. Mather, however, scrambled atop the pile of logs, where he sat for six hours while his companions trudged back to Fort Steele to borrow another boat and return to pluck him from his perilous position.

Finally, one month later, some Indians found Charles Clark's body. James Clark, his brother, took material to build a coffin at the river's edge where Charles was found. Dr. Watt walked down to inspect the battered body and decided it was unnecessary to hold an inquest. James paid the Indians $150 for finding his brother and carrying the coffin containing the remains to Fort Steele's Anglican Church. James stayed beside the coffin until the funeral at twelve noon the next day. J.F. Armstrong conducted the funeral.[103]

On August 17, 1901, *The Prospector* concluded, "It is presumed that heat stroke caused him to lose his balance. IT IS PERFECTLY CLEAR THIS IS NOT A CASE OF SUICIDE."

The immediate consequence of the passing of Charles Clark was that his only child, Herbert, could not afford to attend the University of Toronto as planned. Herbert was taken on staff as a junior clerk at the government office. He also assumed the vacated position of customs officer, at reduced pay because there were no riverboats bringing large shipments upriver from Montana.

The fall term in the senior room at Fort Steele School was interrupted when William Tompkins resigned due to ill health. The young gentleman, aged 30, was hospitalized briefly, and then left with his wife to visit relatives in the east. Mrs. Tompkins was in Ontario when her husband went to Kentucky, where he died shortly after reaching Louisville. The first suggested replacement declined to move to Fort Steele, so the Presbyterian minister, Reverend Read, came to assist Miss Bailey. Mr. Hislop commenced as principal in January 1902; the registration was noted as 54 students.

Government Agent J.F. Armstrong and his wife were transferred to Fort Steele in 1897. They decided this community was too tough for their daughters Winnifred, aged fifteen, and Marjorie, aged eight; the girls were sent to All Hallows, an Anglican boarding school in Yale. Music lessons were part of the curriculum, and academic standards were high when the Armstrong girls attended. Winnifred finished school in 1901 and came to live in Fort Steele, where she frequently participated in musical performances or went on outings with groups of younger citizens.

Winnifred's uncle, Captain Frank Armstrong, took the *North Star* out of mothballs and arranged an excursion trip on the Kootenay River. The cruise left Steele at 1:30 p.m., Monday, May 19, having delayed departure due to a thunderstorm. It took two hours to reach Wasa, where they walked to the attractive Wasa Hotel. They received a genuine old-fashioned welcome from Nils Hanson, played games, were fed, and sailed at 6:45 p.m. for a speedier trip downriver.

That outing was so enjoyable that a second one was scheduled for the following week. A goodly crowd from Cranbrook accompanied the "pleasure seekers from Fort Steele." Nils Hanson opened the drawbridge, and then rushed to the wharf upstream to personally escort the crowd to his parklike property. The guests played ball, or went fishing, or rowed boats on Wasa Lake. They were shown the electric plant at Lewis Creek, and treated to music, good food, and games of ping-pong inside the hotel.

Armstrong's *North Star* was better employed on the Upper Columbia than the Upper Kootenay River, so Captain Armstrong watched for highest water, and on June 4 put the ship into Grohman's canal, squeezed her into the lock, and found his vessel stuck. He sent the passengers, including his wife and two daughters, to Grohman's Hotel while the crew and a few Chinese workers filled sandbags to improvise a dam. He blasted away part of the lock, waited for the water to rise behind the new dam, then blasted that, and the *North Star* rode the wave into marshy Columbia Lake. With considerable difficulty the crew worked the vessel down to Mud Lake and then to Lake

Windermere. The *North Star* berthed at Windermere while the crew removed the tramway rails between the lakes. The rails were loaded aboard, sold, and delivered to R.R. Bruce's Paradise Mine landing at Wilmer. The Upper Columbia had many new obstructions on its course so progress was slow, taking over two weeks en route. When the *North Star* finally tied up in Golden, some bureaucrat checking records discovered that no import tax had been collected on this vessel, which had been built in the U.S. Captain Armstrong refused to pay. He looked at the now battered *North Star*, told the customs officer that she was no longer a working vessel, and henceforth she was a source of spare parts used to keep his other Columbia River crafts operational.

The staff at Fort Steele Jubilee Hospital changed frequently. The first matron set up her own nursing home in another community. Another returned to the U.S. to be married. Miss Folsom, too, followed her fiancé and eventually married. The incumbent felt much more comfortable when she moved into a newly built matron's quarters. This nurses' residence adjacent to the hospital building was by 1902 the home of Mrs. Anderson, widow of the late Constable Anderson of Wild Horse, and Ainsworth, who stayed on staff for almost a year. She, too, resigned and moved. Miss Moss replaced her.

A.B. Grace, the editor of *The Prospector*, was an enthusiastic promoter of Fort Steele. He proudly announced that "a lovely new cottage was built for Mrs. Grace" despite the looming depression. Grace also delighted in sparring verbally about politics. Election after election he seemed to back the loser. During the era he reported the provincial factions as either "Government" or "Opposition" until about 1900 when the parties adopted the traditional titles of Liberals, Conservatives, and even Labor. Grace became a naturalized Canadian so that he could work very closely with Conservative riding committees. One local political hothead was Dr. Hugh Watt, a Liberal, who thought he was better informed than Grace (and most East Kootenay citizens), because he had sat in the legislature for eighteen months, following a by-election in Barkerville.

Grace tucked this bit of philosophy in the May 17, 1902, paper: "If talking politics sometimes makes men fight, what would be the result if women were allowed to vote?"

Lawyer J.A. Harvey and his wife pose in their Fort Steele home in 1903. Ruth, age four, stands beside their secretary, and Marguerite, born in Fort Steele, sits on her mother's lap.

Across the river, an experimental steam-powered excavator arrived, destined for Perry Creek. It was unloaded in Wycliffe before being moved to a claim some fourteen miles farther away. This wood-guzzling machine was set on railway wheels. The speculator had to hire a large crew to lay a temporary track. The crew set four lengths of track in place, moved the machine to the other end, ripped up three sets and laid these ahead, transferred the back track to the way ahead, and repeated the process. *The Prospector* reported on November 15, 1902, "The steamshovel is almost at its destination at Perry Creek." The boiler unit was comparable to that of a locomotive. The appendages were indeed able to lift huge amounts of gravel out of the creek and surrounding banks, but the machine had to be perched on rails that sank into the muddy approaches to Perry Creek. It was operated for two seasons, then left to provide scrap metal for scavengers in later years. The huge boiler still sits there, partly submerged in mud.

The Fort Steele Board of Trade was still active. Delegates eagerly participated in a Kootenay Board of Trade convention in Fernie, where one of the hosts was former Steelite W.R. Ross. Delegates attending represented Rossland, Nelson, Trail, Kaslo, Fort Steele, Cranbrook, Grand Forks, and Greenwood. George Buchanan of Kaslo was elected president for 1903 with H.W. Jackson of Rossland as secretary. The group then authorized four of its members as delegates to the Fifth Congress of the Chamber of Commerce of the Empire to be held in Montreal on August 17. The nominated delegates were J.A. Harvey, Dr. Hugh Watt, J.T. Laidlaw, and A.B. Grace.

Citizens of East Kootenay travelled not only within Canada but beyond, viewing international horizons far from their Rocky Mountain trench. Many of Fort Steele's citizens made pilgrimages to "the old country," be it England, Scotland, Norway, or Switzerland. While en route home to Canada or on leave, the boys from the Strathcona Horse and other subsequent groups of Canadian volunteers who served their year in the Boer War visited the Paris Exposition. (Mineral specimens from mines both in the East and West Kootenays were proudly exhibited at the Paris Exposition.) A later destination for interested travellers was the World's Fair in St. Louis, opened on May 1, 1903, by President Teddy Roosevelt and former President Grover Cleveland. Fort Steele residents connected by horse-drawn stage with ever improving passenger service on whichever railway gave them the most convenient route to their destination. Telegraph messages brought news items from around the world to *The Prospector*.

Echoing throughout the history of Wild Horse, Galbraith's Ferry, and Fort Steele was the refrain, "We want better mail service." In January 1903 this complaint was well documented by *The Prospector*.

> Since the southern railway went into service a letter from Fort Steele to Windermere is routed east to Calgary, west to Golden and then south to Windermere. The letter travels 560 miles—taking nine to sixteen days—when it really needs to travel 80 miles. *The Prospector* arrives usually 16 days late; the *Cranbrook Herald* 10 days late.

Later the newspaper made a long-awaited announcement.

Postmaster Kershaw has been notified of new mail routes commencing April 2nd, 1903.

Lv. Golden Sunday a.m. Arrive Windermere Monday 6 p.m.
Lv. Wilmer Monday eve. For Windermere.
Lv. Windermere Tuesday a.m. Arrive Cranbrook Wednesday eve. 5 o'clock.
Lv. Cranbrook Friday a.m. Arrive Wilmer Saturday 6 p.m.
Lv. Windermere Thursday a.m. Arrive Golden Friday 5 p.m.

This will supersede all other services between Golden, Windermere, main post road, Thunder Hill, Wasa, Fort Steele, Cranbrook, and St. Eugene Mission.

Editor Grace revised his publishing timetable so that *The Prospector* could be delivered on Fridays with the northbound mail to Wasa, Canal Flats, and Windermere.

There were minor disruptions to the new mail schedule during exceptionally high water in June, but it was "business as usual" for Fort Steele merchants and the government office staff for the rest of 1903.

Chapter 25

Cranbrook Gains, Fort Steele Loses (1904–1906)

The year 1904 dawned clear and cold. The future of the district, however, was not clear. Optimism was muted because all the working mines had closed down the previous fall and the managers were unsure when—or even if—they would reopen.

Townsite owner Robert Galbraith had employed a series of agents over the years to sell his lots and collect payments for mortgages. When Beale and Elwell moved their own businesses, first to Moyie and Kimberley, then as a joint enterprise to Cranbrook, Robert became his own agent with his name on the attractive advertisement that ran in *The Prospector* from November 1903 to December 1904. This time he not only advertised lots for sale, but also advertised "Businesses, Good Homes, Garden Properties."

Guy Frank Pawnell moved to the district and prepared to run Norbury's Fish Lake ranch as an experimental farm. This gentleman must have been well connected because he was appointed Justice of the Peace in and for the province of British Columbia within three months of settling here. To introduce themselves, Mr. and Mrs. Pawnell hosted an evening of dancing at the Opera House with a midnight banquet at the Imperial Hotel, followed by more dancing until "the wee small hours." A. Grez and H. Kershaw provided the music.

The Prospector reported that "the sleighing was excellent and a large number of invited guests came over from Cranbrook." Twenty-five Cranbrook guests were named, five of whom had until recently lived in Fort Steele. The Fort Steele guest lists showed all the prominent citizens still in town: Mr. and Mrs. J.F. Armstrong, Mr. and Mrs. J.A. Harvey, Mr. and

Mrs. A.B. Fenwick, Mr. and Mrs. N.A. Wallinger, Mr. and Mrs. T.T. McVittie, Mr. and Mrs. A.B. Grace, Colonel and Mrs. Hendersen, Mr. and Mrs. A.C. Nelson, Mr. and Mrs. Fred Binmore, Mr. and Mrs. E.C. Miller, Mrs. H. Reineman, Mrs. T. Fenwick, Mrs. Levett, Miss Winnie Armstrong, Miss A. Bailey, Miss Clark, Mr. George Watson, J.T. Laidlaw, V. Bannister, John Smith, Allister Robinson, Harold Nation, and William Carlin.[104]

This was the last big social event reported in the Fort Steele newspaper.

Fort Steele's claim to fame of having the government offices located there was about to vanish. The provincial government decreed that commencing in 1904 all business must be done in Cranbrook. J.F. Armstrong, the harried government agent, went into Cranbrook frequently. No further instructions came from Victoria, so on April 12, 1904, Armstrong penned a "private" letter to the Honourable Richard McBride, premier.

I have the honour to address you on the subject of moving the offices from Fort Steele. The location of the offices in that place entails much extra labour and much loss of my time and interferes with a prompt and thorough collection of revenue. During last year I found it impossible to properly supervise the public works and the result was the increase of the cost. Ninety-five percent of the population of South East Kootenay live on the line of railway and of the public works needed during the next summer ninety per cent will be near the railway. To keep the office here therefore means more expense and less revenue. I have never written before because many persons have told me that you informed them the move would be made soon. But the working season has now come and no move has been made. The officials do not know whether to make their garden and I think this is due to them and to me that we should now be told what will be done. I can see no object in retaining them here, I myself am willing to go either to Fernie or to Cranbrook as the Government may prefer but I think that some of the offices should go to each place, certainly a more capable man than Mr. Foster should be retained at Fernie.

Even if buildings have to be rented, it will cost less to have the offices on the line of the railway as there would be a gross saving in the travelling expenses of the Assessor, the Road Superintendent, Constables and myself.[105]

Word came through from Victoria as quickly as could be expected with the existing mail service. On May 4 Armstrong wrote again, referring to the government's "letter of 30th April instructing [him] that all public offices at Fort Steele be moved to Cranbrook on 16th May." His new office was a 26- by 40-foot vacant schoolhouse. It was necessary to rent space elsewhere to store files and some of the office furniture.

Armstrong had compassion for his staff, first shown by the reference about planting gardens, then in a later letter appealing for an increase in salary for two young people: "Miss Taenhauser and Mr. Clark may not move to Cranbrook as their pay is too small to enable them to pay board. Both are currently with their parents." He pointed out that "Miss Taenhauser is a good typewriter and a useful office hand. Her services are worth $50.00 a month." He lamented, "I doubt that I could secure a replacement for her at the $30.00 a month." Finally, he stated, "In case they leave Government employ, please authorize me to employ temporary assistance until their places are filled."

Herbert Clark was appointed Deputy Mining Recorder with instruction to remain in the Fort Steele office. Miss Taenhauser moved to Cranbrook, but she threatened to quit if the pay increase was

F.S. 419 - 01

James Ferguson Armstrong, Government Agent, first in Golden, then at Fort Steele and Cranbrook. This portrait was taken before he came to British Columbia.

14/4/04	
Office Administrator	*Attorney General's Office*
Deputy Clerk of the Peace	*Attorney General's Office*
Gold Commissioner	*Mining*
Government Agent Assistant Commissioner of Lands & Works	*Lands & Works*
Applications under "Land Registry Act"	*Attorney General's Office*
Deputy Coroner Registrar of County Court at Fort Steele	*Attorney General*
To hold Small Debts Court	*Attorney General*
Marriage Registrar	*Provincial Secretary*
Deputy Registrar, Births, Deaths & Marriages	
Court of Revision & Appeal	*Finance*
Registrar of Voters	*Provincial Secretary*

not forthcoming. She was upgraded to "Salary 3 on the pay list for 18 months."

Government Agent Armstrong had a new home built in Cranbrook and moved his family there in August. Victoria then magnanimously offered to expand his responsibilities to include the West Kootenay. Armstrong declined the offer by listing the duties he now carried, which involved communicating with five provincial ministries [see above].

An unsympathetic bureaucrat noted, "Deputy Attorney General suggests that Supreme and Family Court Registries at Fort Steele now be disestablished." Fort Steele had lost all but the mining recorder. It also meant that eight citizens, some with families, moved to Cranbrook.

The attendance at the Fort Steele schools was down. Tupper Blakeny commenced in January as principal of a two-roomed school. On February 22, Miss Bailey departed for Ashcroft, and Blakeny had to combine primary and senior classes. It is doubtful that Miss Bailey could find a buyer for her neat little home in Fort Steele. *The Prospector*, surprisingly, offered no explanation for Miss Bailey's departure. John Fingal Smith was no doubt urging her to wed and to move to his new home in Cranbrook, but Miss Bailey seemed to vanish from the East Kootenay scene.

At this time, T.T. McVittie had a survey party out on the snowy mountainside behind Wasa. The Tracy Creek townsite was to be expanded to serve as a home for workers in the new Alice Mine as well as accommodate the existing residents dependent upon the nearby Estella Mine. Unhappily, a snowslide came down and caught Peter Raymer and Frank Williams. Williams, buried up to his neck, was rescued quickly, but Raymer died. His body was not recovered for several weeks.[106]

The new sawmill at Wardner was gearing up to be a major producer of lumber. By March, logs were piled near the edge of the Kootenay River, ready to float down to Wardner once the ice went out. Tom Fenwick had 500,000 feet of logs ready, E.J. Cann also had 500,000 feet of logs at his place, and R.D. Mather had 150,000 feet at the mouth of Cherry Creek. In April there was blasting on St. Mary's River to clear obstructions and allow for the log drive to take logs to the Crow's Nest Lumber Company. The lumber produced in the region earlier had relied on adjacent stands of timber where horses could drag logs into the designated mill yard. When the timber crop had been harvested, the mill machinery was moved to a new site. The Wardner Mill was much, much larger than its predecessors.

Fort Steele waterworks were still operational. "Mr. James Clark is now engaged in repairing water mains and putting them in first class condition." The piping of that era was made of wooden staves held by coils of very heavy wire.

Once the winter snows melted, the fields and forests were very dry. There were many fires in the district in 1904. Early in May 1904, the business section in Fernie was ravaged by fire. A.W. Bleasdell, for example, reported losses of $10,000 in supplies from his drugstore, plus the building. His insurance coverage was only $4,000. Bleasdell sent his son William to Cranbrook to get a stock of drugs from R.E. Beattie to tide him over until more supplies arrived from the East for his new premises.[107]

In June and July forest fires raged within the district. At one point a fire was reported just two miles from Fort Steele. The July 30, 1904, *Prospector's* front page reported fires between Morrisey and Fernie, one up the St. Mary's, and one on Fisher Creek, up the Wild Horse Canyon. On the newpaper's back page was a welcome last-minute item: "Heavy rain has reduced fires and cleared the smoke." By August 27 Dave Griffiths reported that the water was too low for hydraulic operations to continue and that even placer work was difficult. James Cronin, the manager of the St. Eugene Mine in Moyie, reported shutting down in August as there was no water for the concentrator.

The St. Louis World's Fair was opened in May 1903 and ran right through 1904. Mrs. J.F. Armstrong, Mrs. H. Reineman, and several other East Kootenay citizens visited the fair. In December 1904, *The Prospector* reported, "Dr. A.T. Watt, son of Dr. Hugh Watt, visited his father Saturday and Sunday last, having come in on his way back from the St. Louis Exhibition. Dr. Watt Jr. holds the very responsible position of chief quarantine officer at William Head near Victoria, B.C."

One optimistic note in this less than productive season at Fort Steele came with the arrival of a survey crew assigned to lay out the route of the Kootenay Central Railway (KCR) between Golden and Colvalli near Elko. Editor A.B. Grace excitedly predicted that construction would begin in 90 days. The survey took all of September and most of October. George Geary and Alf Doyle profited by renting horses and supplying teams when necessary. Fort Steele was represented at meetings by C. Hungerford Pollen, chairman; J.A. Harvey, solicitor; and Dr. Hugh Watt, a shareholder in KCR. But despite the survey and the meetings, there was no action, no clearing, no construction, and only further speculation.

Grace's newspaper was losing business. More than once a week he inserted this thought: "Trying to run a business without advertising is like trying to run a machine or a lamp without oil." Indeed, he was losing advertising revenue. The businessmen and women had moved away. Albert Grez, the barber, decided to retire to Victoria. Leon Cohn, a tailor, moved to Cranbrook. The butchers had moved to one or another of the new communities. A Chinese man, Chin Lum, became the owner of the McInnes Meat Market, serving the district until his health failed in 1920. Even the brewery was closing down.

A.B. Grace produced the Fort Steele *Prospector* until December 31, 1904. He suffered considerable anguish. Not only was his business lost, his only daughter had died, and he and his wife were now raising Gracie Higgins, their lovely little granddaughter. Most cruel were the memories of his repeated condemnations of Cranbrook. He had to "eat humble pie" and move to Cranbrook. Editor Simpson of the *Cranbrook Herald* kindly offered Grace the use of his print shop while a move was being arranged. Grace was very appreciative of this offer, but chose to wait until he was completely relocated. The *Prospector Cranbrook* first appeared on June 3, 1905, with an editorial promising loyalty to the editor's new hometown.

> The aim of *The Prospector* will be to promote the growth and progress as much as it can, of Cranbrook, encouraging mining in all its branches, lumbering and agriculture and all other industries of this district.
>
> We regret the necessity which compelled us to leave Fort Steele, but the old town, beautiful in its isolation, has not the necessary means of communication to enable the management to keep up to date.

Readers of *The Prospector* who knew Grace would have been weeping, or perhaps laughing, at this major change in his life.

One facet of Fort Steele life that carried on was attendance at the Masonic Lodge meetings. Despite the fact that more than half the members had moved, the gentlemen came back to Fort Steele for several meetings a year. When J.F. Armstrong was district deputy he conducted the installation of his future son-in-law, Myles Beale, as Master of the North Star Lodge. The Lodge kept going until the 1940s with its handful of members stubbornly refusing to merge with the Cranbrook Lodge.

The citizens remaining in Fort Steele could not afford to keep the pumps running to fill the water tank in the tower above Wild Horse Creek. This water system was designed for fire protection only, not for household consumption. This

Courtesy Martin Ross

This view from the Masonic Lodge shows the Cohn house and the Anglican Church in the foreground, with the Anglican vicarage and Hanson and Hoffman houses behind. The town office sits beneath snow-capped Mount Fisher (on left).

omission would spell disaster to the old town, as *The Prospector* reported on December 1, 1906.

Big Fire at Fort Steele

Almost the entire business section was wiped out by fire Tuesday. At 1:15 p.m. B.P. Cooke of Bull River moved into the Andrew Neidig home. He lit a fire in the Queen heater and went out back to put his horse in the stable. When he returned the house was in flames. The fire alarm was sounded and the fire brigade arrived in good time. Two hoses were laid out. Water in the tank was low and no steam was ready to start the pump. Teams were quickly brought in to help demolish the Lewis building on the north and the King building on the south. By this time the pumps were started and water directed to limit the fire to that block.

The Imperial Hotel, on the opposite side of Riverside Avenue was on fire several times. It had its own standpipe and several hundred feet of hose. The Imperial was scorched. Not a pane of glass remains in the front of the building. The proprietor, with all available force succeeded in saving the building.

The following buildings were totally destroyed

Monte Carlo Restaurant, formerly owned by Wm. Robinson, now E.C. Miller valued at $1,000.

Fort Steele Townsite Building, two stories, one half occupied by the townsite company, the other by E.C. Miller as a flour and feed store, telephone exchange and express office—value $2,000. Contents were saved by volunteers moving them to a safe distance.

The Kershaw Building, owned by D. Griffiths, two stores, occupied by H. Kershaw Jr., General Merchant, was a total loss. It is thought that Griffiths has $1,000 insurance but the building was valued at $2,500. The post office was in the building. Mail and appurtenances were saved as was most of the stock.

The next building, a vacant double store owned by W.R. Rogers of Fernie, $2,000 was not insured.

Neidig building, formerly occupied by A. Grez as a Barber Shop—total loss—no insurance.

Strathcona Hotel, owned by D. Griffiths. Value $4,000—totally destroyed—insurance $1,000.

H.S. Clark owned the next. [Text now not readable]

A double building vacant. Total loss. No insurance.

Imperial Hotel, leased by Ben Werden from owner Nils Hanson and R.L.T. Galbraith was on fire several times. Damage $1,000.

Thus was recorded a dramatic event, typical of episodes in communities with wooden buildings and little or no fire protection. The once booming town of Fort Steele was reduced to a smouldering shadow of its former self.

Epilogue
(1906–1961)

The boom may have passed, but Fort Steele did not deserve "ghost town" designation. It had some loyal citizens who remained for the rest of their lives. A post office served the community until 1997. The school, still Grades One to Eight, graduated its last class in 1954. The school's closing coincided with the introduction of school busses to take both elementary and high school students into Cranbrook. The town had a grocery store until shortly after the heritage park was declared in 1961. One or more hotels remained open. Geary and Doyle's livery stable was modified to become a garage, with a hand-operated gas pump standing out front.

The Levetts sold their Steele House hotel at the beginning of the boom because Mr. Levett was diagnosed with progressive muscular deterioration. Mrs. Levett opened a boarding house intended for better-class patrons, guaranteed to be clean and attractive. Indeed, she had cared for lawyer John Campbell even to preparing his body for his funeral. Mr. Levett died in 1930. Mrs. Levett carried on, keeping her house sparkling clean, just in case any guests chose to stop over, until 1942. The first public health nurse in the East Kootenay remembers assisting Mrs. Levett to apply for the 1935 version of government old age pension, given only to the destitute, poor, or sick. Having to admit that she was penniless was a major psychological blow to her.

St. John's Anglican Church never had another resident minister after Reverend Procunier and his family left Fort Steele. The vicarage was considered one of the nicer homes in town. It was rented and eventually sold, and the Anglican congregation retired the mortgage early in the 1900s.

St. Eugene Mission School was always important to the citizens of the fading community across the river. The frame and log buildings were replaced in 1910 by a sturdy stone structure with running water, lots of room, and central heating. Students from beyond Kootenay territory were added to the roster. The Sisters of Providence staffed the school until 1929. For seven years lay teachers were employed to educate the 150 pupils. Then, in 1936, Father Scannell invited the Sisters of Charity of Halifax to take charge over St. Eugene Residential School. In 1970 the school was closed, and the children were integrated with local schools in their home communities.

The water system had intermittent problems from the time of its inception. Locals had to find their own supply by various means. Long ditches were dug by Chinese market gardeners. These ditches required considerable maintenance and sometimes went dry in times of low water. They were soon lost once the market gardeners left. Wells were dug and water raised by hand pumps. The most reliable source of potable water was a spring in Westport on Tom Fenwick's property. Many householders resorted to filling their barrels there once a week and transporting these home on a horse-drawn trailer or an early truck. It was a boon to Fort Steele residents when the provincial government assumed responsibility for the historic townsite. One of the early projects was to build a reservoir and pipelines.

Miss Adelaide Bailey and John Fingal Smith

Miss Adelaide Bailey, Fort Steele's first schoolteacher, chose to undertake one more challenge before she said, "I do" to her patient suitor. First she spent several weeks in Ashcroft with her brothers, where her nephews enjoyed the visit from "Aunt Addie." Next she dutifully spent time in Victoria with her mother. Then she became the first teacher in a new school at Isabella Point on Salt Spring Island. Her pupils were almost all Kanakas, children of Hawaiian immigrants.

Back in Cranbrook, John Fingal Smith was preparing a home for his bride. The house faced Baker Park. It was a few steps from downtown stores to the north, and from the Anglican Church to the south. Smith had become a member of the congregation at the Anglican Christ Church, as well as maintaining his ties with the Presbyterian Church. Finally Miss

Courtesy Salt Spring Island Archives

Miss Adelaide Bailey (tall woman on left) was the first teacher at Isabella Point on Salt Spring Island. Her pupils were mainly Kanakas, families of immigrants from Hawaii. She is shown here with her students on a family outing in 1905. The tall boy (left) holds a scroll marking his graduation from Grade 8.

Bailey said, "Yes" and set the date for the wedding on her 48th birthday, December 11, 1905.

They were married in St. Barnabus Anglican Church in Victoria. Adelaide Susan Steinburg Bailey, eldest daughter of the late Benjamin Bailey, was given in marriage by her brother-in-law, J.P. Burgess. Addie wore a navy blue suit and her attendant, sister Annie Bailey, was attired in a very pretty dress of cream crepe with a cream velvet collar. The groom was supported by Arthur Bailey, and Little Nellie Sinclair, niece of the bride, acted as flower girl. The service was choral. The popular couple received many gifts. They left that evening to travel to Cranbrook, where they were feted by friends who had been their neighbours in Fort Steele.

The new Mrs. Smith seemed to drop her ingrained inhibitions. She capitalized on her freedom from 30 years of the responsibilities in various classrooms by dressing fashionably, visiting on weekdays, walking, or enjoying outdoor sports. Addie was a graceful skater; teenaged girls and boys vied for turns to skate with her. The following summer Addie signed up for swimming lessons in Baker Park. (Winnifred Weir remembers the good lady as one of her class of twelve-year-olds.) The Smiths enjoyed gardening, with flower borders in the front and the kitchen garden behind. John Fingal purchased one of the earliest cars in Cranbrook, and then discovered he disliked motorization. His wife, with traditional correctness, did not undertake to learn to drive. The car would be rolled out of the garage at intervals so that John Fingal could wash and polish every feature. A Cranbrook senior citizen, "Bud" Caldwell, remembers joining other boys to admire the car when it came out for cleaning. He swears that the Ford Motor Company made an offer to buy it back after Smith died. "It was in mint condition."[108]

Addie gave piano lessons to children of some of her Fort Steele friends, and for a time was a Sunday school teacher. The couple regularly attended Anglican service on Sunday mornings and Presbyterian service in the evenings. Long-time Presbyterians were impressed with John Fingal's intensity within the church (he interrupted a youth choir singing what he declared was "A Roman Catholic hymn"), and the pleasure he obtained from playing the bagpipes. It was traditional for him to play at the annual Presbyterian picnic at Moyie Lake, marching back and forth along the beach with a file of small boys behind him. John Fingal also served as Cranbrook's representative to the national church congresses that created the United Church of Canada by merging the Presbyterian, Methodist, and Congregational churches.

The Smiths' orderly life together came to a sudden end when fire destroyed the wing of their home that contained their prized library. They were pulled from the flames by helpful neighbours, and taken to the Anglican vicarage for sanctuary. John Fingal died in hospital on November 12. Addie was cared for by the Reverend and Mrs. Harrison for several weeks until carpenters restored the damaged house. Adelaide placed a marker for her husband in the cemetery.

John Fingal Smith
Born P.E.I. 1846
Died Cranbrook, B.C. 1936
A Faithful Lover for 18 years
A Devoted Husband for 31 years

The plot beside John Fingal Smith remains empty, however, as Adelaide moved away and eventually died at her sister's home in White Rock in January 1949. She was buried in the Surrey Centre Cemetery.

Robert Leslie Thomas Galbraith

Robert Leslie Thomas Galbraith lived most of his life in the community founded by his brother. His name headed the petition to Ottawa to allow the change from Galbraith's Ferry to Fort Steele. The Galbraith presence was reinforced with their two sisters Maria and Catherine and their spouses, James and Charles Clark. Maria died in 1909. James and Catherine died in 1911. Robert gave up his position as Indian agent in 1912. The Kootenay Club was disbanded. There were fewer neighbours to visit. Robert left the Indian Agency buildings and moved to a modest home next to Mrs. Levett on Riverside. He met Ella Jessie Balfour Flemying when she came to Cranbrook as a governess/lady's companion. He decided he had been a bachelor too long. The lady returned to England to see her family and attend the burial of her father.

Then on October 16, 1913, the *Cranbrook Herald* printed this eye-opening report.

Nakusp, B.C., October 14, 1913

A wedding took place here today of special interest to old timers throughout the province. When Robert Leslie Thomas Galbraith, pioneer merchant, ex MPP, prominent churchman, and for many years Indian agent for the Kootenay under the Dominion government, arrived in town yesterday, his visit was looked upon as a periodical one. His true mission, however, was secret until the arrival of the steamer *Rossland* from the north, when a lady disembarked at the wharf and was met by Mr. Galbraith and a few friends. The party went to St. Mark's Church, entering that edifice to the strain of "The Wedding March" from Lohengrin, played by Dr. Lavelle. The marriage service of the Episcopal Church was conducted by Rev. S.H. Phillmore, with Mr.

Courtesy Shelagh Dehart

Indian Agent "Bob" Galbraith visits with Chief Pierre Kinbasket and his wife Marian. A summer kitchen is in the foreground. This log house stood near Radium until 1999.

Galbraith and Miss Ella Balfour Fleyming, late of Torquay, England, as principals.

The bride was given away by J.L. Edwards, while Miss Florence Edwards acted as bridesmaid, there being present also H.L. Rothwell and Mrs. Edwards, all old friends of the groom in early Kootenay days. Immediately after the ceremony the church bells pealed forth the news and the happy couple returned to the waiting steamer and proceeded on their way to Fort Steele, where they will reside, amid the deafening noises of steamer whistles, which were repeated by the whistles of mills and other tugs around the bay.

Mr. Galbraith is a pioneer of pioneers in Kootenay, having lived at Fort Steele 43 years, and represented the district in the provincial legislature in the third and fourth parliaments from 1878 to 1886.

The groom was 72 and the bride 33 years younger. They lived happily at Fort Steele, maintaining a big vegetable garden with some help from a Chinese neighbour. There were visits from former students at the Indian school, or their elders. "Bob" Galbraith had been a kind friend during his eighteen years as Indian agent, so many paused to sit on his doorstep and chat for awhile. Robert attended lodge meetings as regularly as his health would permit. He basked in the loving attention of his Ella until May 1924. Ella lived in Fort Steele for the rest of her life, assisted when necessary by neighbour Isabel Barr. She died in 1966 at the ripe old age of 92, the last Galbraith to live at "Galbraith's Ferry."

Chin Lum's Family

The Chinese neighbours who helped Galbraith with the gardening were members of the Lum family. Chin Lum had "worked his way with a gold pan" from California to B.C., where he made his home in Rock Creek. Lum ran a store for prospectors. His supplies came from Hope brought in by a packer who had a lovely daughter, Lucy, who was part Shuswap. Lum and Lucy married and had seven children. The family moved to Cranbrook in 1907 and to Fort Steele the following year. The youngest boys, Pete and Jimmy, took all their schooling at Fort Steele. Chin Lum ran the Fort Steele butcher shop until 1920. At that time Lum felt he was nearing death, so he asked his son George to escort him back to China. First, however, he collected whatever outstanding payments he could, then burned his books so that other debtors were freed. Chin died in China, where George saw him buried before hurrying back to Canada.

Lum's eldest daughter, Maggie, married Hop Yuen, a market gardener at Fort Steele. Lillian married Chu Ban Quon, operator of the Invicta Mine up the Wild Horse, and her sister Caroline was hired as camp cook. George worked driving team and breaking horses for Alf Doyle, then aided big-game guide Arthur Nicol. During the late 1920s and early 1930s George, assisted by brothers Pete and Dick (who was assisted by son Ira), ran pony stands and trail rides at Lake Louise. In 1931 George met and married Beryl Kibble, an English girl working on summer staff at Chateau Lake Louise. The couple settled in Fort Steele, returning to Lake Louise each summer until 1939. Beryl and George had seven children who were raised in the former Indian agency building, attended school at Fort Steele, and attained professional status as teachers, accountants, or social workers.

Pete Lum worked at a variety of jobs, commencing as a log driver on the Bull River, then running a hydraulic monitor up the Wild Horse for William Astor Drayton. He apprenticed as a big-game guide with Arthur Nicol before obtaining his own licence. In 1948 his home and pastures in Westport were flooded out, so he moved to near Premier Lake. Pete died in 1999 at the age of 101.[109]

Robert and Mary Jane Mather

Robert and Mary Jane Mather had sent six children to school in Fort Steele. Their seventh child, a twelve-pound baby boy born in June 1900, died in infancy. Once they became teenagers the girls were able to help in the hotel, but brother Earl was barely out of Grade Eight when he died. He drowned when he tried to round up the family cows that had gone to an island southwest of town. Earl was on horseback and attempted a shortcut that took horse and rider into a very deep pool. Two women from the St. Mary's Reserve saw Earl's hat floating downstream, his horse shaking dry on the beach, and his dog barking excitedly. The women led the horse into town. A crowd rushed downriver to see if they could help. When the body was found, the coroner declared that the struggle for life had been brief and no inquest was necessary.

The tragic accident prompted *The Prospector* to publish this admonition: "This should teach us a lesson that every boy or girl in this community should be taught to be a good swimmer."[110]

Robert ran the bar in the Windsor Hotel with the help of his brother Harry. Mary Jane hired a couple of girls to help in the dining room and upstairs, while a Chinese man did the cooking. When the recession hit Fort Steele the older Mather girls replaced the hired help, and Mary Jane took over the kitchen herself.

Robert died in 1908. Brother Harry assumed management and later married Mary Jane. The family grew up and moved away, so the Mathers sold the hotel and moved to Penticton around 1920. Harry died in 1940. Mary Jane died at the age of 96, after receiving a Centennial Year (1958) Pioneer's Scroll.[111]

Dr. Hugh Watt

Dr. Hugh Watt stayed in Fort Steele long enough to see one of his advocated projects serve the community. The spur railway, promised by some since 1898, arrived on October 1, 1912. On that date the first of daily passenger trains chugged into the station adjacent to Wild Horse Creek, very close to the intake for Fort Steele's water system. The railway did not attract sufficient ridership to keep on daily runs, so service was cut to twice a week, then once a week or for special events. The Kootenay Central did not connect with Golden until 1915. Again, passenger service was offered once a week going north on Mondays, returning south on Saturdays.

Watt had been a bouncing single male while in Barkerville and during his early years at Fort Steele. Occasionally he bragged about his sons, one a corporation lawyer in Toronto, or Dr. Alfred Tennyson Watt, medical chief at William Head near Victoria. The mother of his two sons died in Ontario shortly after Watt moved to Barkerville. In September 1912, Watt married Alice, widow of the late John Nicholson of Morden. The wedding took place in Trail, B.C., and the couple honeymooned at the new luxury CPR hotel at Balfour before returning to Fort Steele. The newlyweds later moved to Elko, where Watt bestirred the new business community to form the Elko Board of Trade. He was saddened when his son Herbert fell ill in Toronto and died on May 15, 1913, then shocked when Alfred committed suicide on July 27, 1913. Watt's new wife supported him until he died on March 21, 1914. Members of North Star Lodge buried him in the Fort Steele cemetery.

The Fort Steele Diamond Jubilee Hospital had nursing staff and patients as long as Watt was a resident in the community. The nurses seldom stayed more than a year. It was difficult to finance the institution that limped along on subscriptions (call it health insurance) paid by some mine operators or logging camps for their crews. The provincial government reluctantly allocated funding here, generally tendering one-half to two-thirds the amount requested. Indigents found it difficult to pay the dollar per day requested for hospital care, and an additional fee for the doctor's treatment. The hospital property remained in Robert Galbraith's name for 80 years, so it appears that he must have quietly subsidized the institution ... or perhaps the nurses went unpaid.

Kershaw Family

The Kershaw family had a presence in the village for many years after the senior Kershaws died. Henry Jr.'s two sons were valued citizens in their respective roles. Alfred Kershaw ran the jitney mail service to Cranbrook for 28 years. Gordon Kershaw and his wife ran the store and post office until 1954.

William Adolph Baillie-Grohman

William Adolph Baillie-Grohman, the man who had attempted to change the flow of the Kootenay River at Canal Flats and Creston, died in Austria in 1921. His widow wrote to Guy Constable of Creston.

> You will I'm sure regret to hear that my dear husband W.A. Baillie-Grohman died suddenly on 27th of November last.
> I had many interviews with Mr. X, then Commissioner of Works, so am pretty well initiated into all that went before and behind the scenes. I might still be up for libel if I wrote all, I fear. (I only hope the present administration is less corrupt.) Mr. X told me that my husband was not free enough with his money. It's the way things are done out there.[112]

William Astor Drayton

A New York socialite and mining magnate, William Astor Drayton, discovered the East Kootenay with its tantalizing prospects of gold. Drayton, backed by the Astor family's millions, built a comfortable cabin above Wild Horse Creek in 1924, with a bunkhouse for staff on the old Fisherville flat below. One spring he directed that a giant flume be built to carry the total flow of water, baring the creek bed for approximately half a mile. A giant steam engine with a claw crane was brought in and "walked" up Wild Horse Canyon from the Fort Steele railway station. All summer the creekbed and nearby banks were excavated, and the gravel sluiced by water from China Ditch (or Victoria Ditch). Late in the season, while trying to move the crane under the flume round an "S" turn in the river, the flume was knocked down. Drayton, satisfied with that experiment, did not rebuild it. He returned in later summers and had his crews operating hydraulic monitors.

Drayton's wife agreed to move to the Kootenays. William purchased about a third of the Fort Steele townsite and had a ten-room mansion built in 1930. They employed several servants who were quartered in comfortable cabins close by. There was a tennis court for summer entertainment, and a pasture for their thoroughbred horses, and goodwill for their neighbours. This great-nephew of John Jacob Astor IV (who drowned when the *Titanic* sank) and his Australian wife created employment for dozens of locals during the "Dirty Thirties" Depression. The Draytons sold Wild Horse Farm in 1944.

Wild Horse Creek continues to draw prospectors as if by magnet. There are serious searchers who still register their placer claims. There are the curious who try their luck with a pan for a few hours. The old creek, serene and secretive, may allow today's seeker to find a small nugget or a glitter of gold dust. Or the Wild Horse may roar and rampage and attempt to wash out yet another bridge on the road to Bull River.

The town of Fort Steele now dozes in the winter and dances in the summer. There are the ghosts of the gruff and the great, the good pioneer women, and the ladies of the night. One can hear music that might have been played by the Fort Steele Brass Band, or the fiddlers accompanying barbers Highwarden and Grez. There is the clip-clop of horses' hooves with the sound of wagons rolling along the street. The heritage town is a happy place where today's visitor can experience the past as it was when Fort Steele was the centre of the East Kootenays.

Endnotes

Chapter 1

1. Historians claim that horses were introduced to North America in 1519 by Spanish invaders to Mexico, from where their descendants spread northward as wild horses, ranging mainly on the prairies.

Chapter 2

2. Gold Fields Act, page 533.
3. Ibid., page 535.
4. O'Reilly Diary, 1865. Provincial Archives of British Columbia.
5. Quotes from *Building the Dewdney Trail*, by Edgar Dewdney as told to R.E. Gosnell, *Vancouver Province*, November 14 and 21, 1908.
6. Ibid.

Chapter 3

7. Duncan, Janet Catherine (neé Mather), *Cominco Magazine*, April 1961.
8. Norbury's presence in the East Kootenays is well documented with letters written to his family between 1887 and 1898. These letters are stored in the British Columbia Archives in Victoria with copies held in the archives in Fort Steele Heritage Town.
9. Crow's Nest Pass is the spelling used at the time; today it is spelled Crowsnest Pass.

Chapter 4

10. Gurney William C. Seminar at Libby, Montana, September 20, 1978.
11. Ibid.

Chapter 5

12. Farwell, A.S. Report on the Kootenay Indians.

Chapter 6

13. Powell I.W., Report to Superintendent of Indian Affairs, Ottawa, August 1, 1887.
14. Steele, Samuel Benfield, NWMP Report, December 1887.
15. Ibid.
16. Ibid.
17. Joseph's Prairie became Colonel Baker's townsite of Cranbrook.
18. Steele, Colonel Samuel B., *Forty Years in Canada—Reminiscences of the Great Northwest*, 1915.
19. Ibid.
20. North-West Territories was the spelling used before 1905, when Alberta and Saskatchewan were formed from part of the area. The remaining northern territory was then called the Northwest Territories.

21. Steele, Colonel Samuel B., *Forty Years in Canada—Reminiscences of the Great Northwest*, 1915.

Chapter 7
22. Steele, Major Samuel Benfield, NWMP Report, 1888, p. 87.

Chapter 8
23. Lees J.A. and W.J. Clutterbuck, *A Ramble in British Columbia, 1887*, p.148.
24. Ibid., p. 203.
25. Ibid., p. 204.
26. Ibid.
27. Ibid., p. 205.
28. Ibid., p. 222.
29. Ibid., p. 224.
30. Ibid., Preface.
31. Ibid., p. 137.
32. Ibid., Preface.

Chapter 9
33. Whitehead, Margaret, *They Call Me Father: Memoirs of Father Nicolas Coccola*, p. 91.
34. Ibid., p. 15.
35. Ibid., p. 113.
36. Ibid., p. 113.
37. La Bissoniere, Sister Jean P., *Providence Trail Blazers*, pps. 4–5.
38. Information from Amelia Kinbasket's daughter, Shelagh Dehart, of Radium, B.C.
39. La Bissoniere, Sister Jean P., *Providence Trail Blazers*, p. 5.
40. Whitehead, Margaret, *They Call Me Father: Memoirs of Father Nicolas Coccola*, pps.111–112.
41. Ibid., p. 6
42. Ibid., p.
43. bid., p.119.

Chapter 11
44. Humphreys, J.E., *Indians and Whites*, unpublished diary.
45. Norbury Files, February 10, 1892.
46. Norbury Files, August 1892.
47. Recounted by Edna Whalen, daughter of Alice (Phillipps) Parnell.
48. Kimberley Seniors Society, *Mountain Treasures: The History of Kimberley*, pps 9–11.
49. Johnson, Olga, *The Story of Tobacco Plains Country*, p. 24.
50. Ibid.
51. "Waggon" is old spelling.

Chapter 12
52. Sessional Papers, Province of British Columbia, 1896.

Chapter 13
53. Affleck, E.L., *Sternwheelers, Sandbars and Switchbacks*, pps. 24 and 132.
54. Indian Affairs, RG10, Volume 3855, File 80,143 (this copy from the Kinbasket Estate; courtesy of Shelagh Dehart).

55. White, Derryll, *Fort Steele: Here History Lives*, p.105.

Chapter 14

56. *The Prospector*. February 22, 1896.
57. *Mrs. Beeton's Everyday Cookery*, 1923 Revision, p. 328.
58. La Bissoniere, Sister Jean P., *Providence Trail Blazers*, p. 11.
59. *The Prospector*, July 18, 1896.
60. La Bissoniere, Sister Jean P., *Providence Trail Blazers*, p. 11.
61. *The Prospector*, October 10, 1896.
62. Ibid., November 17, 1896.

Chapter 15

63. A cord is a pile of wood four feet wide, four feet high, and eight feet long.
64. Interview with Joe Ban Quan, 1987.

Chapter 16

65. *The Prospector*, January 30, 1897.
66. *Kamloops Inland Sentinel*, June 11, 1897.
67. *The Prospector*, May 15, 1897.
68. Ibid., May 29, 1897.

Chapter 17

69. *The Prospector*, June 26, 1897.
70. Ibid., September 3, 1897.
71. Ibid., September 11, 1897.

Chapter 18

72. Whitehead, Margaret, *They Call Me Father: Memoirs of Father Nicolas Coccola*, pps. 128–9.
73. *The Prospector*, June 12, 1897.
74. Ibid., July 17, 1897.
75. Jackman, S.W., *Portraits of the Premiers*, pps. 32–33.
76. *The Prospector*, December 18, 1897.
77. Ibid., December 25, 1897.

Chapter 19

78. *Provincial Mineralogist*, Report of the Minister of Mines, 1898.
79. *The Prospector*, September 25, 1897.

Chapter 20

80. White, Derryll, *Fort Steele: Here History Lives*, p. 113.
81. Chernoff, Lee, "Fort Steele's Presbyterian Church MS," *British Columbia Historical News*, Summer 1994.
82. *The Prospector*, February 12, 1898.
83. Ibid., April 30, 1898.
84. Ibid., May 14, 1898.
85 Story told to the author by Cecil Parson of Golden, B.C. in 1969.

Chapter 21

86. *The Prospector*, January 1, 1898.
87. Ibid., April 30, 1898.

88. Casselman, Verdun, *Ties To Water*, pps. 71–73.
89. White, Derryll, unpublished manuscript.
90. *The Prospector*, November 26, 1898.

Chapter 22

91. *The Prospector*, May 6, 1899.
92. Ibid., May 27, 1899.
93. Ibid., February 11, 1899.
94. Ibid., April 8, 1899.
95. Ibid., April 22, 1899.
96. Ibid.
97. Ibid., June 10, 1899.
98. Ibid., October 30, 1897.

Chapter 23

99. Wragge, E.C., unpublished memoirs.
100. Ibid.

Chapter 24

101. *The Prospector*, June 1, 1901.
102. Ibid., July 20, 1901.
103. House, Candace, Letter from Maria Clark to Candace L. House, 1902, from *The Galbraiths and the Kootenays*, p. 60.

Chapter 25

104. *The Prospector*, February 6, 1904.
105. Government agents' file of 1904, letter "5."
106. Ibid., February 20, 1904.
107. *Cranbrook Herald*, May 5, 1904.

Epilogue

108. Interview with Bud Caldwell, February 1999.
109. Information supplied by Pete Lum in 1988, and Florence (Ban Quon) Hucklack in 1996.
110. *The Prospector*, September 10, 1904.
111. Duncan Janet (Mather), "A Fort Steele Family's Story," *Cominco Magazine*, April 1961.
112. Constable, William. Quotes at the opening of Libby Dam, September 20, 1978.

Bibliography

Affleck, Edward L. *Sternwheelers, Sandbars and Switchbacks*. Privately printed: 1973.

Barman, Jean. *The West Beyond the West*. Toronto, ON: University of Toronto Press, 1991.

Casselman, Verdun. *Ties to Water: The History of Bull River in the East Kootenay*. Privately printed: 1988.

Downs, Art. *Paddlewheels on the Frontier*. Vancouver, BC: Evergreen Press 1972.

Graham, Clara. *Kootenay Mosaic*. Vancouver, BC: Evergreen Press, 1971.

Graham, Clara. *This Was the Kootenay*. Vancouver, BC: Evergreen Press, 1963.

House, Candace L. *The Galbraiths and the Kootenays*. New York, NY: Vantage Press, 1969.

Inwood, Damian. *Fort Steele: The Golden Era*. Langley, BC: Sunfire Publications, 1986.

Jackman, S.W. *Portraits of the Premiers*. Sidney, BC: Gray's Publishing, 1969.

Kimberley Seniors Association. *Mountain Treasures: The History Of Kimberley B.C.* Kimberley, BC: 1979.

LaBissoniere, Sister Jean S.P. *Providence Trail Blazers*. Edmonton, AB: Jasper Printing, 1978.

Lees, J.A. and W.J. Clutterbuck. *A Ramble in British Columbia, 1887*. London and New York: Longman, Green and Company, 1888.

Scott, David and Edna Hanic. *East Kootenay Chronicle*. Mr. Paperback, 1979.

Steele, Samuel Benfield. *Reminiscences of the Great Northwest: Forty Years in Canada*. New York, NY: Dodd, Mead and Company, 1915. Reprinted by Coles, 1973.

White, Derryll. *Fort Steele : Here History Lives*. Surrey, BC: Heritage House, 1988.

Whitehead, Margaret. *They Call Me Father: Memoirs of Father Nicolas Coccola*. Vancouver, BC: University of BC Press, 1988.

Periodicals and Other Sources

Anglican Church Records, Diocese of Kootenay, Fort Steele Parish 1899–1962.

The Cranbrook Herald newspaper.

Fenwick, Arthur B. *Reminiscences of Kootenay, 1940*. MSS 219. Fort Steele Heritage Archives.

Geological Survey of Canada. Annual reports 1885,1887, 1894, 1902–03.

Gold Fields Act – 1859. Revision February 26,1864. Re: Placer Mines (amended 1898 and 1899).

Indian Agency, Reel B1893 (1892 to 1898). BC Archives, Victoria, BC.

Kootenay Reclamation Scheme: The Resources of British Columbia 1883–84.

Minister of Mines Annual Reports 1898–1901, 1904, 1907.

Norbury, Frederick Paget. *Norbury Letters 1887–1899*. Fort Steele Archives.

Oblates. *A Short Account of the Work of the Oblates of Mary Immaculate 1860–1910*. Vancouver, BC: Bagley & Sons, 1910.

The Prospector newspaper, Fort Steele 1895–1904; Cranbrook 1905–06.

Wragge, E.C. Unpublished memoirs.

Index

Index

The Author

Naomi Miller was born and grew up in the West Kootenay town of Kaslo, B.C. She received a degree in nursing from the University of British Columbia, and then worked as a nurse before marrying and moving to eastern Canada. While raising six children she enjoyed 26 years with the Girl Guides of Canada as a leader, administrator, and trainer.

In 1968 her family moved to Golden, B.C., where she and her husband worked as directors to build and establish the Golden and District Museum. Naomi volunteered as curator for twelve years. Her interest expanded to include history province-wide. She served as president of the B.C. Historical Federation, and then became the editor of the *British Columbia Historical News* quarterly for over ten years. She was also a director of the British Columbia Heritage Trust and was honoured in 1999 with the British Columbia Heritage Award.

Since moving to the district in 1987, Naomi has delighted in sharing stories of its history each summer with hundreds of tourists at Fort Steele Heritage Town.